"THERE CAN BE NO DOUBT THAT THIS IS THE BEST TEXT OF THE HISTORY OF PHILOSOPHY NOW AVAILABLE IN ENGLISH"
The Historical Bulletin

"Fr. Copleston presents in this volume a comprehensive survey of ancient philosophy . . . He discusses the matter at hand in a fresh and interesting as well as in an accurate and authoritative manner . . . This work is highly recommended."
The Catholic Historical Review

"A detailed, clear and judicious account of ancient philosophy from the Pre-Socratics down to Neoplatonism, based on adequate knowledge of the sources and of the most important secondary material."
The Journal of Philosophy

"Fr. Copleston writes with ease and lucidity, and his book should be valuable not merely as a text book but as an introduction to Christian philosophy for the general reader."
Pax

". . . broad-minded and objective, comprehensive and scholarly, unified and well-proportioned . . . No thinker with any claim to distinction in ancient philosophy is dismissed. . . We cannot recommend too highly the adoption of Fr. Copleston's book as a manual in Catholic seminaries, colleges and universities."
Thought

"Fr. Copleston has written an authoritative, well documented history which the reader can trust. Although his work is far from being a 'popularization', it is not ponderous and has an easy style which makes for pleasant reading."
TheThomist

"The author's desire to be objective and fair is evidenced throughout by his painstaking recourse to primary sources and by a spirit of impartiality and tolerance in his critical appraisals."
Theological Studies

A History of Philosophy

VOLUME I

Greece and Rome

PART II

by Frederick Copleston, S.J.

NEW REVISED EDITION

IMAGE BOOKS
A Division of Doubleday & Company, Inc.
Garden City, New York

Image Books Edition 1962
by special arrangement with The Newman Press

PRINTING HISTORY
The Newman Press Edition published December, 1946

1st printing	December, 1946
2nd printing	September, 1948
3rd printing	December, 1950
4th printing	July, 1953
5th printing	October, 1955
6th printing	July, 1957
7th printing	July, 1959
8th printing	October, 1960

Image Books Edition published February, 1962

DE LICENTIA SUPERIORUM ORDINIS:
Franciscus Mangan, S.J., Praep. Prov. Angliae
NIHIL OBSTAT:
C. Lattey, S.J., Censor Deputatus
IMPRIMATUR:
✠ Thomas, Archiepiscopus Birmingamiensis
Die 17 Martii 1944

CONTENTS

Part Four
ARISTOTLE

Chapter	Page
Twenty-Seven: LIFE AND WRITINGS OF ARISTOTLE	9
Twenty-Eight: LOGIC OF ARISTOTLE	20
Twenty-Nine: THE METAPHYSICS OF ARISTOTLE	30
Thirty: PHILOSOPHY OF NATURE AND PSYCHOLOGY	62
Thirty-One: ARISTOTLE'S ETHICS	74
Thirty-Two: POLITICS	92
Thirty-Three: AESTHETICS OF ARISTOTLE	100
NOTE ON THE OLDER PERIPATETICS	110
Thirty-Four: PLATO AND ARISTOTLE	113

Part Five
POST-ARISTOTELIAN PHILOSOPHY

Thirty-Five: INTRODUCTORY	123
Thirty-Six: THE EARLY STOA	129
Thirty-Seven: EPICUREANISM	145
NOTE ON CYNICISM IN THE FIRST PERIOD OF THE HELLENISTIC EPOCH	156
Thirty-Eight: THE OLDER SCEPTICS, THE MIDDLE AND NEW ACADEMIES	157

Chapter	Page
Thirty-Nine: THE MIDDLE STOA	165
NOTE ON THE PERIPATETIC SCHOOL IN THE HELLENISTIC-ROMAN PERIOD	169
Forty: THE LATER STOA	172
Forty-One: CYNICS, ECLECTICS, SCEPTICS	182
Forty-Two: NEO-PYTHAGOREANISM	190
NOTE ON APOLLONIUS OF TYANA	193
Forty-Three: MIDDLE PLATONISM	195
Forty-Four: JEWISH-HELLENISTIC PHILOSOPHY	201
Forty-Five: PLOTINIAN NEO-PLATONISM	207
Forty-Six: OTHER NEO-PLATONIC SCHOOLS	219
Forty-Seven: CONCLUDING REVIEW	229

APPENDICES

One: SOME ABBREVIATIONS USED IN THIS VOLUME	251
Two: A NOTE ON SOURCES	254
Three: A FEW BOOKS	257
NOTES	262
INDEX	274

Part Four

ARISTOTLE

Chapter Twenty-Seven

LIFE AND WRITINGS
OF ARISTOTLE

Aristotle was born in 384/3 B.C. at Stageira in Thrace, and was the son of Nicomachus, a physician of the Macedonian king, Amyntas II. When he was about seventeen years old Aristotle went to Athens for purposes of study and became a member of the Academy in 368/7 B.C., where for over twenty years he was in constant intercourse with Plato until the latter's death in 348/7 B.C. He thus entered the Academy at the time when Plato's later dialectic was being developed and the religious tendency was gaining ground in the great philosopher's mind. Probably already at this time Aristotle was giving attention to empirical science (i.e. at the time of Plato's death), and it may be that he had already departed from the Master's teaching on various points; but there can be no question of any radical break between Master and pupil as long as the former was still alive. It is impossible to suppose that Aristotle could have remained all that time in the Academy had he already taken up a radically different philosophical position to that of his Master. Moreover, even after Plato's death Aristotle still uses the first person plural of the representatives of the Platonic doctrine of Ideas, and soon after Plato's death Aristotle eulogises him as the man "whom bad men have not even the right to praise, and who showed in his life and teachings how to be happy and good at the same time." [1] The notion that Aristotle was in any real sense an opponent of Plato in the Academy and that he was a thorn in the side of the Master, is scarcely tenable: Aristotle found in Plato a guide and friend for whom he had the greatest admiration,

and though in later years his own scientific interests tended
to come much more to the fore, the metaphysical and religious teaching of Plato had a lasting influence upon him. Indeed, it was this side of Plato's teaching that would have
perhaps a special value for Aristotle, as offsetting his own
bent towards empirical studies. "In fact, this myth of a cool,
static, unchanging and purely critical Aristotle, without il-
lusions, experiences, or history, breaks to pieces under the
weight of the facts which up to now have been artificially
suppressed for its sake." [2] As I shall briefly indicate, when
considering Aristotle's writings, the Philosopher developed
his own personal standpoint only gradually; and this is,
after all, only what one would naturally expect.

After Plato's death Aristotle left Athens with Xenocrates
(Speusippus, Plato's nephew, had become head of the
Academy, and with him Aristotle did not see eye to eye;
in any case he may not have wished to remain in the
Academy in a subordinate position under its new head), and
founded a branch of the Academy at Assos in the Troad.
Here he influenced Hermias, ruler of Atarneus, and married
his niece and adopted daughter, Pythias. While working
at Assos, Aristotle no doubt began to develop his own independent views. Three years later he went to Mitylene
in Lesbos, and it was there that he was probably in intercourse with Theophrastus, a native of Eresus on the same
island, who was later the most celebrated disciple of Aristotle. (Hermias entered into negotiations with Philip of
Macedon, who conceived the idea of an Hellenic defeat
of the Persians. The Persian general, Mentor, got hold of
Hermias by treachery and carried him off to Susa, where
he was tortured but kept silence. His last message was:
"Tell my friends and companions that I have done nothing
weak or unworthy of philosophy." Aristotle published a
poem in his honour.[3])

In 343/2 Aristotle was invited to Pella by Philip of
Macedon to undertake the education of his son Alexander,
then thirteen years old. This period at the court of Macedon
and the endeavour to exercise a real moral influence on the
young prince, who was later to play so prominent a part on
the political stage and to go down to posterity as Alexander
the Great, should have done much to widen Aristotle's horizon and to free him from the narrow conceptions of the
ordinary Greek, though the effect does not seem to have
been so great as might have been expected: Aristotle never

ceased to share the Greek view of the City-State as the centre of life. When Alexander ascended the throne in 336/5, Aristotle left Macedon, his pedagogical activity being now presumably at an end, and probably went for a time to Stageira, his native city, which Alexander rebuilt as payment of his debt to his teacher. After a time the connection between the philosopher and his pupil became weaker: Aristotle, though approving to a certain extent of Macedonian politics, did not approve of Alexander's tendency to regard Greeks and "barbarians" as on an equal footing. Moreover, in 327, Callisthenes, nephew of Aristotle, who had been taken into the service of Alexander on Aristotle's recommendation, was suspected of taking part in a conspiracy and was executed.

In 335/4 Aristotle had returned to Athens, where he founded his own School. Apart from the fact of his absence from Athens for some years, the development of his own ideas no doubt precluded any return to the Athenian Academy. The new School was in the north-east of the city, at the Lyceum, the precincts of Apollo Lyceus. The School was also known as the Περίπατος, and the members as οἱ Περιπατητικοί, from their custom of carrying on their discussions while walking up and down in the covered ambulatory or simply because much of the instruction was given in the ambulatory. The School was dedicated to the Muses. Besides educational and tuitional work the Lyceum seems to have had, in a more prominent way than the Academy, the character of a union or society in which mature thinkers carried on their studies and research: it was in effect a university or scientific institute, equipped with library and teachers, in which lectures were regularly given.

In 323 B.C. Alexander the Great died, and the reaction in Greece against Macedonian suzerainty led to a charge of ἀσέβεια against Aristotle, who had been so closely connected with the great leader in his younger days. Aristotle withdrew from Athens (lest the Athenians should sin against philosophy for the second time, he is reported to have said) and went to Chalcis in Euboea, where he lived on an estate of his dead mother. Shortly afterwards, in 322/1 B.C., he died of an illness.

The Works of Aristotle

The writings of Aristotle fall into three main periods, (i) the period of his intercourse with Plato; (ii) the years of

his activity at Assos and Mitylene; (iii) the time of his
headship of the Lyceum at Athens. The works fall also into
two groups or kinds, (i) the exoteric works—ἐξωτερικοί,
ἐκδεδομένοι λόγοι—which were written for the most
part in dialogue form and intended for general publication; and (ii) the pedagogical works—ἀκροαματικοὶ λόγοι,
ὑπομνήματα, πραγματεῖα—which formed the basis of
Aristotle's lectures in the Lyceum. The former exist only in
fragments, but of the latter kind we possess a large number.
These pedagogical works were first made known to the public in the edition of Andronicus of Rhodes (c. 60-50 B.C.),
and it is these works which have earned for Aristotle a
reputation for baldness of style unembellished by literary
graces. It has been pointed out that, though a great in-
ventor of philosophical terms, Aristotle was neglectful of style
and of verbal beauty, while his interest in philosophy
was too serious to admit of his employing metaphor instead
of clear reason or of relapsing into myth. Now, this is true
of the pedagogical works—that they lack the literary graces,
but it is also true that the works which Aristotle himself
published, and of which we possess only fragments, did not
disdain the literary graces: their fluent style was praised by
Cicero,[4] and even myths were occasionally introduced. They
do, however, represent Aristotle's earlier work, when he
was under direct Platonic influence or working his way
towards his own independent position.

(i) In Aristotle's *first period* of literary activity he may be
said to have adhered closely to Plato, his teacher, both in
content and, in general at least, in form, though in the
Dialogues Aristotle seems to have appeared himself as the
leader of the conversation. "... *sermo ita inducitur ceterorum,
ut penes ipsum sit principatus.*" (So Cic. *Ad Att.* 13, 19, 4.)
It is most probable that in the Dialogues Aristotle held
the Platonic philosophy, and only later changed his mind.
Plutarch speaks of Aristotle as changing his mind
(μετατίθεσθαι).[5] Moreover, Cephisodorus, pupil of Isocrates, saddles Aristotle with Plato's theories, e.g. concerning
the Ideas.[6]

(*a*) To this period belongs the dialogue of *Eudemus,*
or *On the Soul,* in which Aristotle shares Plato's doctrine of
recollection and the apprehension of the Ideas in a state
of pre-existence, and is in general dominated by the Master's
influence. Aristotle argues for the immortality of the soul
on lines suggested by the *Phaedo*—the soul is not a mere

harmony of the body. Harmony has a contrary, namely, disharmony. But the soul has no contrary. Therefore the soul is not a harmony.[7] Aristotle supposes pre-existence and the substantiality of the soul—also Forms. Just as men who fall ill may lose their memories, so the soul, on entering this life, forgets the state of pre-existence; but just as those who recover health after sickness remember their suffering, so the soul after death remembers this life. Life apart from the body is the soul's normal state (κατὰ φύσιν); its inhabitation of the body is really a severe illness.[8] This is a very different view from that afterwards put forward by Aristotle when he had taken up his own independent position.

(b) The *Protrepticus* also belongs to this period of Aristotle's development. This appears to have been an epistle to Themison of Cyprus and not a dialogue. In this work the Platonic doctrine of Forms is maintained, and the philosopher is depicted as one who contemplates these Forms or Ideas and not the imitations of them (αὐτῶν γάρ ἐστι θεατής ἀλλ᾽ οὐ μιμημάτων).[9] Again Phronesis retains the Platonic signification, denoting metaphysical speculation, and so having a theoretical meaning and not the purely practical significance of the *Nichomachean Ethics*. In the *Protrepticus* Aristotle also emphasises the worthlessness of earthly goods, and depicts this life as the death or tomb of the soul, which enters into true and higher life only through bodily death. This view certainly indicates direct Platonic influence, for in the *Nicomachean Ethics* Aristotle insists on the necessity of earthly goods, in some degree at least, for the truly happy life, and so even for the philosopher.

(c) It is probable that the oldest parts of the Logical Works, of the *Physics*, and perhaps also of the *De Anima* (Book Γ) date back to this period. Thus if a preliminary sketch of the *Metaphysics* (including Book A) dates back to Aristotle's *second* period, it is to be supposed that *Physics* (book 2) dates back to his *first* period, since in the first book of the *Metaphysics* there is a reference to the *Physics*, or at least the setting-out of the theory of the causes is presupposed.[10] It is probable that the *Physics* fall into two groups of monographs, and the first two books and Book 7 are to be ascribed to the earliest period of Aristotle's literary activity.

(ii) In his *second period* Aristotle began to diverge from his former predominantly Platonic position and to adopt a more critical attitude towards the teaching of the Academy.

He still looked on himself as an Academician apparently, but it is the period of criticism or of growing criticism in regard to Platonism. The period is represented by the dialogue *On Philosophy*, Περὶ φιλοσοφίας, a work which combines clear Platonic influence with a criticism of some of Plato's most characteristic theories. Thus although Aristotle represents Plato as the culmination of previous philosophy (and indeed as regards pre-Aristotelian philosophy, Aristotle always held this idea), he criticises the Platonic theory of Forms or Ideas, at least under its later form of development at Plato's hands. "If the Ideas were another kind of number, and not the mathematical, we should have no understanding of it. For who understands another kind of number, at any rate among the majority of us?" [11] Similarly, although Aristotle adopts more or less Plato's stellar theology, the concept of the Unmoved Mover makes its appearance,[12] though Aristotle has not yet adopted the multitudinous movers of his later metaphysics. He applies the term visible god —τοσοῦτον ὁρατὸν θεόν—to the Cosmos or Heaven, a term which is of Platonic derivation.

It is interesting that the argument for the existence of the Divine drawn from the gradations of perfections is found in this dialogue. "In general, wherever there is a better there is also a best. Now, since among the things that are one is better than another, there is also a best thing, and this would be the divine." Aristotle supposes apparently the gradation of real forms.[13] The subjective belief in God's existence is derived by Aristotle from the soul's experience of ecstasies and prophecies in e.g. the state of sleep, and from the sight of the starry heavens, though such recognition of occult phenomena is really foreign to Aristotle's later development.[14] In this dialogue, then, Aristotle combines elements that can have no other source than Plato and his circle with elements of criticism of the Platonic philosophy, as when he criticises the Platonic theory of Ideas or the doctrine of "creation" as given in the *Timaeus*, asserting the eternity of the world.[15]

It appears that a first sketch of the *Metaphysics* goes back to this second period in Aristotle's development, the period of transition. This would comprise Book A (the use of the term "we" denoting the transitional period), Book B, Book K, 1-8, Book Λ (except C 8), Book M, 9-10, Book N. According to Jaeger the attack in the original *Metaphysics* was directed mainly against Speusippus.[16]

The *Eudemian Ethics* are sometimes thought to belong to this period, and to date from Aristotle's sojourn at Assos. Aristotle still holds to the Platonic conception of Phronesis, though the object of philosophic contemplation is no longer the Ideal World of Plato but the transcendent God of the *Metaphysics*.[17] It is also probable that an original *Politics* dates from this second period, including Books 2, 3, 7, 8, which deal with the Ideal State. Utopias on the style of the Platonic Republic are criticised by Aristotle.

The writings *De Caelo* and *De Generatione et Corruptione* (Περὶ οὐρανοῦ and Περὶ γενέσεως καὶ φθορᾶς) are also ascribed to this period with probability.

(iii) Aristotle's *Third Period* (335-322) is that of his activity in the Lyceum. It is in this period that there appears Aristotle the empirical observer and scientist, who is yet concerned to raise a sure philosophical building upon a firm foundation sunk deep in the earth. We cannot but marvel at the power of organising detailed research in the provinces of nature and history that is shown by Aristotle in this last period of his life. There had, indeed, been in the Academy a practice of classification, mainly for logical purposes, that involved a certain amount of empirical observation, but there was nothing of the sustained and systematic investigation into details of nature and history that the Lyceum carried out under the direction of Aristotle. This spirit of exact research into the phenomena of nature and history really represents something new in the Greek world, and the credit for it must undoubtedly go to Aristotle. But it will not do to represent Aristotle as merely a Positivist in the last phase of his life, as is sometimes done, for there is really no evidence to show that he ever abandoned metaphysics, in spite of all his interest in exact, scientific research.

Aristotle's lectures in the School formed the basis of his "pedagogical" works, which were circulated among the members of the School, and were, as already mentioned, first given to the public by Andronicus of Rhodes. Most of the pedagogical works belong to this period, except, of course, those portions of works which are probably to be ascribed to an earlier phase. These pedagogical works have offered many difficulties to scholars, e.g. because of the unsatisfactory connections between books, sections that appear to break the logical succession of thought, and so on. It now appears probable that these works represent lectures of Aristotle which were equivalently published—so far as the School was concerned—by being given as lectures. But this does not imply that each work represents a single lecture or a continuous course of lectures: rather are they different sections or lectures which were later put together and given an external unity by means of a common title. This work of composition can have been only in part accomplished by Aristotle himself: it continued in the following generations of the School and was first completed by Andronicus of Rhodes, if not later.

These works of Aristotle's third period may be divided into:

(a) *Logical Works* (combined in Byzantine times as the *Organon*). The *Categories* or κατηγορίαι (Aristotelian in content at least), the *De Interpretatione* or Περὶ ἑρμηνείας (on proposition and judgment), the *Prior Analytics* or 'Αναλυτικὰ Πρότερα (two books on inference), the *Posterior Analytics* or 'Αναλυτικὰ Ὕστερα (two books on proof, knowledge of principles, etc.), the *Topics* or Τοπικά (eight books on dialectic or probable proof), the *Sophistical Fallacies* or Περὶ σοφιστικῶν ἐλέγχων.

(b) *Metaphysical Works.*
The *Metaphysics*, a collection of lectures of different dates, so called from its position in the Aristotelian Corpus, probably by a Peripatetic before the time of Andronicus.

(c) Works on Natural Philosophy, Natural Science, Psychology, etc. The *Physics* or φυσικὴ ἀκρόασις or φυσικά or τὰ περὶ φύσεως. This work consists of eight books, of which the first two must be referred to Aristotle's Platonic period. *Metaphysics* A 983 a 32-3 refers to the *Physics*, or rather presupposes explicitly the setting-out of the theory of causes in *Physics* 2. Book 7 of the *Physics* probably belongs also to the earlier work of Aristotle, while Book 8 is really not part of the *Physics* at all, since it quotes the *Physics*, with the remark "as we have previously shown in the *Physics*." [18] The total work would then appear to have consisted originally of a number of independent monographs, a supposition borne out by the fact that the *Metaphysics* quotes as "Physics" the two works *De Caelo* and *De Generatione et Corruptione*.[19]

The *Meteorology* or Μετεωρολογικά or Περὶ μετεώρων (four books).

The *Histories of Animals* or Περὶ τὰ ζῷα ἱστορίαι (ten books on comparative anatomy and physiology, of which the last is probably post-Aristotelian).

The 'Ανατομαί in seven books, which is lost.

The *De Incessu Animalium* or Περὶ ζῴων πορείας (one book) and the *De Motu Animalium* or Περὶ ζῴων κινήσεως (one book).

The *De Generatione Animalium* or Περὶ ζῴων γενέσεως (five books).

The *De Anima* or Περὶ ψυχῆς, Aristotle's Psychology in three books.

The *Parva Naturalia*, a number of smaller treatises dealing with such subjects as perception (Περὶ αἰσθήσεως καὶ αἰσθητῶν), memory (Περὶ μνήμης καὶ ἀναμνήσεως), sleep and waking (Περὶ ὕπνου καὶ ἐγρηγόρσεως), dreams (Περὶ ἐνυπνίων), long life and short life (Περὶ μακροβιότητος καὶ βραχυβιότητος), life and death (Περὶ ζωῆς καὶ θανάτου), breathing (Περὶ ἀναπνοῆς), divination in sleep (Περὶ τῆς καθ' ὕπνον μαντικῆς).

The *Problemata* (Προβλήματα) seems to be a collection of problems, gradually formed, which grew up round a nucleus of notes or jottings made by Aristotle himself.

(d) *Works on Ethics and Politics.*

The *Magna Moralia* or 'Ηθικὰ μεγάλα, in two books, which would seem to be a genuine work of Aristotle, at least so far as the content is concerned.[20] Part would appear to date from a time when Aristotle was still more or less in agreement with Plato.

The *Nicomachean Ethics* ('Ηθικὰ Νικομάχεια) in ten books, a work which was edited by Aristotle's son Nicomachus after the philosopher's death.

The *Politics* (Πολιτικά), of which Books 2, 3, 7, 8, would appear to date from the second period of Aristotle's literary activity. Books 4-6 were, thinks Jaeger, inserted before the first book was prefixed to the whole, for Book 4 refers to 3 as the beginning of the work—'ἐν τοῖς πρώτοις λόγοις."The contents of 2 are merely negative." [21]

Collection of Constitutions of 158 States. That of Athens was found in papyrus in 1891.

(e) *Works on Aesthetics, History and Literature.*

The *Rhetoric* (Τέχνη ῥητορική) in three books.

The *Poetics* (Περὶ ποιητικῆς), which is incomplete, part having been lost.

Records of dramatic performances at Athens, collection of Didascalia, list of victors at Olympic and Pythian games. Aristotle was engaged on a work concerning the Homeric problem, a treatise on the territorial rights of States (Περὶ τῶν τόπων δικαιώματα πόλεων), etc.

There is no need to suppose that all these works, for example the collection of the 158 Constitutions, were by Aristotle himself, but they would have been initiated by him and carried out under his superintendence. He entrusted others with the compilation of a history of natural philosophy (Theophrastus), of mathematics and astronomy (Eudemus of Rhodes), and medicine (Meno). One can but marvel at the catholicity of his interests and the scope of his aims.

The mere list of Aristotle's works shows a rather different spirit to that of Plato, for it is obvious that Aristotle was drawn towards the empirical and scientific, and that he did not tend to treat the objects of this world as semi-illusory or as unfitted to be objects of knowledge. But this difference in tendency, a difference which was no doubt accentuated as time went on, has, when coupled with consideration of such facts as the Aristotelian opposition to the Platonic theory of Ideas and to the Platonic dualistic psychology, led to the popular conception of a radical contrast between the two great philosophers. There is, of course, truth in this view, since there are clear cases of opposition between their tenets and also a general difference in atmosphere (at least if we compare Plato's exoteric works —and we have no other—with Aristotle's pedagogical works), but it can easily be exaggerated. Aristotelianism, historically speaking, is not the opposite of Platonism, but its development, correcting one-sided theories—or trying to do so—such as the theory of Ideas, the dualistic psychology of Plato, etc., and supplying a firmer foundation in physical fact. That something of value was omitted at the same time is true, but that simply shows that the two philosophies should not be considered as two diametrically opposed systems, but as two complementary philosophical spirits and bodies of doctrine. A synthesis was later attempted in Neo-Platonism, and mediaeval philosophy shows the same synthetic spirit. St. Thomas, for instance, though speaking of Aristotle as "the Philosopher," could not, and would not have wished to, cut himself off entirely from the Platonic tradition, while in the Franciscan School even St. Bonaventure, who awarded the palm to Plato, did not disdain to make use of Peripatetic doctrines, and Duns Scotus carried much further the impregnation of the Franciscan spirit with Aristotelian elements.

And it should not be supposed that Aristotle, in his enthusiasm for facts and his desire to set a firm empirical and scientific foundation, was lacking in systematic power or ever renounced his metaphysical interest. Both Platonism and Aristotelianism culminate in metaphysics. Thus Goethe can compare Aristotle's philosophy to a pyramid rising on high in regular form from a broad basis on the earth, and that of Plato to an obelisk or a tongue of flame which shoots up to heaven. Nevertheless, I must admit that, in my opinion, the direction of Aristotle's thought was increasingly directed away from the Platonic position to which he at first adhered, while the results of his new orientation of thought do not always combine harmoniously with those elements of the Platonic legacy which he seems to have retained to the last.

Chapter Twenty-Eight

LOGIC OF ARISTOTLE

1. Although Aristotle divides philosophy systematically in different ways on different occasions,[1] we may say that the following is his considered view of the matter.[2] (i) *Theoretical* Philosophy,[3] in which knowledge as such is the end in view and not any practical purpose, is divided into (*a*) Physics or Natural Philosophy, which has to do with material things which are subject to motion; (*b*) Mathematics, which has to do with the unmoved but unseparated (from matter); (*c*) Metaphysics, which has to do with the separated (transcendent) and unmoved. (Metaphysics would thus include what we know as Natural Theology.[4]) (ii) *Practical* Philosophy (πρακτική) deals principally with Political Science, but has as subsidiary disciplines Strategy, Economics and Rhetoric, since the ends envisaged by these disciplines are subsidiary to and depend on that of Political Science.[5] (iii) *Poetical* Philosophy (ποιητική) has to do with production and not with action as such, as in the case with Practical Philosophy (which includes ethical action in the wider or political sense), and is to all intents and purposes the Theory of Art.[6]

2. The Aristotelian Logic is often termed "formal" logic. Inasmuch as the Logic of Aristotle is an analysis of the forms of thought (hence the term *Analytic*), this is an apt characterisation; but it would be a very great mistake to suppose that for Aristotle logic concerns the forms of human thinking in such an exclusive way that it has no connection with external reality. He is chiefly concerned with the forms of proof, and he assumes that the conclusion of a scientific proof gives certain knowledge concerning reality. For ex-

ample, in the syllogism "All men are mortal, Socrates is a man, therefore Socrates is mortal," it is not merely that the conclusion is deduced correctly according to the formal laws of logic: Aristotle assumes that the conclusion is verified in reality. He presupposes, therefore, a realist theory of knowledge and for him logic, though an analysis of the forms of thought, is an analysis of the thought that thinks reality, that reproduces it conceptually within itself, and, in the true judgment, makes statements about reality which are verified in the external world. It is an analysis of human thought in its thought about reality, though Aristotle certainly admits that things do not always exist in extramental reality precisely as they are conceived by the mind, e.g. the universal.

This may be clearly seen in his doctrine of the Categories. From the logical viewpoint the Categories comprise the ways in which we think about things—for instance, predicating qualities of substances—but at the same time they are ways in which things actually exist: things are substances and actually have accidents. The Categories demand, therefore, not only a logical but also a metaphysical treatment. Aristotle's Logic, then, must not be likened to the Transcendental Logic of Kant, since it is not concerned to isolate *a priori* forms of thought which are contributed by the mind alone in its active process of knowledge. Aristotle does not raise the "Critical Problem": he assumes a realist epistemology, and assumes that the categories of thought, which we express in language, are also the objective categories of extramental reality.

3. In the *Categories* and in the *Topics* the number of Categories or Praedicamenta is given as ten: οὐσία or τί ἐστι (man or horse); ποσόν (three yards long); ποιόν (white); πρός τι (double); ποῦ (in the market-place); πότε (last year); κεῖσθαι (lies, sits); ἔχειν (armed, with shoes); ποιεῖν (cuts); πάσχειν (is cut or burnt). But in the *Posterior Analytics* they appear as eight, κεῖσθαι or *Situs* and ἔχειν or *Habitus* being subsumed under the other categories.[7] Aristotle, therefore, can hardly have looked upon the deduction of the Categories as definitive. Nevertheless, even if the tenfold division of the Categories was not looked upon as definitive by Aristotle, there is no reason to suppose that he regarded the list of Categories as a haphazard list, devoid of structural arrangement. On the contrary, the list of the Categories constitutes an orderly arrangement, a

classification of concepts, the fundamental types of concepts governing our scientific knowledge. The word κατηγορεῖν means to predicate, and in the *Topics* Aristotle considers the Categories as a classification of predicates, the ways in which we think of being as realised. For example, we think of an object either as a substance or as a determination of substance, as falling under one of the nine categories that express the way in which we think of substance as being determined. In the *Categories* Aristotle considers the Categories rather as the classification of genera, species and individuals from the *summa genera* down to individual entities. If we examine our concepts, the ways in which we represent things mentally, we shall find, for example, that we have concepts of organic bodies, of animals (a subordinate genus), of sheep (a species of animal); but organic bodies, animals, sheep, are all included in the category of substance. Similarly, we may think of colour in general, of blueness in general, of cobalt; but colour, blueness, cobalt, all fall under the category of quality.

The Categories, however, were not in Aristotle's mind simply modes of mental representation, moulds of concepts: they represent the actual modes of being in the extramental world, and form the bridge between Logic and Metaphysics (which latter science has Substance as its chief subject).[8] They have, therefore, an ontological as well as a logical aspect, and it is perhaps in their ontological aspect that their orderly and structural arrangement appears most clearly. Thus, in order that being may exist, substance must exist: that is, as it were, the starting-point. Only singulars actually exist outside the mind, and for a singular to exist independently in this way it must be a substance. But it cannot exist merely as a substance, it must have accidental forms. For instance, a swan cannot exist unless it has some colour, while it cannot have colour unless it has quantity, extension. At once, then, we have the first three Categories—substance, quantity, quality, which are intrinsic determinations of the object. But the swan is the same in specific nature as other swans, is equal in size or unequal in size to other substances; in other words, it stands in some relation to other objects. Moreover, the swan as a physical substance, must exist in a certain *place* and at a certain *period,* must have a certain *posture.* Again, material substances, as belonging to a cosmic system, *act* and are *acted upon.* Thus some of the Categories belong to the object considered in itself, as its *intrinsic* determinations, while others belong to it as *extrinsic* determinations, affecting it as standing in relation to other material objects. It will be seen, therefore, that even if the number of the Categories could be reduced by subsuming certain Categories under others, the principle whereby the Categories are deduced is by no means merely a haphazard principle.

In the *Posterior Analytics* (in connection with definition) and in the *Topics*, Aristotle discusses the *Predicables* or various relations in which universal terms may stand to the subjects of which they are predicated. They are *genus* (γένος), *species* (εἶδος), *difference* (διαφορά), *property* (ἴδιον), *accident* (συμβεβηκός). In the *Topics* (I, c. 8), Aristotle bases his division of the predicables on the relations between subject and predicate. Thus if the predicate is co-extensive with the subject, it either gives us the essence of the subject or a property of the subject; while if it is not co-extensive with the subject, it either forms part of the attributes comprised in the definition of the subject (when it will be either a genus or a difference) or it does not do so (in which case it will be an accident).

Essential definitions are strict definitions by genus and difference, and Aristotle considered definition as involving a process of division down to the *infimae species* (cf. Plato).[9] But it is important to remember that Aristotle, aware that we are by no means always able to attain an essential or real definition, allows for nominal or descriptive definitions,[10] even though he had no high opinion of them, regarding as he did essential definitions as the only type of definition really worthy of the name. The distinction, however, is of importance, since in point of fact, we have to be content, in regard to the natural objects studied by physical science, with distinctive or characteristic definitions, which even if they approach the ideal more closely than Aristotle's nominal or descriptive definition, do not actually attain it.

(Some writers have emphasised the influence of language on philosophy. For instance, because we speak of the rose as being red (and this is necessary for purposes of social life and communication), we are naturally inclined to think that in the actual objective order there is a quality or accident, "redness," which inheres in a thing or substance, the rose. The philosophical categories of substance and accident can thus be traced back to the influence of words, of language. But it should be remembered that language follows thought,

is built up as an expression of thought, and this is especially true of philosophical terms. When Aristotle laid down
the ways in which the mind thinks about things, it is true that
he could not get away from language as the medium of
thought, but the language follows thought and thought
follows things. Language is not an *a priori* construction.)

4. Scientific knowledge *par excellence* means for Aristotle,
deducing the particular from the general or the conditioned
from its cause, so that we know both the cause on which
the fact depends and the necessary connection between the
fact and its cause. In other words, we have scientific knowledge when we know the cause on which the fact depends,
as the cause of that fact and of no other, and further, that
the fact could not be other than it is." [11]

But though the premisses are prior to the conclusion from
the logical viewpoint, Aristotle clearly recognises that there
is a difference between logical priority or priority *in se* and
epistemological priority *quoad nos*. He expressly states that
" 'prior' and 'better known' are ambiguous terms, for there
is a difference between what is prior and better known in
the order of being and what is prior and better known to
man. I mean that objects nearer to sense are prior and better
known to man; objects without qualification prior and better
known are those further from sense." [12] In other words, our
knowledge starts from sense, i.e. from the particular, and
ascends to the general or universal. "Thus it is clear that
we must get to know the primary premisses by induction;
for the methods by which even sense-perception implants
the universal is inductive." [13] Aristotle is thus compelled
to treat not only of deduction, but also of induction. For
instance, in the aforementioned syllogism the major premiss,
"All men are mortal," is founded on sense-perception, and
Aristotle has to justify both sense-perception and memory,
since both are involved. Hence we have the doctrine that
the senses *as such* never err: it is only the judgment which
is true or false.

Thus if a patient who is suffering from *delirium tremens*
"sees" pink rats, the senses as such do not err; error arises
when the patient judges that the pink rats are "out there,"
as real extramentally-existing objects. Similarly, the sun *appears* smaller than the earth, but this is not an error on
the part of the senses; indeed if the sun appeared as *larger*
than the earth, the senses would be out of order. Error
arises when, through a lack of astronomical knowledge, a

man *judges* that the sun is objectively smaller than the earth.

5. In the *Analytics*, therefore, Aristotle treats, not only of scientific proof, demonstration or deduction, but also of induction (ἐπαγωγή). Scientific induction means for him *complete* induction, and he expressly states that "induction proceeds through an enumeration of all the cases." [14] *Incomplete* induction is of use especially to the orator. Aristotle used experiment but did not elaborate a scientific methodology of induction and the use of hypothesis. Although he admits that "syllogism through induction is clearer to us," [15] his ideal remains that of deduction, of syllogistic demonstration. The analysis of deductive processes he carried to a very high level and very completely; but he cannot be said to have done the same for induction. This was no doubt only natural in the Ancient World, where mathematics was so much more highly developed than natural science. Nevertheless, after stating that sense-perception as such cannot attain the universal, Aristotle points out that we may observe groups of singulars or watch the frequent recurrence of an event, and so, by the use of the abstract reason, attain to knowledge of a universal essence or principle.[16]

6. In the *Prior Analytics* Aristotle inquires into the forms of inference, and he defines the syllogism as "discourse in which certain things being stated, something other than what is stated follows of necessity from their being so." [17] He discusses the three figures of the syllogism, etc.

(i) The Middle Term is Subject in one premiss and Predicate in the other. Thus: M is P, S is M, therefore S is P. Every animal is a substance. Every man is an animal. Therefore every man is a substance.

(ii) The Middle Term is Predicate in both premisses. P is M, S is not M, therefore S is not P. Every man is risible. But no horse is risible. Therefore no horse is a man.

(iii) The Middle Term is Subject in both premisses. Thus: M is P, M is S, therefore S is P. Every man is risible. But every man is an animal. Therefore some animals are risible.

In the *Topics*[18] Aristotle distinguishes *demonstrative* reasoning (i.e. "when the premisses from which the reasoning starts are true and primary, or are such that our knowledge of them has originally come through premisses which are primary and true") from *dialectical* reasoning (i.e. reasoning "from opinions that are generally accepted," i.e. "by all, or by the majority, or by the most notable and illustrious of them"). He adds a third kind of reasoning, eristic or "contentious" reasoning (which "starts from opinions that seem to be generally accepted, but are not really such"). This third is dealt with at length in the *De Sophisticis Elenchis*, where Aristotle examines, classifies and solves the various kinds of fallacy.

7. Aristotle saw clearly that the premisses in deduction themselves need proof, while on the other hand if *every* principle needs proof, we shall be involved in a *processus in infinitum* and *nothing* will be proved. He held, therefore, that there are certain principles which are known intuitively and immediately without demonstration.[19] The highest of these principles is the *principle of contradiction*. Of these principles no proof can be given. For example, the logical form of the principle of contradiction—"Of two propositions, one of which affirms something and the other denies the same thing, one must be true and the other false"—is not a proof of the principle in its metaphysical form—e.g. "The same thing cannot be an attribute and not an attribute of the same subject at the same time and in the same way." It simply exhibits the fact that no thinker can question the principle which lies at the basis of all thinking and is presupposed.[20]

We have, therefore, (i) first principles, perceived by νοῦς; (ii) what is derived necessarily from first principles, perceived by ἐπιστήμη; and (iii) what is contingent and could be otherwise, the subject of δόξα. But Aristotle saw that the major premiss of a syllogism, e.g. All men are mortal, cannot be derived immediately from the first principles: it depends also on induction. This involves a realist theory of universals, and Aristotle declares that induction exhibits the universal as implicit in the clearly known particular.[21]

8. In a book of this nature it would scarcely be desirable to enter upon a detailed exposition and discussion of the Aristotelian logic, but it is necessary to emphasise the very great contribution that Aristotle made to human thought in this branch of science, especially in regard to the syllogism. That logical analysis and division had been pursued in the Academy, in connection with the theory of Forms, is quite true (one has only to think of the discussions in the *Sophist*); but it was Aristotle who first constituted logic ("Analytics") as a separate science, and it was Aristotle

who discovered, isolated and analysed the fundamental form of inference, namely, the syllogism. This is one of his lasting achievements, and even if it were his only positive achievement, it would still be one for which his name would rightly be held in lasting memory. One could not justifiably assert that Aristotle made a complete analysis of all deductive processes, for the classical syllogism supposes (i) three propositions, each in subject and predicate form; (ii) three terms, from which each proposition takes both subject and predicate, and, given this situation, determines the cases in which two of the propositions entail the third in virtue, either (a) of logical form only, or (b) of an adjoined existence assertion, as with *Darapti*. Aristotle, for instance, did not consider that other form of inference discussed by Cardinal Newman in his *Grammar of Assent,* when the mind derives conclusions, not from certain propositions but from certain concrete facts. The mind considers these facts and, after forming a critical estimate of them, infers a conclusion, which is not a general proposition (as in induction proper), but a particular conclusion such as, e.g. "The prisoner is innocent." It is certainly true that general propositions are implied (e.g. evidence of a certain type is compatible, or incompatible, with the innocence of an accused man), but the mind is not actually concerned to elicit the implication of presupposed propositions so much as to elicit the implications of a number of concrete facts. St. Thomas Aquinas recognised this type of reasoning, and attributed it to the *vis cogitativa,* also called *ratio particularis.*[22] Moreover, even in regard to that form of inference which Aristotle analysed, he did not really consider the question, whether these general principles from which it starts are simply formal principles or have ontological import. The latter view seems to be assumed for the most part.

But it would be absurd to criticise Aristotle adversely for not having made a complete study of all the forms of inference, and for not having clearly raised and solved all the questions that might be raised in connection with the forms of human thought: the task that he did undertake to accomplish, he accomplished very well, and the group of his logical treatises (later termed the *Organon*) constitute a masterpiece of the human mind. It is not without reason, we may be sure, that Aristotle represents himself as being a pioneer in logical analysis and systematisation. At the close of the *De Sophisticis Elenchis* he remarks, that while much

had been said by others before him on the subject of
Rhetoric, for instance, he had no anterior work to speak
of on the subject of reasoning, which he might have used
as a foundation, but was compelled to break what was
practically new ground. It was not the case that systematic
analysis of the reasoning-processes had been already completed in part: nothing at all existed in this line. The professors of rhetoric had given their pupils an empirical training in "contentious arguments," but they never worked out a
scientific methodology or a systematic exposition of the subject: he had had to start from the beginning by himself.
Aristotle's claim in reference to the particular subject-matter
of the *De Sophisticis Elenchis* is doubtless substantially just
in regard to the discovery and analysis of the syllogism in
general.

Occasionally one hears people speak as though modern
logical studies had deprived the traditional Aristotelian logic
of all value, as though one could now relegate the traditional
logic to the lumber-room of museum pieces, of interest only
to the philosophical antiquarian. On the other hand, those
who have been brought up according to the Aristotelian
tradition may be tempted to display a mistaken loyalty to
that tradition by attacking, e.g. modern symbolic logic. Either
extreme is in fact unwarranted, and it is necessary to adopt
a sane and balanced position, recognising indeed the in-
completeness of the Aristotelian logic and the value of
modern logic, but at the same time refusing to discredit the
Aristotelian logic on the ground that it does not cover
the whole province of logic. This sane and balanced position is the position maintained by those who have made a
deep study of logic, a point that needs to be emphasised
lest it be thought that it is only Scholastic philosophers,
speaking *pro domo sua*, who in the present age still attach
any value to the logic of Aristotle. Thus, while affirming,
and rightly affirming, that "it is no longer possible to regard
it as constituting the whole subject of deduction," Susan
Stebbing admits that "the traditional syllogism retains its
value";[23] while Heinrich Scholz declares that "the Aristotelian *Organon* is to-day still the most beautiful and instruc-
tive introduction to logic ever written by man." [24] Modern
symbolic logic may be an addition, and a very valuable addition, to the logic of Aristotle, but it should not be regarded
as a completely opposite counter thereto: it differs from

non-symbolic logic by its higher degree of formalisation, e.g. by the idea of propositional functionality.

9. This necessarily brief and curtailed treatment of the Aristotelian logic may profitably be concluded by a summary of a *few characteristic topics* discussed in the *Organon,* a summary from which will appear the wide range of the Aristotelian logical analysis. In the *Categories,* Aristotle treats of the range of variability of Subject and Predicate, in the *De Interpretatione* of the opposition of propositions, modal and assertoric, which leads him into an interesting discussion of excluded middle in Chapters 7 and 10. In the first book of the *Prior Analytics* he discusses the conversion of pure propositions and of necessary and contingent propositions, analyses the syllogisms in the three figures, and gives rules for constructing or discovering syllogisms dealing with, e.g. oblique inference (Ch. 36), negation (Ch. 46), proofs *per impossibile* and *ex hypothesi* (Chs. 23 and 44). In the second book Aristotle deals with the distribution of truth and falsity between premisses and conclusion, the defects in the syllogism, induction in a narrow sense, through "enumeration of all the cases" (Ch. 23), the enthymeme, etc.

The first book of the *Posterior Analytics* treats of the structure of a deductive science and its logical starting-point, the unity, diversity, distinction and logical ranking of sciences, ignorance, error and invalidity; while the second book is concerned with definitions, essential and nominal, the difference between definition and demonstration, the indemonstrability of the essential nature, the way in which basic truths become known, etc. The *Topics* is concerned with the predicables, definition, the technique of proof or the practice of dialectic, the *De Sophisticis Elenchis* with the classification of fallacies and their solutions.

Chapter Twenty-Nine

THE METAPHYSICS
OF ARISTOTLE

1. "All men by nature desire to know." [1] So does Aristotle optimistically begin the *Metaphysics*, a book, or rather collection of lectures, which is difficult to read (the Arabian philosopher Avicenna said that he had read the *Metaphysics* of Aristotle forty times without understanding it), but which is of the greatest importance for an understanding of the philosophy of Aristotle, and which has had a tremendous influence on the subsequent thought of Europe. [2] But though all men desire to know, there are different degrees of knowledge. For example, the man of *mere experience,* as Aristotle calls him, may know that a certain medicine had done good to X when he was ill, but without knowing the reason for this, whereas the man of *art* knows the reason, e.g. he knows that X was suffering from fever, and that the medicine in question has a certain property which abates fever. He knows a universal, for he knows that the medicine will tend to cure all who suffer from that complaint. Art, then, aims at production of some kind, but this is not Wisdom in Aristotle's view, for the highest Wisdom does not aim at producing anything or securing some effect—it is not utilitarian—but at apprehending the first principles of Reality, i.e. at knowledge for its own sake. Aristotle places the man who seeks for knowledge for its own sake above him who seeks for knowledge of some particular kind with a view to the attainment of some practical effect. In other words, that science stands higher which is desirable for its own sake and not merely with a view to its results.

This science, which is desirable for its own sake, is the science of first principles or first causes, a science which took its rise in wonder. Men began to wonder at things, to desire to know the explanation of the things they saw, and so philosophy arose out of the desire of understanding, and not on account of any utility that knowledge might possess. This science, then, is of all sciences to be called free or liberal, for, like a free man, it exists for its own sake and not for the sake of someone else. Metaphysics is thus, according to Aristotle, Wisdom *par excellence*, and the philosopher or lover of Wisdom is he who desires knowledge about the ultimate cause and nature of Reality, and desires that knowledge for its own sake. Aristotle is therefore a "dogmatist" in the sense that he supposes that such knowledge is attainable, though he is not of course a dogmatist in the sense of advancing theories without any attempt to prove them.

Wisdom, therefore, deals with the first principles and causes of things, and so is universal knowledge in the highest degree. This means that it is the science which is furthest removed from the senses, the most abstract science, and so is the hardest of the sciences as involving the greatest effort of thought. "Sense-perception is common to all and therefore easy and no mark of Wisdom." [3] But, though it is the most abstract of the sciences, it is, in Aristotle's view, the most *exact* of the sciences, "for those which involve fewer principles are more exact than those which involve additional principles, e.g. arithmetic than geometry." [4] Moreover, this science is in itself the most knowable, since it deals with the first principles of all things, and these principles are in themselves more truly knowable than their applications (for these depend on the first principles, and not vice versa), though it does not follow that they are the most knowable in regard *to us*, since we necessarily start with the things of sense and it requires a considerable effort of rational abstraction to proceed from what is directly known to us, sense-objects, to their ultimate principles.

2. The causes with which Wisdom or philosophy deals are enumerated in the *Physics* and are four in number: (i) the substance or essence of a thing; (ii) the matter or subject; (iii) the source of motion or the efficient cause; and (iv) the final cause or good. In the first book of the *Metaphysics* Aristotle investigates the views of his predecessors, in order, he says, to see if they discussed any other kind of cause

besides the four he has enumerated. In this way he is led
to give a brief sketch of the history of Greek philosophy up
to his time, but he is not concerned to catalogue all their
opinions, whether relevant or irrelevant to his purpose, for
he wishes to trace the evolution of the notion of the four
causes, and the net result of his investigation is the conclusion, not only that no philosopher has discovered any
other kind of cause, but that no philosopher before himself
has enumerated the four causes in a satisfactory manner.
Aristotle, like Hegel, regarded previous philosophy as leading up to his own position; there is none of the parapher-
nalia of the dialectic in Aristotle, of course, but there is the
same tendency to regard his own philosophy as a synthesis
on a higher plane of the thought of his predecessors. There
is certainly some truth in Aristotle's contention, yet it is by
no means completely true, and he is sometimes far from
just to his predecessors.

Thales and the early Greek philosophers busied themselves
with the material cause, trying to discover the ultimate
substratum of things, the principle that is neither generated
nor destroyed, but from which particular objects arise and
into which they pass away. In this way arose, e.g. the
philosophies of Thales, Anaximenes, Heraclitus, who posited
one material cause, or Empedocles, who postulated four
elements. But even if elements are generated from one
material cause, why does this happen, what is the source
of the movement whereby objects are generated and destroyed? There must be some cause of the becoming in the
world, even the very facts themselves must in the end impel
the thinker to investigate a type of cause other than the
material cause. Attempted answers to this difficulty we find in
the philosophies of Empedocles and Anaxagoras. The latter
saw that no material element can be the reason why objects manifest beauty and goodness, and so he asserted the
activity of Mind in the material world, standing out like
a sober man in contrast with the random talk of his predecessors.[5] All the same, he uses Mind only as a *deus ex
machina* to explain the formation of the world, and drags
it in when he is at a loss for any other explanation: when
another explanation is at hand, he simply leaves Mind out.[6]
In other words, Anaxagoras was accused by Aristotle of
using Mind simply as a cloak for ignorance. Empedocles,
indeed, postulated two active principles, Friendship and
Strife, but he used them neither sufficiently nor consistently.[7]

These philosophers, therefore, had succeeded in distinguishing two of Aristotle's four causes, the material cause and the source of movement; but they had not worked out their conceptions systematically or elaborated any consistent and scientific philosophy.

After the philosophy of the Pythagoreans, who cannot be said to have contributed very much, came the philosophy of Plato, who evolved the doctrine of the Forms, but placed the Forms, which are the cause of the essence of things (and so, in a sense, the cause), apart from the things of which they are the essence. Thus Plato, according to Aristotle, used only two causes, "that of the essence and the material cause." [8] As to the final cause, this was not explicitly, or at least not satisfactorily, treated by previous philosophers, but only by the way or incidentally.[9] As a matter of fact, Aristotle is not altogether just to Plato, since the latter, in the *Timaeus*, introduces the concept of the Demiurge who serves as an efficient cause, and also makes use of the star-gods, besides maintaining a doctrine of finality, for the final cause of becoming is the realisation (in the sense of imitation) of the Good. Nevertheless, it is true that Plato, through the *chorismos*, was debarred from making the realisation of its immanent form or essence the final cause of the concrete substance.

3. After stating some of the main problems of philosophy in Book 3 (B) of the *Metaphysics*, Aristotle declares at the beginning of Book 4 (Γ) that metaphysical science is concerned with being as such, is the study of being *qua* being. The special sciences isolate a particular sphere of being, and consider the attributes of being in that sphere; but the metaphysician does not consider being of this or that particular characteristic, e.g. as living or as quantitative, but rather being itself and its essential attributes as being. Now, to say that something is, is also to say that it is *one*: unity, therefore, is an essential attribute of being, and just as being itself is found in all the categories, so unity is found in all the categories. As to goodness, Aristotle remarks in the *Ethics* (*E.N.* 1096) that it also is applicable in all the categories. Unity and goodness are, therefore, transcendental attributes of being, to use the phraseology of the Scholastic philosophers, inasmuch as, applicable in all the categories, they are not confined to any one category and do not constitute genera. If the definition of man is "rational animal," animal is the genus, rational the specific difference;

but one cannot predicate animality of rationality, the genus of the specific difference, though one can predicate being of both. Being, therefore, cannot be a genus, and the same holds good of unity and goodness.

The term "being," however, is not predicated of all existent things in precisely the same sense, for a substance is, possesses being, in a way that a quality, for instance, which is an affection of substance, cannot be said to be. With what category of being, then, is metaphysics especially concerned? With that of substance, which is primary, since all things are either substances or affections of substances. But there are or may be different kinds of substances, and with which kind does first philosophy or metaphysics deal? Aristotle answers that, if there is an unchangeable substance, then metaphysics studies unchangeable substance, since it is concerned with being *qua* being, and the true nature of being is shown in that which is unchangeable and self-existent, rather than in that which is subject to change. That there is at least one such unchangeable being which causes motion while remaining itself unmoved, is shown by the impossibility of an infinite series of existent sources of movement, and this motionless substance, comprising the full nature of being, will have the character of the divine, so that first philosophy is rightly to be called theology. Mathematics is a theoretical science indeed and deals with motionless objects, but these objects, *though considered in separation from matter,* do not exist separately: physics deals with things that are both inseparable from matter and are subject to movement: it is only metaphysics that treats of that which both exists in separation from matter and is motionless.[10]

(In Book E of the *Metaphysics* Aristotle simply divides substances into changeable and unchangeable substances, but in Book Λ he distinguishes three kinds of substances, (i) sensible and perishable, (ii) sensible and eternal, i.e. the heavenly bodies, (iii) non-sensible and eternal.)

Metaphysical science is, therefore, concerned with being, and it studies being primarily in the category of substance, not "accidental being," which is the object of no science,[11] nor being as truth, since truth and falsity exist in the judgment, not in things.[12] (It also establishes the first principles or axioms, especially the principle of contradiction, which, though not of course deducible, is the ultimate principle governing all being and all knowledge.[13]) But, if metaphysics studies substance, non-sensible substance, it is ob-

viously of importance to determine what non-sensible substances there are. Are the objects of mathematics substances,
or universals, or the transcendental ideas of being and unity?
No, replies Aristotle, they are not: hence his polemic against
the Platonic theory of ideas, of which a summary will now
be given.

4. (i) The argument for Plato's theory that it makes scientific knowledge possible and explains it, proves, says
Aristotle, that the universal is real and no mere mental
fiction; but it does not prove that the universal has a sub-
sistence apart from individual things. And, indeed, on Plato's
theory, strictly applied, there should be Ideas of negations
and relations. For if, whenever we conceive a common concept in relation to a plurality of objects, it is necessary to
postulate a Form, then it follows that there must be Forms
even of negations and relations. "Of the ways in which we
prove that the Forms exist, none is convincing, for from some
no inference necessarily follows, and from some it follows
that there are Forms of things of which we think there are
no Forms." [14]

(ii) The doctrine of Ideas or Forms is *useless*.

(*a*) According to Aristotle, the Forms are only a purpose-
less doubling of visible things. They are supposed to explain
why the multitude of things in the world exist. But it does
not help simply to suppose the existence of another multitude of things, as Plato does. Plato is like a man who, unable
to count with a small number, thinks that he will find it
easier to do so if he doubles the number. [15]

(*b*) The Forms are useless for our knowledge of things.
"They help in no wise towards the knowledge of the other
things (for they are not even the substance of these, else
they would have been in them. [16])" This seems to be an
expression of Aristotle's interest in the visible universe, whereas Plato was not really concerned with the things of this
world for their own sake, but as stepping-stones to the
Forms; though, by getting to know the Types, at which
phenomena are, as it were, aiming or which they are trying
to realise, we can, inasmuch as we are efficient causes, contribute to this approximate realisation. To this consideration
Plato attached very considerable importance. For example,
by coming to know the ideal Type of the State, to which
actual States are, in a greater or less degree, approximations,
we are enabled to contribute to the elevation of the actual
State—for we know the goal.

(c) The Forms are useless when it comes to explaining the movement of things. Even if things exist in virtue of the Forms, how do the latter account for the movement of things and for their coming-to-be and passing-away? "Above all one might discuss the question what on earth the Forms contribute to sensible things, either to those that are eternal or to those that come into being and cease to be." [17] The Forms are motionless, and the objects of this world, if they are copies of the Forms, should be motionless too; or, if they move, as they do, whence their motion?

Aristotle would not seem to be altogether just to Plato in pursuing this line of criticism, since Plato fully realised that the Forms are not moving causes, and it was precisely on this account that he introduced the concept of the Demiurge. The latter may be a more or less mythological figure, but, however that may be, it is clear that Plato never considered the Forms to be principles of motion and that he made an attempt to account for the dynamism of the world on other lines.

(d) The Forms are supposed to explain sensible objects. But they will themselves be sensible: the Ideal Man, for instance, will be sensible, like Socrates. The Forms will resemble the anthropomorphic gods: the latter were only eternal men, and so the Forms are only "eternal sensibles." [18]

This is not a very telling criticism. If the Ideal Man is conceived as being a replica of concrete man on the ideal plane, in the common sense of the word "ideal," as being actual man raised to the highest pitch of development, then of course Ideal Man will be sensible. But is it at all likely that Plato himself meant anything of this kind? Even if he may have implied this by the phrases he used on certain occasions, such an extravagant notion is by no means essential to the Platonic theory of Forms. The Forms are subsistent concepts or Ideal Types, and so the subsistent concept of Man will contain the idea of corporeality, for instance, but there is no reason why it should itself be corporeal: in fact, corporeality and sensibility are *ex hypothesi* excluded when it is postulated that the Ideal Man means an *Idea*. Does anybody suppose that when later Platonists placed the Idea of man in the Divine Mind, they were positing an actual concrete man in God's Mind? The objection seems really to be a debating point on Aristotle's part, i.e. so far as it is supposed to touch Plato personally, and that not a particularly fair one. It would be conclusive against a very gross rendering of the theory of Forms; but it is useless to read into Plato the most gross and crude interpretation possible.

(iii) The theory of Ideas or Forms is an *impossible* theory. (*a*) "It must be held to be impossible that the substance, and that of which it is the substance, should exist apart; how, therefore, can the Ideas, being the substance of things, exist apart?" [19] The Forms contain the essence and inner reality of sensible objects; but how can objects which exist apart from sensibles contain the essence of those sensibles? In any case, what is the relation between them? Plato tries to explain the relation by the use of terms such as "participation" and "imitation," but Aristotle retorts that "to say that they (i.e. sensible things) are patterns and the other things share in them, is to use empty words and poetical metaphors." [20]

This criticism would certainly be a very serious one if separation meant local separation. But does separation, in the case of the Forms, necessarily imply local separation? Does it not rather mean independence? Literal local separation would be impossible if the Forms are to be looked on as subsistent concepts or Ideas. It seems that Aristotle is arguing from the point of view of his own theory, according to which the form is the immanent essence of the sensible object. He argues that participation can mean nothing, unless it means that there is a real immanent form, co-constitutive of the object with matter—a conception not admitted by Plato. Aristotle rightly points out the inadequacy of the Platonic theory; but, in rejecting Platonic exemplarism, he also betrays the inadequacy of his own (Aristotle's) theory, in that he provides no real transcendental ground for the fixity of essences.

(*b*) "But, further, all things cannot come from the Forms in any of the usual senses of 'from'." [21] Here Aristotle again touches on the question of the relation of the Forms to that of which they are said to be Forms, and it is in this connection that he objects that the explanatory phrases used by Plato are merely poetical metaphors. This is of course one of the crucial points of the Platonic theory, and Plato himself seems to have felt the inadequacy of the attempted explanation. He cannot be said to have cleared up in any satisfactory manner what he actually meant by the metaphors he used and what the relation of sensible objects to the Forms really is. But it is curious that Aristotle, in his

treatment of the Platonic theory in the *Metaphysics,* neglects
the Demiurge altogether. One might suggest as a reason for
this neglect, that the ultimate cause of motion in the world
was, for Aristotle, a *Final* Cause. The notion of a super-ter-
restrial *efficient* Cause was for him unacceptable.

(*c*) The Forms will be individual objects like those other
objects of which they are the Forms, whereas they should
be not individuals but *universals*. The Ideal Man, for instance,
will be an individual like Socrates. Further, on the supposition that when there is a plurality of objects possessing a
common name, there must be an eternal pattern or Form,
we shall have to posit a third man (τρίτος ἄνθρωπος),
whom not only Socrates imitates, but also the Ideal Man.
The reason is that Socrates and the Ideal Man have a
nature in common, therefore there must be a subsistent universal beyond them. But in this case the difficulty will always
recur and we shall proceed to infinity.[22]

This criticism of Aristotle would hold good if Plato held
that the Forms are things. But did he? If he held them to
be subsistent concepts, they do not turn into individual
objects in the same sense that Socrates is an individual object. Of course they are individual concepts, but there are
signs that Plato was trying to systematise the whole world
of concepts or Ideas, and that he envisaged them as forming
one articulated system—the rational structure of the world,
as we might say, that the world, to speak metaphorically,
is always trying to embody, but which it cannot fully embody, owing to the contingency which is inevitable in all
material things. (We are reminded of Hegel's doctrine of the
universal Categories in relation to the contingent objects of
Nature.)

(iv) Against the theory that the Forms are Numbers.

(*a*) It scarcely seems necessary to treat of Aristotle's objections and criticisms in detail, since the Form-Number
theory was perhaps an unfortunate adventure on Plato's part.
As Aristotle remarks, "mathematics has come to be the whole
of philosophy for modern thinkers, though they say that it
should be studied for the sake of other things."[23]

For Aristotle's general treatment of number and pertinent
questions, one should see *Metaphysics* A, 991 b 9 to
993 a 10 and M and N.

(*b*) If the Forms are Numbers, how can they be causes?[24]
If it is because existing things are other numbers (e.g. "one
number is man, another is Socrates, another Callias"), then

why "are the one set of numbers causes of the other set"?
If it is meant that Callias is a numerical ratio of his elements,
then his Idea will also be a numerical ratio of elements, and
so neither will be, properly speaking, a number. (Of course,
for Plato the Forms were exemplary causes, but not efficient
causes.)

(c) How can there be two kinds of numbers?[25] If besides
the Form-numbers it is also necessary to posit another kind
of numbers, which are the mathematical objects, then what is
the basis of differentiation between the two kinds of numbers? We only know one kind of numbers, thinks Aristotle,
and that is the kind of numbers with which the mathema-
tician deals.

(d) But whether there are two classes of numbers, i.e.
Forms and mathematical objects (Plato) or simply one
class, i.e. mathematical numbers existing, however, apart
from sensible objects (Speusippus), Aristotle objects (i) that
if the Forms are numbers, then they cannot be unique, since
the elements of which they are composed are the same (as
a matter of fact, the Forms were not supposed to be
unique in the sense that they were without inner relation
to one another); and (ii) that the objects of mathematics
"cannot in any way exist separately." [26] One reason for the
latter assertion is that a *processus in infinitum* will be un-
avoidable if we accept the separate existence of mathematical objects, e.g. there must be separate solids corresponding to the sensible solids, and separate planes and lines
corresponding to the sensible planes and lines. But there
must also be other separate planes and lines corresponding
to the planes and lines of the separate solid. Now, "the
accumulation becomes absurd, for we find ourselves with
one set of solids apart from the sensible solids; three sets
of planes apart from the sensible planes—those which exist
apart from the sensible planes, and those in the mathematical
solids, and those which exist apart from those in the mathematical solids; four sets of lines; and five sets of points. With
which of these, then, will the mathematical sciences deal?" [27]

(e) If the substance of things is mathematical, then what
is the source of movement? "If the great and the small are to
be movement, evidently the Forms will be moved; but if they
are not, whence did movement come? If we cannot answer
this, the whole study of Nature has been annihilated." [28] (As
already remarked, Plato tried to provide a source of movement other than the Forms themselves, which are motionless.)

(v) Some of what Aristotle has to say on the subject of Plato's mathematical objects and the Form-numbers implies a rather crude interpretation of Platonic doctrine, as though for example Plato imagined that mathematical objects or the Forms are things. Moreover, Aristotle has himself to meet the great difficulty against the abstraction theory of mathematics (for Aristotle the geometrician, for instance, considers, not separate mathematical objects but sensible things abstractly, i.e. according to one particular point of view), namely, that we cannot abstract e.g. the perfect circle from nature, since there is no perfect circle in nature which we could abstract, while on the other hand it is difficult to see how we could form the idea of a perfect circle by "correcting" the imperfect circles of nature, when we should not know that the circles of nature *were* imperfect unless we *previously* knew what a perfect circle was. To this Aristotle might answer either that, though perfect circles are not given really, i.e. as regards measurement, in nature, yet they are given *quoad visum,* and that this is sufficient for the abstraction of the idea of the perfect circle, or that mathematical figures and axioms are more or less arbitrary hypotheses, so that the cardinal requisite in mathematics is to be consistent and logical, without its being necessary to suppose that e.g. every type of geometry will fit the "real" world, or, on the other hand, that it has an ideal world corresponding to it, of which it is the mental reflection or perception.

In general, we would point out that we cannot well dispense with either Plato or Aristotle, but that the truth in both of them has to be combined. This the Neo-Platonists attempted to do. For example, Plato posited the Forms as Exemplary Causes: the later Platonists placed them in God. With due qualifications, this is the correct view, for the Divine Essence is the ultimate Exemplar of all creatures.[29] On the other hand, Plato assumes that we have, or can have, direct knowledge of the Forms. Now, we certainly have not got a direct knowledge of the Divine Ideas, as Malebranche supposed we have. We have direct knowledge only of the expressed universal, and this expressed universal exists externally, i.e. as universal, only in the particulars. We have therefore the external exemplary Idea in God, the foundation in the particular object, i.e. its specific essence, and the abstract universal in our minds. From this point of view Aristotle's criticism of Plato would seem to be justified, for the universal, of which we have direct knowledge, simply is the nature of the individual thing. It would appear, therefore, that we require both Plato and Aristotle in order to form anything like a complete philosophical view. Plato's Demiurge must be identified with the Aristotelian νόησις νοήσεως, the eternal Forms must be referred to God, and Aristotle's doctrine of the concrete universal must be accepted, together with the Aristotelian doctrine of abstraction. Neither of these two great thinkers can be accepted precisely as he stands, and while it is right to value Aristotle's criticism of the Platonic theory of Forms, it is a great mistake to suppose that that theory was a mass of crude absurdity, or that it can be dispensed with altogether. The Augustinian philosophy was, through Neo-Platonism, strongly impregnated with the thought of Plato.

Although it has been admitted that Aristotle's fundamental criticism of the Platonic theory of Forms, that the theory involves the *chorismos,* is justified, and that the Platonic theory cannot stand by itself but needs to be supplemented by Aristotle's doctrine of the immanent Form (which we consider abstractly in its universality), we have not given an altogether sympathetic treatment of Aristotle's criticisms. "How, then," it might be asked, "can you say that Aristotle's statements concerning what Plato taught must be taken seriously? If Aristotle's account of what Plato taught is correct, then his criticisms of the Platonic theory were perfectly justified, while if his criticisms misrepresent the Platonic theory, then he either deliberately misrepresented that theory or he did not understand it."

First of all, it must be admitted that Aristotle was attacking, in his own mind at least, the theory of Plato himself, and not merely that of some Platonists as distinct from Plato: a careful reading of the *Metaphysics* hardly permits any other supposition. Secondly, it must be admitted that Aristotle, though primarily perhaps attacking the form of the Platonic theory that was taught in the Academy, was perfectly well acquainted with the content of the published dialogues, and knew that some of his own criticisms had already been raised in the *Parmenides.* Thirdly, there is no real reason for supposing that the Platonic theory as taught in the Academy involved a retraction or rejection of the theory developed in the published works of Plato: if this had been the case, we might reasonably have expected Aristotle to make some reference to the fact; while conversely, if he makes no reference to such a change of view on Plato's part, we have no right to affirm such a change without better evidence than can be offered. The mathematical form of the theory was probably meant to be a supplement to the theory, or, rather, a speculative justification and elucidation of it, an "esoteric" version of it (if one may use a word with somewhat unfortunate associations, without at the same time wishing to imply that the mathematical version was *another* and *different* theory). Aristotle, therefore, was attacking, under both its aspects, what he regarded as the *Platonic* theory of Ideas. (It must, however, be remembered that the *Metaphysics* is not a continuous book, written for publication, and that we cannot assume without more ado that all the objections raised against the Platonic theory in Aristotle's lectures were regarded with equal seriousness by Aristotle himself. A man may say things in his lectures that he would not say, in the same form at least, in a work intended for publication.)

It would seem, then, that we are faced by an awkward dilemma. Either Plato, in spite of the difficulties that he himself saw and proposed in the *Parmenides,* held the theory in the exact form under which it was attacked by Aristotle (in which case Plato appears in a foolish light), or Aristotle grossly misunderstood the Platonic theory (in which case it is Aristotle who appears as the fool). Now, we are not willing to admit that either Plato or Aristotle was a fool, and any treatment of the problem that necessarily involves either supposition is to our mind thereby ruled out of court. That Plato on the one hand never really solved satisfactorily the problem of the *chorismos,* and that Aristotle on the other hand was not perfectly *au fait* with contemporary higher mathematics, does not show either of them to be a fool and can easily be admitted; but this admission obviously does not dispose of the difficulty involved by Aristotle's criticisms, that the Platonic theory is therein depicted as excessively naïve, and that Aristotle makes little reference to the dialogues and is silent as to the Demiurge. But perhaps a way out of the difficulty can be found. Aristotle, well aware that Plato had not satisfactorily solved the problem of the *chorismos,* had broken away from his Master's theory and adopted a quite different standpoint. When he regarded the theory *from that standpoint,* it could not but appear to him as extravagant and bizarre under any form: he might, therefore, have easily considered himself justified in attempting to put this bizarre character of the theory in an exaggerated light for polemical purposes. One might cite as a parallel the case of Hegel. To one who believes that the Hegelian system is a mere intellectual *tour de force* or an *extravaganza*, nothing is easier than to overstate and even to misrepresent the undoubtedly weak elements in that system for polemical purposes, even though the critic, believing the system to be fundamentally false, could not be justly accused of deliberate misrepresentation. We would wish that the critic had acted otherwise in the interests of historical accuracy, but we could hardly dub him an imbecile because he had chosen to overdo the rôle of critic. While refusing to believe that Aristotle felt towards Plato any of the animus that Schelling and Schopenhauer felt towards Hegel, I would suggest that Aristotle overdid the rôle of critic and exaggerated weak points in a theory that he considered false. As to his silence concerning the Demiurge, that can be explained, in part at least, if we remember that Aristotle was criticising Plato from his own (i.e. Aristotle's) standpoint, and that the conception of the Demiurge was unacceptable to him: he did not take it seriously. If, in addition, Aristotle had reason to believe that the actual Demiurge of the *Timaeus* was largely a symbolic figure, and *if* Plato never worked out thoroughly, even in the Academy, the precise nature or status of Mind or Soul, then it is not so difficult to understand how Aristotle, who did not believe in any formation of the world *a tergo*, could neglect the figure of the Demiurge altogether in his criticism of the Ideal Theory. He may have been unjustified in neglecting it to the extent that he did, but the foregoing considerations may make it easier to understand how he could do so. The suggestions we have made may not be altogether satisfactory, and no doubt remain open to serious criticism, but they have at least this advantage, that they make it possible for us to escape from the dilemma of holding either Plato or Aristotle to have been a fool. And after all, Aristotle's root criticism of Plato's theory is perfectly justified, for by using the terms "imitation" and "participation," Plato clearly implies that there is some formal element, some principle of comparative stability, in material things, while on the other hand, by failing to provide a theory of substantial form, he failed to explain this immanent formal element. Aristotle rightly provided this element, but, seeing (rightly again) that the Platonic Forms, being "separate," *could not* account for this element, he unfortunately went too far by rejecting the Platonic exemplarism altogether: looking on the Platonic theory from the point of view of a *biologist* primarily (with a biologist's insistence on the immanent entelechy) and from the theological standpoint envisaged in the *Metaphysics* (xii), he had no use for Platonic exemplarism, Platonic mathematicism and the Platonic Demiurge. Thus, when regarded in the light of his own system, Aristotle's attitude towards Plato's theory is quite understandable.

5. But although Aristotle passes an adverse criticism on the Platonic theory of separate Ideas or Forms, he is in full agreement with Plato that the universal is not merely a subjective concept or a mode of oral expression (*universale post rem*), for to the universal in the mind there corresponds the specific essence in the object, though this essence does not exist in any state of separation *extra mentem:* it is separated only in the mind and through the mind's activity. Aristotle was convinced, as Plato was, that the universal is the object of science: it follows, then, that if the universal is in no way real, if it has no objective reality whatsoever, there is no scientific knowledge, for science does not deal with the individual as such. The universal is real, it has reality not only in the mind but also in the things, though the existence in the thing does not entail that formal universality that it has in the mind. Individuals belonging to the same species are real substances, but they do not partake in an objective universal that is numerically the same in all members of the class. This specific essence is numerically different in each individual of the class, but, on the other hand, it is specifically the same in all the individuals of the class (i.e. they are all alike in species), and this objective similarity is the real foundation for the abstract universal, which has numerical identity in the mind and can be predicated of all the members of the class indifferently. Plato and Aristotle are, then, at one as to the character of true science, namely, that it is directed to the universal element in things, i.e. to the specific similarity. The scientist is not concerned with individual bits of gold as individual, but with the essence of gold, with that specific similarity which is found in all individual bits of gold, i.e. supposing that gold is a species. "Socrates gave the impulse to this theory" (i.e. the Platonic theory) "by means of his definitions, but he did not separate them" (i.e. the universals) "from the particulars; and in this he thought rightly in not separating them. This is plain from

the results, for without the universal it is not possible to get knowledge, but the separation is the cause of the objections that arise with regard to the Ideas." [30] *Strictly* speaking, therefore, there is no objective Universal for Aristotle, but there is an objective foundation in things for the subjective universal in the mind. The universal "horse" is a subjective concept, but it has an objective foundation in the substantial forms that inform particular horses.

The individuals are truly substance (οὐσία). Are the universals substances, i.e. is the specific element, the formal principle, that which places the individual in its specific class, to be called substance? No, says Aristotle, except in a secondary and derived sense. It is the individual alone which is the subject of predication and is itself not predicated of others. The species may, however, be called substance in a secondary sense and it has a claim to this title, since the essential element has a higher reality than the individual *qua* individual and is the object of science. Aristotle, therefore, terms the individuals πρῶται οὐσίαι and the species δεύτεραι οὐσίαι.[31] In this way Aristotle has brought upon himself the charge of contradiction. The alleged contradiction consists in this, that if only the individual is truly substance and if science is concerned with the οὐσία, it necessarily follows that the individual is the true object of science, whereas Aristotle teaches in point of fact the very opposite, namely, that science is not concerned with the individual as such but with the universal. In other words, Aristotle teaches that science is concerned with substance and that the individual is substance in the primary sense, while on the other hand he teaches that the universal is of superior quality and is the true object of science, which would seem to be the exact opposite of what he should teach on his premisses.

In answer to this accusation of self-contradiction, we might answer two things. (i) There is no real contradiction, if we consider what Aristotle *means*. When he says that the individual is truly substance and that it alone is truly substance, he means to reject Plato's doctrine that the universal is a separate substance on its own, but he does not mean to deny that the universal, in the sense of the formal or specific element in things, is real. The individual is truly substance, but that which makes it a substance of this or that kind, that which is the chief element in the thing and is the object of science, is the universal element, the form of the thing, which the mind abstracts and conceives in formal

universality. So when he says that the universal is the object
of science he is not contradicting himself, for he has not
denied that the universal has some objective reality but only
that it has a separate existence. It is real in the individual:
it is not transcendent, if considered in its objective reality,
but immanent, the concrete universal. The individual alone
is substance in the true sense, but the individual sensible
thing is compound, and the intellect, in scientific knowledge,
goes straight to the universal element, which is really there,
though existing only concretely, *as an element of the individual*. Aristotle was no doubt influenced by the fact that
individuals perish, while the species persists. Thus individual
horses perish, whereas the nature of horses remains the same
(specifically, though not numerically) in the succession of
horses. It is the nature of horses that the scientist considers,
and not merely Black Beauty or any other individual horse.
(ii) Nor does Aristotle really contradict himself even in
terminology, for he expressly distinguishes the two meanings
of οὐσία or substance. Substance in the primary sense is the
individual substance, composed of matter *and* form: substance in the secondary sense is the formal element or
specific essence that corresponds to the universal concept.
πρῶται οὐσίαι are objects which are not predicated of
another, but of which something else (i.e. accident or
τὸ συμβεβηκός) is predicated. Substances in the secondary
sense (δεύτεραι οὐσίαι) are the nature, in the sense of
specific essence, that which corresponds to the universal
concept ἡ κατὰ τὸν λόγον οὐσία. Moreover, when Aristotle speaks of primary and secondary substances, he does
not mean primary and secondary in nature, dignity, or time,
but primary and secondary in regard to us.[32]

The individual substance, οὐσία αἰσθητή, is a compound
(σύνολον) of the subject or substratum (ὑποκείμενον or
ὕλη) and the essence of form. To the individual substance
belong the conditions (πάθη) and the relations (πρός τι),
which are distinguished according to the nine accidental
categories. The universal becomes pre-eminently the object
of science, because it is the essential element and so has
reality in a higher sense than what is *merely* particular. The
universal certainly exists only in the particular, but from this
it follows, not that we are unable to make the universal
an object of science in its universality, but that we cannot
apprehend the universal except through apprehension of the
individual.

Is it true, as Aristotle thinks it is true, that universals are
necessary for science? (i) If by science is meant knowledge
of the universal, the answer is obvious. (ii) If by science is
meant Wisdom in the sense in which Aristotle uses the term,
then it is perfectly true to say that the philosopher is not
concerned with the particular as particular. If, for example,
the philosopher is arguing about contingent being, he is not
thinking of this or that particular contingent being as such,
but with contingent being in its essential nature, even if he
uses particular contingent beings as an illustration. If he
were confined to the particular contingent beings that have
actually been experienced, either by himself or by others
whose testimony he could trust, then his conclusion would
be limited to those particular beings, whereas he desires as
philosopher to reach a universal conclusion which will apply
to all possible contingent beings. (iii) If by science is meant
"science" in the sense in which we use the term generally to-
day, then we must say that, although knowledge of the true
universal essence of a class of beings would certainly be
desirable and remains the ideal, it is hardly *necessary*. For
example, botanists can get along very well in their classification of plants without knowing the essential definition of
the plants in question. It is enough for them if they can
find phenomena which will suffice to delimit and define a
species, irrespective of whether the real specific essence is
thereby defined or not. It is significant that when Scholastic
philosophers wish to give a definition which is representative
they so often say "Man is a rational animal." They would
scarcely take it upon themselves to give an essential definition of the cow or the buttercup. We frequently have to
be content with what we might call the "nominal" essence as
opposed to the real essence. Yet even in this case knowledge of *some* universal characteristics is necessary. For even
if you cannot assign the difference of some species, yet you
have got to define it, if you define it at all, in function of
some universal characteristics possessed by the whole class.
Suppose that "Rational Animal" is the real definition of man.
Now, if you could not attain this definition but had to
describe man as e.g. a featherless significantly-speaking bi-
ped, you imply a knowledge of the universals "featherless-
ness" and "significantly-speaking." So even classification or
description by accidental characteristics would seem to imply
a discerning of the universal in some way, for one discerns
the type even if one cannot adequately define it. It is as

though one had a dim realisation of the universal, but could not adequately define or grasp it clearly. Universal definition, in the sense of real essential definition, would thus remain the ideal at any rate, even if in practice empirical science can get along without attaining the ideal, and Aristotle is of course speaking of science in its ideal type. He would never agree with the empiricist and nominalist views of e.g. J. S. Mill, although he would doubtless admit that we often have to content ourselves with description instead of true definition.

6. Aristotle, therefore, refuses to admit that the objects of mathematics or universals are substances. In the *Metaphysics*, where he wishes to refute the Platonic theory, he simply denies flatly that they are substances, though in the *Categories*, as we have seen, he called them secondary substances or substances in a secondary and derived sense. In any case, it is the individual that is truly substance, and only the individual. There is, however, this further point to be observed. According to Aristotle,[33] the sensible individuals cannot be defined owing to the material element in them, which renders them perishable and makes them obscure to our knowledge. On the other hand, substance is primarily the definable essence or form of a thing, the principle in virtue of which the material element is some definite concrete object.[34] It follows from this that substance is primarily form which is, in itself, immaterial, so that if Aristotle begins by asserting that individual sensible objects are substances, the course of his thought carries him on towards the view that pure form alone is truly and primarily substance. But the only forms that are really independent of matter are God, the Intelligences of the spheres and the active intellect in man, so that it is these forms which are primarily substance. If metaphysics studies substance, then, it is easily seen that it is equivalent to "theology." It is certainly not unreasonable to discern here the influence of Platonism, since, in spite of his rejection of the Platonic theory of Ideas, Aristotle evidently continued to look on matter as the element which is impenetrable to thought and on pure form as the intelligible. It is not suggested that Aristotle was wrong in thinking this, but, right or wrong, it is clearly a legacy of Platonism.

7. Aristotle, as we have seen, gives four principles: ὕγρ ῃ or matter, τὸ εἶδος or the form, τὸ ὅθεν ἡ κίνησις—the source of movement or the efficient cause, and τὸ οὖ ἕνεκα

or the final cause. Change or motion (i.e. motion in the general sense of the term, which includes every passage from a *terminus a quo* to a *terminus ad quem,* such as the change of the colour of a leaf from green to brown) is a fact in the world, in spite of the dismissal of change as illusory by Parmenides, and Aristotle considered this fact of change. He saw that several factors are involved, to each of which justice must be done. There must, for example, be a substratum of change, for in every case of change which we observe there is something that changes. The oak comes from the acorn and the bed from the wood: there is something which is changed, which receives a new determination. First of all, it is in potentiality (δύναμις) to this new determination; then under the action of some efficient cause (τὸ ὅθεν ἡ κίνησις) it receives a new actualisation (ἐντελέχεια). The marble upon which the sculptor works is in potency to receiving the new form or determination which the sculptor gives it, namely, the form of the statue.

Now, when the marble receives the form of the statue, it is indeed changed, but this change is only accidental, in the sense that the substance is still marble, but the shape or figure is different. In some cases, however, the substance by no means remains the same: thus when the cow eats grass, the grass is assimilated in the process of digestion and takes on a new substantial form. And since it would seem that, absolutely speaking, anything might ultimately change into anything else, it would appear that there is an ultimate substratum which has no definite characteristics of its own, but is simply potentiality as such. This is what Aristotle means by ἡ πρώτη ἑκάστῳ ὑποκειμένη ὕλη[35]— the *materia prima* of the Scholastics—which is found in all material things and is the ultimate basis of change. Aristotle is, of course, perfectly aware that no efficient agent ever acts directly on prime matter as such: it is always some definite thing, some already actualised substratum, that is acted upon. For example, the sculptor works upon the marble; this is his matter, the substratum of the change which he initiates: he does not act upon prime matter as such. Similarly, it is grass which becomes cow, and not prime matter as such. This means that prime matter never exists precisely as such—as bare prime matter, we might say—but always exists in conjunction with form, which is the formal or characterising factor. In the sense that prime matter cannot exist by itself, apart from all form, it is only

logically distinguishable from form; but in the sense that
it is a real element in the material object, and the ultimate
basis of the real changes that it undergoes, it is really
distinguishable from form. We should not, therefore, say
that prime matter is the simplest body in the material universe, for it is not a body at all, but an element of body,
even of the simplest body. Aristotle teaches in the *Physics*[36]
that the apparently simplest bodies of the material sublunary
world, the four elements, earth, air, fire and water, themselves contain contraries and can be transmuted into one
another. But if they can change, then they presuppose composition of potentiality and act. Air, for instance, *is* air, but
can become fire. It has the form or *actuality* of air, but has
also the *potentiality* of becoming fire. But it is logically necessary to presuppose, prior to the potentiality of becoming fire
or any other particular and definite kind of thing, a potentiality of becoming at all, i.e. a bare potentiality.

Now, change is the development of a previously existing
body, not precisely as that definite body, but as a body
capable of becoming something else, though as not yet that
something else. It is the actualisation of a potentiality; but
a potentiality involves an actual being, which is not yet that
which it could be. Steam, for example, does not come
from nothing, it comes from water. But it does not come
from water precisely as water: water precisely as water is
water and nothing else. Steam comes from water, which
could be steam and "demands" to be steam, having been
heated to a certain temperature, but is not yet steam, which
is as yet "deprived" of the form of steam—not merely in
the sense that it has not got the form of steam, but in the
sense that it could have the form of steam and ought to
have it but has not yet got it. There are, then, three, and
not merely two, factors in change, since the product of
change contains two positive elements—form and matter—and
presupposes a third element—privation (στέρησις). Privation
is not a positive element in the same sense that matter
and form are positive elements, but it is, nevertheless, necessarily presupposed by change. Aristotle accordingly gives
three presuppositions of change, matter, form and privation
or exigency.[37]

8. The concrete sensible substance is thus an individual
being, composed of matter and form. But the formal element in such a being, that which makes it this definite
thing, is specifically the same in all the members of an

infima species. For instance, the specific nature or essence of man is the same (though not, of course, numerically the same) in Socrates and in Plato. This being so, it cannot be that the formal element renders the concrete sensible substance this individual, i.e. form cannot be the principle of individuation in sensible objects. What is the individuating principle according to Aristotle? It is matter. Thus Callias and Socrates are the same in form (i.e. the human form or nature), but they are different in virtue of the different matter that is informed.[38] This view of the principle of individuation was adopted by St. Thomas Aquinas, but seeing the difficulty involved in holding that completely characterless prime matter is the principle of individuation, he said that it is *materia signata quantitate* which individualises matter considered as having an anticipatory exigency for the quantity that it will afterwards actually possess in virtue of its union with form. This theory, that it is matter that individualises, would appear to be a consequence or legacy of Platonism, according to which Form is the universal.

From this theory it logically follows that each pure form must be the only member of its species, must exhaust the possibilities of its species, since there is no matter which can act as a principle of individuation within the species. St. Thomas Aquinas drew this conclusion, and did not hesitate to say (a point in which he was at variance with St. Bonaventure) that the pure intelligences or angels constitute so many species, that there cannot be a plurality of angels or immaterial forms belonging to one species. This conclusion was one that had already occurred to Aristotle himself, for, after observing that plurality depends on matter, he goes on to comment that the immovable first mover, having no matter, must be numerically one, and not only one in formula or definition.[39] It is true that the passage in question seems to be by way of objection against Aristotle's theory of a plurality of unmoved movers, but it is at least clear that he was not unaware of the consequence that follows from his doctrine of matter as principle of individuation within the species.

There is a further and a more serious consequence, which would appear to follow from this doctrine. According to Aristotle, matter is at once the principle of individuation and unknowable in itself. Now, from this it appears to follow, that the individual concrete thing is not fully knowable.

Moreover, Aristotle, as has been mentioned, explicitly stated that the individual cannot be defined, whereas science is concerned with the definition or essence. The individual as such, therefore, is not the object of science and is not fully knowable. Aristotle does indeed remark[40] concerning individual intelligible (i.e. mathematical circles) and sensible circles (e.g. of bronze or wood) that, though they cannot be defined, they are apprehended by intuition (μετὰ νοήσεως) or perception (αἰσθήσεως); but he did not elaborate this hint or work out any theory of the intuition of the individual. Yet such a theory is surely necessary. For example, we are fully convinced that we can and do know an individual person's character, but we do not arrive at the knowledge by discursive and scientific reasoning. In fact, one can hardly avoid the impression that Aristotle's exaltation of scientific definition, of knowledge of substance in the sense of specific essence, and his depreciation of knowledge of the sensible individual, were little more than a relic of his Platonic education.

9. In the ninth book of the *Metaphysics* Aristotle discusses the notions of potency and act. This is an extremely important distinction, as it enables Aristotle to admit a doctrine of real development. The Megaric School had denied potentiality, but, as Aristotle remarks, it would be absurd to say that the builder who is not actually building cannot build. It is true, of course, in one sense, that he cannot build when he is not actually building, i.e. if "cannot build" be understood as "cannot be actually building" (that is an obvious application of the principle of contradiction); but he has a potentiality for building, a power to build, even when he is not actually employing that power. That potentiality is not simply the negation of actuality can be shown by a simple illustration. A man in a state of deep sleep or coma is not actually thinking, but, being a man, he has the potentiality of thinking, whereas a stone, though it is not actually thinking, has no potentiality for thinking. A natural object is in potency in regard to the full realisation of its form, e.g. an acorn or a small tree in regard to its full development. This potency may be the power to effect a change in another or it may be a power of self-realisation: in either case it is something real, something between not-being and actuality.

Actuality, says Aristotle, is prior to potency.[41] The actual is always produced from the potential, the potential is always reduced to act by the actual, that which is already in act, as man is produced by man. In this sense the actual is *temporally* prior to the potential. But the actual is also prior to the potential *logically*, in principle, since the actuality is the end, that for the sake of which the potency exists or is acquired. Thus, although a boy is temporally prior to his actualisation as man, his manhood is logically prior, since his boyhood is for the sake of his manhood. Moreover, that which is eternal is prior in substance to that which is perishable; and that which is eternal, imperishable, is in the highest sense actual. God, for example, exists necessarily, and that which exists necessarily must be fully actual: as the eternal Source of movement, of the reduction of potentiality to act, God must be full and complete actuality, the Unmoved First Mover. Eternal things, says Aristotle,[42] must be good: there can be in them no defect or badness or perversion. Badness means defect or perversion of some kind, and there can be no defect in that which is fully actual. It follows that there can be no separate bad principle, since that which is without matter is pure form. "The bad does not exist apart from bad things." [43] It is clear from this that God, in the thought of Aristotle, took on something of the character of Plato's Idea of the Good, and indeed he remarks that the cause of all goods is the good itself.[44] The First Unmoved Mover, being the source of all movement, as *final* cause, is the ultimate cause why potentiality is actualised, i.e. why goodness is realised.

It is through the distinction between potency and act that Aristotle answers Parmenides. Parmenides had said that change is impossible, because being cannot come out of not-being (out of nothing comes nothing), while equally it cannot come from being (for being already *is*). Thus fire could not come out of air, since air is air and not fire. To this Aristotle would reply that fire does not come out of air as air, but out of air which can be fire and is not yet fire, that has a potentiality to become fire. Abstractly put, a thing comes into being from its privation. If Parmenides were to object that this is tantamount to saying that a thing comes into being from not-being, Aristotle would answer that it does not come into being from its privation merely (i.e. from bare privation), but from its privation *in a subject*. Were Parmenides to retort that in this case a thing comes into being from being, which is a contradiction, Aristotle could answer that it does not come into being from being precisely as such, but from being which is also not-being, i.e. not the thing which it comes to be. He thus answers the Parmenidean difficulty by recourse to the distinction between form, matter and privation, or (better and more generally), between act, potency and privation.[45]

10. The distinction of potency and act leads to the doctrine of the hierarchy or scale of existence, for it is clear that an object which is in act as regards its own *terminus a quo* may be in potency as regards a further *terminus ad quem*. To use a hackneyed illustration, the hewn stone is in act as regards the unhewn stone—in respect to the latter's potentiality of being hewn—but in potency as regards the house, in respect to the part it will play in the house that is yet to be built. Similarly, the soul or ψυχή, i.e. the soul in its sensitive aspect and functions, is act in regard to the body, but potency in respect to the higher function of νοῦς. At the bottom of the ladder, so to speak, is prime matter, in itself unknowable and never actually existing apart from form. In union with the contraries, with heat or cold and with dryness or wetness, it forms the four bodies—earth, air, water and fire. These relatively, though not absolutely, simple bodies form in turn inorganic bodies, such as gold, and the simple tissues of living beings (both together called homoemerous bodies). Anomoemerous beings, organisms, are formed of homoemerous bodies as their material. Thus the rungs of the ladder are gradually ascended, until we come to the active intellect of man, unmixed with matter, the separate intelligence of the spheres and finally God. (The doctrine of the scale of existence should not, of course, be understood as involving "evolution." Pure forms do not evolve out of matter. Moreover, Aristotle held that species are eternal, though individual sensible objects perish.)

11. How is change initiated? Stone that is unhewn remains unhewn so far as the stone itself is concerned: it does not hew itself. No more does hewn stone build itself into a house. In both cases an external agent, source of the change or movement, is required. In other words, besides the formal and material causes an *efficient* cause is requisite, τὸ ὅθεν ἡ κίνησις. But this is not necessarily *external* to the thing that undergoes the change: for instance, according to Aristotle, each of the four elements has a natural movement towards its own proper place in the universe (e.g. fire goes "up"), and the element in question will move in accord with its natural motion unless it is hindered. It be-

longs to the form of the element to tend towards its natural region,[46] and thus the formal and efficient causes coincide. But this does not mean that the efficient cause is always identical with the formal cause: it is identical in the case of the soul, formal principle of the organism, regarded as initiator of movement; but it is not identical in the case of the builder of the house, while in that of the generation of the human being, for example, the efficient cause, the father, is only specifically, and not numerically, the same as the formal cause of the child.

12. It will be remembered that Aristotle thought of himself as being the first thinker to give real consideration to the final cause, τὸ οὗ ἕνεκα. But though he lays great stress on finality, it would be a mistake to suppose that finality, for Aristotle, is equivalent to *external* finality, as though we were to say, for instance, that grass grows in order that sheep may have food. On the contrary, he insists much more on internal or immanent finality (thus the apple tree has attained its end or purpose, not when the fruit forms a healthy or pleasant food for man or has been made into cider, but when the apple tree has reached that perfection of development of which it is capable, i.e. the perfection of its form), for in his view the formal cause of the thing is normally its final cause as well.[47] Thus the formal cause of a horse is the specific form of horse, but this is also its final cause, since the individual of a species naturally strives to embody as perfectly as may be the specific form in question. This natural striving after the form means that the final, formal and efficient causes are often the same. For example, in the organic substance the soul or ψυχή is the formal cause or determining element in the *compositum*, while at the same time it is also the efficient cause, as source of movement, and final cause, since the immanent end of the organism is the individual embodiment of the specific form. Thus the acorn, in the whole process of its development into a full-grown tree, is tending towards the full realisation of its final cause. In Aristotle's view it is the final cause itself which moves, i.e. by attraction. In the case of the oak tree its final cause, which is also its formal cause, causes the development of the acorn into the oak-tree by drawing up, as it were, the acorn towards the term of its process of development. It might of course be objected that the final cause, the perfected form of the oak, does not as yet exist and so cannot cause, while on the

other hand it cannot cause as conceived in the mind (as the idea of the picture in the artist's mind is said to have a causal action), since the acorn is without mind and power of reflection. He would answer, no doubt, by recalling the fact that the form of the acorn is the form of the oak in germ, that it has an innate and natural tendency towards its own full evolution. But difficulties might arise for Aristotle if one were to continue asking questions.

(Of course, in spite of the tendency to run the causes together, Aristotle does not deny that the causes may be physically distinct from one another. For instance, in the building of a house, the formal cause of the house—so far as one can talk of the formal cause of a house—is not only conceptually but also physically distinct from the final cause, the idea or plan of the house in the architect's mind, as also from the efficient cause or causes. In general, however, one can say that the efficient, final, formal and material causes tend to melt, into two, that Aristotle inclines to reduce the four causes to two, namely, the formal cause and the material cause (though in our modern use of the term "cause" we naturally think first of all of efficient causality, and then perhaps of final causes).

This emphasis on finality does not mean that Aristotle excludes all mechanical causality, and this in spite of the anthropomorphic language he uses concerning teleology in nature, e.g. in his famous saying that "Nature does nothing in vain, nothing superfluous," [48] language which is scarcely consistent with the theology of the *Metaphysics* at least. Sometimes finality and mechanism combine, as in the fact that light cannot but pass through the lantern, since its own particles are finer than those of the horn, though it thereby serves to preserve us from stumbling;[49] but in other cases there may be, he thinks, only mechanical causality at work (as in the fact that the colour of the eyes of the animal has no purpose, but is due simply to circumstances of birth).[50] Moreover, Aristotle says explicitly that we must not always look for a final cause, since some things have to be explained only by material or efficient causes.[51]

13. Every motion, every transit from potentiality to act, requires some principle in act, but if every becoming, every object in movement, requires an actual moving cause, then the world in general, the universe, requires a First Mover.[52] It is important, however, to note that the word "First" must

not be understood temporally, since motion, according to Aristotle, is necessarily eternal (to initiate it or cause it to disappear would itself require motion). Rather is it to be understood as meaning *Supreme:* the First Mover is the eternal source of eternal motion. Moreover, the First Mover is not a Creator-God: the world existed from all eternity without having been created from all eternity. God forms the world, but did not create it, and He forms the world, is the source of motion, by *drawing* it, i.e. by acting as *final* cause. In Aristotle's view, if God caused motion by efficient physical causation—"shoving" the world, as it were—then He Himself would be changed: there would be a reaction of the moved on the mover. He must act, therefore, as Final Cause, by being the object of desire. To this point we shall return in a moment.

In *Metaphysics,* Λ 6 ff., Aristotle shows that this moving Principle must be of such a kind that it is pure act, ἐνέργεια, without potentiality. Presupposing the eternity of the world (if time could come into being there would, he thinks, be a time before time was—which is contradictory—and since time is essentially connected with change, change too must be eternal) he declares that there must be a First Mover which causes change without itself being changed, without having any potentiality, for if, for instance, it could cease from causing motion, then motion or change would not be necessarily eternal—which it is. There must accordingly be a First Mover which is pure act, and if it is pure act, then it must be immaterial, for materiality involves the possibility of being acted upon and changed. Moreover, experience, which shows that there exists the ceaseless, circular motion of the heavens, confirms this argument, since there must be a First Mover to move the heavens.

As we have seen, God moves the universe as Final Cause, as being the object of desire. Apparently God is conceived as moving directly the first heaven, causing the daily rotation of the stars round the earth. He moves by inspiring love and desire (the desirable and the intelligible are the same in the immaterial sphere), and so there must be an Intelligence of the first sphere, and other Intelligences in the other spheres. The Intelligence of each sphere is spiritual, and the sphere desires to imitate the life of its Intelligence as closely as may be. Not being able to imitate it in its spirituality, it does the next best thing by performing a circular movement. In an earlier period Aristotle maintained the Platonic conception of star souls, for in the Περὶ Φιλοσοφίας the stars themselves possess souls and move themselves; but he abandoned the conception in favour of that of the Intelligences of the spheres.

It is a curious fact that Aristotle does not seem to have had any very definite conviction as to the *number* of un-moved movers. Thus in the *Physics* there are three passages which refer to a plurality of unmoved movers,[53] while in the *Metaphysics* a plurality also appears.[54] According to Jaeger, chapter eight of *Metaphysics*, Λ is a later addition on Aristotle's part. In chapters seven and nine (continuous and forming part of the "original" *Metaphysics*) Aristotle speaks of the One Unmoved Mover. But in chapter eight the fifty-five transcendent movers make their appearance. Plotinus afterwards objected that the relation of these to the First Mover is left wholly obscure. He also asks how there can be a plurality of them, if matter is the principle of in-dividuation—as Aristotle held it to be. Now, Aristotle him-self saw this last objection, for he inserts the objection in the middle of chapter eight without giving a solution.[55] Even in Theophrastus' time some Aristotelians clung to *one* Un-moved Mover—not seeing how the independent movements caused by the plurality of movers could be harmonised.

It was ultimately due to this notion of a plurality of movers that mediaeval philosophers supposed there were In-telligences or Angels that move the spheres. By making them subordinate to and dependent on the First Mover or God, they were taking up the only possible position, since, if any harmony is to be achieved, then the other movers must move in subordination to the First Mover and should be related by intelligence and desire to Him, whether directly or indirectly, i.e. hierarchically. This the Neo-Platonists saw.

The First Mover, being immaterial, cannot perform any bodily action: His activity must be purely spiritual, and so intellectual. In other words, God's activity is one of thought. But what is the object of His thought? Knowledge is intellectual participation of the object: now, God's object must be the best of all possible objects, and in any case the knowledge enjoyed by God cannot be knowledge that in-volves change or sensation or novelty. God therefore knows Himself in an eternal act of intuition or self-consciousness. Aristotle, then, defines God as "Thought of Thought," νόησις νοήσεως.[56] God is subsistent thought, which eternally thinks itself. Moreover, God cannot have any object of thought outside Himself, for that would mean that He had an end outside Himself. God, therefore, knows only Himself. St. Thomas[57] and others, e.g. Brentano, have tried to interpret Aristotle in such a way as not to exclude knowledge of the world and the exercise of Divine Providence; but, though St. Thomas is right as to the true view of God, it does not follow that this was the view of Aristotle. "Aristotle has no theory either of divine creation or of divine providence." [58] He does indeed speak in rather a different strain on occasion, as when he speaks of God as the captain of an army who brings about order in the army, or says that God provides for the continuance of generation in the case of those beings which, unlike the stars, are incapable of permanent existence: but such remarks should hardly be pressed in view of his treatment of the First Mover.[59]

Is the God of Aristotle a Personal God? Aristotle sometimes speaks of God as the First Unmoved Mover (τὸ πρῶτον κινοῦν ἀκίνητον), sometimes as ὁ θεός,[60] while in the *Nicomachean Ethics* he also speaks about οἱ θεοί.[61] Like most Greeks, Aristotle does not seem to have worried much about the number of the gods, but if we are to say that he was definitely and exclusively monotheist, then we would have to say that his God is personal. Aristotle may not have spoken of the First Mover as being personal, and certainly the ascription of anthropomorphic personality would be very far indeed from his thoughts, but since the First Mover is Intelligence or Thought, it follows that He is personal in the philosophic sense. The Aristotelian God may not be personal *secundum nomen*, but He is personal *secundum rem*. We should add, however, that there is no indication that Aristotle ever thought of the First Mover as an object of worship, still less as a Being to Whom prayers might profitably be addressed. And indeed, if Aristotle's God is entirely self-centred, as I believe Him to have been, then it would be out of the question for men to attempt personal intercourse with Him. In the *Magna Moralia* Aristotle says expressly that those are wrong who think that there can be a friendship towards God. For (a) God could not return our love, and (b) we could not in any case be said to love God.[62]

14. Other arguments for the existence of God are found in rudimentary form in Aristotle's works. Thus in the fragments of the Περὶ Φιλοσοφίας he pictures men who behold for the first time the beauty of the earth and sea and the

majesty of the heavens, and conclude that they are the work
of gods. This is an adumbration of the teleological argument.[63] In the same work Aristotle hints at least at a line of
argument which was later to develop into the "fourth way"
of St. Thomas Aquinas (through various intermediaries, of
course). Aristotle there argues that "where there is a better,
there is a best; now, among existing things one is better
than another, therefore there is a best, which must be the
divine." [64] This line of argument leads directly only to a
relatively best: in order to arrive at the absolutely best, or the
Perfect, it is necessary to introduce the idea of causality,
arguing that all finite perfections ultimately spring from or
are "participations" in Absolute Perfection, which is the fount
of all finite perfections. This St. Thomas does, referring to
a passage in the *Metaphysics*,[65] and even making use of
Aristotle's illustration of fire, which is said to be the hottest
of all things, inasmuch as it is the cause of the heat of all
other things.[66] As far as Aristotle himself is concerned, the
use of the degrees of perfection in order to prove God's
existence would seem to be confined to his earlier period,
when he is still strongly under Platonic influence: in the
Metaphysics he does not use this line of argument in reference
to the existence of the divine. In general, we must say that
Aristotle, when he came to compose the *Metaphysics*, had
moved a good way from the popular religious conceptions
that appear, for example, in the fragments of the Περὶ
Φιλοσοφίας. He continued on occasion to use language that
hardly fits the conceptions of *Metaphysics*, Λ; but in any
case we would not expect Aristotle to avoid all popular language, expressions and notions with an absolute and rigorous
consistency, while it is also extremely probable that he never
really attempted any final systematisation of his doctrine
concerning God or to harmonise the expressions he sometimes employs implying Divine Providence and activity
in the world with the speculations of the *Metaphysics*.

15. From what has been said, it should be apparent that
Aristotle's notion of God was far from satisfactory. It is true
that he shows a clearer apprehension of the ultimate Godhead
than Plato does, but in Book Λ of the *Metaphysics* at least,
Aristotle leaves out of account that Divine operation in the
world which was so insisted on by Plato, and which is an
essential element in any satisfactory rational theology. The
Aristotelian God is efficient Cause *only* by being the final
Cause. He does not know this world and no Divine plan

is fulfilled in this world: the teleology of nature can be nothing more than unconscious teleology (at least this is the only conclusion that will really fit in with the picture of God given in the *Metaphysics*). In this respect, therefore, the Aristotelian metaphysic is inferior to that of Plato. On the other hand, while not a few of Aristotle's doctrines must be traced to a Platonic origin, he certainly succeeded, by his doctrine of immanent teleology, of the movement of all concrete sensible objects towards the full realisation of their potentialities, in establishing the reality of the sensible world on a firmer foundation than was possible for his great predecessor, and at the same time attributed a real meaning and purpose to becoming and change, even if in the process he abandoned valuable elements of Plato's thought.

Chapter Thirty

PHILOSOPHY OF NATURE
AND PSYCHOLOGY

1. Nature is the totality of objects which are material and subject to movement. As a matter of fact, Aristotle does not really define what he means by nature, but it is clear from what he writes in the *Physics*[1] that he regards Nature as the totality of natural objects, i.e. of objects which are capable of initiating change and of bringing it to an end, of objects which have an inner tendency to change. Artificial objects, a bed for instance, have not the power of self-movement. The "simple" bodies of which the bed is composed have this power of initiating change or movement, but they do so as natural bodies, not as components of a bed as such. This position has, of course, to be qualified by the doctrine that the passage of lifeless bodies from a state of rest to a state of movement must be initiated by an external agent. But, as we have seen, when the agent removes an obstacle, e.g. makes a hole in the bottom of a cauldron, the water responds with a movement of its own, its natural downward motion. This may seem a contradiction, namely, that natural objects are spoken of as having in themselves a principle of movement; while, on the other hand, Aristotle makes use of the maxim, that whatever is moved is moved in virtue of the action of an external agent.[2] Aristotle, however, holds that the apparent initiation of movement by animals, e.g. when an animal goes for food, is not an absolute initiation, for there would be no movement were the food not an external attractive agent. Similarly, when the water falls through the hole in the cauldron, this

downward movement may indeed be spoken of as though it
were a natural movement of the element, yet it is incidentally caused by the external agent who makes the hole
and so removes the obstacle to the natural motion of the
water, while it is directly caused by that which generated
the water and made it heavy, presumably by the primary
contraries, hot or cold. Aristotle expresses the matter by
saying that inanimate bodies have in themselves "a beginning
of being moved" but not "a beginning of causing movement." [3]

2. Movement in the wider sense is divided into coming-to-
be and passing-away on the one hand, and κίνησις or movement in the narrower sense on the other. This latter (κίνησις)
is to be divided into its three kinds—qualitative movement
(κίνησις κατὰ τὸ ποιὸν or κατὰ πάθος), quantitative
movement (κατὰ τὸ ποσὸν or κατὰ μέγεθος) and local
movement (κίνησις κατὰ τὸ ποῦ or κατὰ τόπον). The first
is ἀλλοίωσις or qualitative change, the second αὔξησις
καὶ φθίσις or quantitative change, the third φορά or motion in our ordinary sense of the word. [4]

3. Presuppositions of local motion, and indeed of all
motion, are Place and Time. That Place (τόπος) exists is
proved [5] (a) by the fact of displacement, e.g. by the fact
that where there is water, there may come to be air; and
(b) by the fact that the four elements have their natural
places. These distinctions of natural place are not simply
relative to us but exist independently: for instance "up"
is the place whither fire moves and "down" the place
whither earth moves. Place, therefore, exists and it is defined by Aristotle as τὸ τοῦ περιέχοντος πέρας ἀκίνητον
πρῶτον, [6] the Terminus continentis immobilis primus of the
Scholastics. Aristotle's τόπος, then, is the limit within which
a body is, a limit considered as immobile. If this definition
is adopted then obviously there can be no empty place nor
any place outside the universe or world, for place is the
inner limit of the containing body. But Aristotle distinguished
between the vessel or container of a body and its place.
In the case of a boat carried down by a stream, the stream
—itself moving—is the vessel rather than the place of the
boat. Place, then, is the first unmoved limit of the container, reckoning outwards. In the actual case in point the
whole river, according to Aristotle, is the place of the boat
and of whoever is in the boat, on the ground that the
whole river is at rest, ὅτι ἀκίνητον ὁ πᾶς. [7] Everything in

the physical universe is thus in a place, while the universe itself is not. Since, therefore, motion occurs through change of place, the universe itself cannot move *forwards,* but only by turning.

4. According to Aristotle a body can only be moved by a present mover in contact with the moved. What, then, are we to say of projectiles?[8] The original mover communicates to the medium, e.g. air or water, not only motion but also the power of moving. The first particles of air moved move other particles *and* the projectiles. But this power of moving decreases in proportion to the distance, so that in the end the projectile comes to rest irrespective of opposing forces. Aristotle is thus no believer in the law of inertia: he thought of compulsory movement as tending to decelerate, whereas "natural" movement tends to accelerate. (Cf. *Physics*, 230 a 18 ff.) In this he was followed by e.g. St. Thomas, who rejected the *impetus* theory of Philoponus, Al Bitrogi, Olivi, etc.

5. In regard to Time, Aristotle points out that it cannot be simply identified with movement or change, for movements are many, while time is one.[9] However, time is clearly connected with movement and change: if we are unaware of change, we are also unaware of time. The definition of time given by Aristotle is ὁ χρόνος ἀριθμός ἐστι κινήσεως κατὰ τὸ πρότερον καὶ ὕστερον.[10] He does not refer in this definition to pure number but to number in the sense of that which is numbered, i.e. to the numerable aspect of movement. Time, however, is a *continuum,* as movement is a continuum: it does not consist of discrete points.

Only things which are in movement or at rest in such a way that they are capable of movement, are in time: what is eternal *and* immobile is not in time. (Movement is eternal but obviously it is not immobile: therefore it is in time, and it necessarily follows that time also is eternal, in the sense that it never first began and will never end.) It is to be noted that the movement referred to is not of necessity local motion, for Aristotle expressly allows that the recognition even of a change in one's own state of mind may enable us to recognise a lapse of time. As to Aristotle's assertion that time is that in movement which is *counted,* it is not meant to be understood as though we could count the *nows* involved in change, as though the period of change were made up of discrete points of time: he means that, when one is conscious of time, one is recognising plurality, i.e.

a plurality of phases. Time, then, is that aspect of element of change or movement, which makes it possible for the mind to recognise a plurality of phases.[11]

If we are to measure time, we must have a standard of measurement. According to Aristotle, movement in a straight line is not satisfactory for this purpose, for it is not uniform. If it is natural movement, it accelerates; if it is unnatural, it decelerates. What movement, then, is both natural and uniform? In Aristotle's view movement in a circle is naturally uniform, and the rotation of the heavenly spheres is a natural movement. So it is thus the best suited for our purpose—and telling time by the sun will be justified.[12]

Aristotle raises the question,[13] though he does not treat it at length, whether there would be time if there were no mind. In other words, as time is the measure of movement or movement *qua* countable, would there be any time if there were no mind to count? He answers that there would be no time, properly speaking, though there would be the substratum of time. Professor Ross comments that this position is consistent with Aristotle's general account of the *continuum*.[14] In the continuum there are no actual parts, but only potential parts. These are brought into actual existence when some event breaks up the *continuum*. So with time or duration. The "nows" within duration are brought into actual existence by a mind which distinguishes the "nows'" within that duration. The difficulty that time may have existed when there were as yet no minds in existence, is at first sight no difficulty for Aristotle, since he thought of animals and men as having always existed. But a more pertinent difficulty is that counting is not the creation of parts, but the recognition of parts already there.[15] In any case, how could there be change if there were no time? We might suggest in answer that since, according to Aristotle, time is not really distinguished from the *prius* and *posterius* of motion, time exists independently of the mind, because motion does, though it receives a complement, as it were, from mind. "Parts" of time are potential in the sense that they are not formally distinguished from one another save by the "counting" mind; but they are not potential in the sense that they have no real existence apart from mind. Aristotle's position is not that of Kant, nor does it, of itself, lead to the position of Kant.

6. Aristotle raises the question of the possibility of the infinite.

(a) An infinite body, he says, is impossible,[16] since every body is bounded by a surface, and no body which is bounded by a surface can be infinite. He also proves the impossibility of an existent actually infinite body by showing that it could be neither composite nor simple. For example, if it is supposed to be composite, the elements of which it is composed are themselves either infinite or finite. Now, if one element is infinite and the other element or elements finite, then the latter are deleted by the first, while it is impossible for both elements to be infinite, since one infinite element would equal the whole body. As to finite elements, composition of such elements would certainly not form one actually infinite body. Aristotle also considered that the existence of absolute "up," "down," etc., which he accepted, shows that there cannot be an existent actually infinite body, for such distinctions would be meaningless in the case of an infinite body. Nor can there be an actual infinite number, since number is that which can be numbered, whereas an infinite number could not be numbered.[17]

(b) On the other hand, though Aristotle rejected an existent actually infinite body or number, he admitted the infinite in another sense.[18] The infinite exists potentially. For example, no spatial extension is an actual infinite, but it is potentially infinite in the sense that it is infinitely divisible. A line does not consist of an actual infinite of points, for it is a *continuum* (it is in this way that Aristotle attempts, in the *Physics,* to meet the difficulties raised by Zeno the Eleatic), but it is infinitely divisible, though this potentially infinite division will never be completely realised in actuality. Time, again, is potentially infinite, since it can be added to indefinitely; but time never exists as an actual infinite, for it is a *successive continuum* and its parts never coexist. Time, therefore, resembles spatial extension in being infinitely divisible (though no actual infinity is ever realised), but is also potentially infinite by way of addition, and in this it differs from extension, since extension, according to Aristotle, has a maximum, even if it has no minimum. A third potential infinity is that of Number, which resembles time in being potentially infinite by way of addition, since you cannot count up to a number beyond which all counting and addition is impossible. Number, however, differs from both time and extension in being insusceptible of infinite division, for the reason that it has a minimum—the unit.

7. According to Aristotle, all natural motion is directed

towards an end.[19] What is the end that is sought in nature?
It is the development from a state of potentiality to one
of actuality, the embodiment of form in matter. With Aristotle, as with Plato, the teleological view of nature prevails
over the mechanical, even if it is difficult to see how Aristotle
could logically admit any conscious teleology in regard to
nature in general. The teleology is not, however, all-pervasive
and all-conquering, since matter sometimes obstructs the
action of teleology (as, for instance, in the production of
monsters, which must be ascribed to defective matter.[20])
Thus the working of teleology in any particular instance
may suffer interference from the occurrence of an event
which does not serve the end in question at least, but the
occurrence of which cannot be avoided owing to certain
circumstances. This is τὸ αὐτόματον or the "fortuitous,"
consisting of those events which are "by nature," though not
"according to nature," e.g. the production of a monster by
generation. Such occurrences are undesirable and are distinguished by Aristotle from luck (τύχη), which denotes
the occurrence of a desirable event, e.g. which might be
the willed end of a purposive agent, as in the case of the
finding of a treasure in a field.[21]

With what justification does Aristotle speak of "Nature"
as having ends? Plato had made use of the conceptions of a
World-Soul and of the Demiurge, and so was enabled to
speak of ends in nature, but Aristotle talks as though there
were some teleological activity inherent in nature itself. He
does indeed speak on occasion of ὁ θεός, but he never
gives any satisfactory treatment of the relation of nature to
God, and what he says about God in the *Metaphysics* would
seem to preclude any purposive activity in nature on the
part of God. Probably it is true to say that Aristotle's increasing interest in empirical science led him to neglect
any real systematisation of his position, and even lays him
open to a justified accusation of inconsistency with his metaphysical presuppositions. While having no wish to reject or
question Aristotle's view that there is teleology in nature, we
are, it seems, compelled to admit that Aristotle's metaphysical system, his theology, gives him little justification for
speaking of nature, as he not infrequently does, as though it
were a consciously operating and organising principle. Such
language bears an unmistakably Platonic flavour.

8. According to Aristotle the universe consists of two distinct worlds—the superlunary and the sublunary. In the

superlunary world are the stars, which are imperishable
and undergo no change other than that of local motion,
their motion being circular and not rectilinear, as is the
natural movement of the four elements. Aristotle concludes
that the stars are composed of a different material element,
aether, which is the fifth and superior element, incapable
of any change other than change of place in a circular
movement.

Aristotle maintained the view that the earth, spherical
in shape, is at rest in the centre of the universe, and that
round it lie the layers, concentric and spherical, of water, air
and fire or the warm (ὑπέκκαυμα). Beyond these lie the
heavenly spheres, the outermost of which, that of the fixed
stars, owes its motion to the First Mover. Accepting from
Calippus the number thirty-three as the number of spheres
which must be presupposed in order to explain the actual
motion of the planets, Aristotle assumed also twenty-two
backward-moving spheres, interposed between the other
spheres, in order to counteract the tendency of a sphere to
disturb the motion of the planet in the next encompassed
sphere. He thus obtained fifty-five spheres, excluding the
outermost sphere; and this is the explanation of his suggestion in the *Metaphysics* that there are fifty-five unmoved
movers, in addition to the First Mover that moves the outermost sphere. (He remarks that if the computation of Eudoxus be accepted instead of that of Calippus, then the number will be forty-nine).[22]

9. Particular things in this world come into being and
pass away, but species and genera are eternal. There is,
therefore, no evolution in the modern sense to be found in
the system of Aristotle. But although Aristotle cannot develop any theory of temporal evolution, an evolution of
species, he can and does develop a theory of what may be
called "ideal" evolution, namely, a theory concerning the
structure of the universe, a theory of the scale of being, in
which form is ever more predominant as the scale is
ascended. At the bottom of the scale comes inorganic matter,
and above this organic matter, the plants being less perfect
than the animals. Nevertheless, even the plants possess soul,
which is the principle of life, and which Aristotle defines as
"the entelechy of a natural body endowed with the capacity of life" or as "the first entelechy of a natural organic
body." (So in *De Anima* B 1, 412 a 27-b 4, ψυχή ἐστιν
ἐντελέχεια ἡ πρώτη σώματος φυσικοῦ δυνάμει ζωὴν

ἔχοντος τοιοῦτον δέ, ὃ ἂν ᾖ ὀργανικόν, or ἐντελέχεια ἡ πρώτη σώματος φυσικοῦ ὀργανικοῦ.) Being the act of the body, the soul is at the same time form, principle of movement, and end. The body is for the soul, and every organ has its purpose, that purpose being an activity.

At the beginning of the De Anima Aristotle points out the importance of an investigation concerning the soul, for the soul is, as it were, the vital principle in living things.[23] This problem is, however, he says, a difficult one, for it is not easy to ascertain the right method to be employed: but he insists—and how wisely—that the speculative philosopher and the naturalist have different standpoints, and so frame their definitions differently. It is not every thinker that has recognised that different sciences have their different methods, and that because a particular science cannot employ the method of the chemist or the natural scientist, it does not follow that all its conclusions must necessarily be vitiated.[24]

The composite substance, says Aristotle,[25] is a natural body endowed with life, the principle of this life being called the soul (ψυχή). Body cannot be soul, for body is not life but what has life. (In the first book of the De Anima, where Aristotle gives a history of Psychology, he remarks, apropos of the views of different philosophers concerning the soul, that "the most far-reaching difference is that between the philosophers who regard the elements as corporeal and those who regard them as incorporeal." Aristotle ranges himself with the Platonists as against the followers of Leucippus and Democritus.) The body, then, must be as matter to the soul, while the soul is as form or act to the body. Hence Aristotle, in his definition of the soul, speaks of it as the entelechy or act of the body that possesses life in potency—"potentiality of life," as he remarks, not referring to a thing which has become dispossessed of soul, but to that which possesses it. The soul is thus the realisation of the body and is inseparable from it (though there may be—as Aristotle held there were—parts which can be separated, because they are not precisely realisations of the body). The soul is thus the cause and principle of the living body, (a) as source of movement,[26] (b) as final cause, and (c) as the real substance (i.e. formal cause) of animate bodies.

The different types of soul form a series of such a kind that the higher presupposes the lower, but not vice versa. The lowest form of soul is the nutritive or vegetative soul, τὸ θρεπτικόν, which exercises the activities of assimilation and reproduction. It is found, not only in plants, but also in animals; yet it can exist by itself, as it does in plants. In order that any living thing should continue to exist, these functions are necessary: they are found, therefore, in all living things, but in plants they are found alone, without the higher activities of soul. For plants sensation is not necessary, for they do not move but draw their nourishment automatically. (The same holds good, indeed, of motionless animals.) But animals endowed with the power of movement must have sensation, for it would be useless for them to move after their food, if they could not recognise it when they found it.

Animals, then, possess the higher form of soul, the sensitive soul, which exercises the three powers of sense-perception (τὸ αἰσθητικόν), desire (τὸ ὀρεκτικόν), and local motion (τὸ κινητικόν κατὰ τόπον).[27] Imagination (φαντασία) follows on the sensitive faculty, and memory is a further development of this.[28] Just as Aristotle has pointed out the necessity of nutrition for the preservation of life at all, so he shows the necessity of touch in order that an animal should be able to distinguish its food, at least when it is in contact with it.[29] Taste, whereby that which is food attracts the animal, and what is not food repels it, is also necessary. The other senses, though not strictly necessary, are for the well-being of the animal.

10. Higher in the scale than the merely animal soul is the human soul. This soul unites in itself the powers of the lower souls, τὸ θρεπτικόν, τὸ αἰσθητικόν, τὸ ὀρεκτικόν, τὸ κινητικόν κατὰ τόπον, but has a peculiar advantage in the possession of νοῦς, τὸ διανοητικόν. The latter is active in two ways, as the power of scientific thought (λόγος, νοῦς θεωρητικὸς = τὸ ἐπιστημονικόν) and as the power of deliberation (διάνοια πρακτική = λογιστικόν). The former has truth as its object, truth for its own sake, while the latter aims at truth, not for its own sake but for practical and prudential purposes. All the powers of the soul, with the exception of νοῦς, are inseparable from the body and perishable: νοῦς, however, pre-exists before the body and is immortal. λείπεται δὲ τὸν νοῦν μόνον θύραθεν ἐπεισιέναι καὶ θεῖον εἶναι μόνον.[30] This νοῦς, however, which enters into the body, requires a potential principle— a *tabula rasa*, on which it may imprint forms; and so we have the distinction between the νοῦς ποιητικός and the νοῦς παθητικός. (Aristotle speaks himself of τὸ ποιοῦν:

the phrase νοῦς ποιητικός is first found in Alexander Aphrodisiensis, c. A.D. 220). The active intellect abstracts forms from the images or *phantasmata*, which, when received in the passive intellect, are actual concepts. (Aristotle considered that the use of imagery is involved in all thinking.) Only the active intellect is immortal. οὗτος ὁ νοῦς χωριστὸς καὶ ἀπαθὴς καὶ ἀμιχὴς τῇ οὐσίᾳ ὢν ἐνέργεια, ἀεὶ γὰρ τιμιώτερον τὸ ποιοῦν τοῦ πάσχοντος καὶ ἡ ἀρχὴ τῆς ὕλης . . . καὶ τοῦτο μόνον ἀθάνατον καὶ ἀΐδιον . . . ὁ δὲ παθητικὸς νοῦς φθαρτός.[31] To this point I shall return in a moment.

11. If we leave out of account the question of the νοῦς ποιητικός, it is clear that Aristotle does not uphold the Platonic dualism in the *De Anima*, for he makes soul to be the entelechy of the body, so that the two form one substance. Altogether Aristotle allows a much closer union between soul and body than did the Platonists: the tendency to look on the body as the tomb of the soul is not that of Aristotle. Rather is it for the good of the soul to be united with the body, since only so can it exercise its faculties. This was the view adopted by the mediaeval Aristotelians, such as St. Thomas, although many great Christian thinkers had spoken and continue to speak, in language very reminiscent of the Platonic tradition—we have only to think of St. Augustine. Aristotle insisted that the Platonic School failed to give any satisfactory explanation of the soul's union with the body. They seem, he says, to suppose that any soul can fit itself into any body. This cannot be true, for every body appears to have a distinct form and character.[32] "A notion like that of Descartes, that the existence of the soul is the first certainty and the existence of matter a later inference, would have struck Aristotle as absurd. The whole self, soul and body alike, is something given and not questioned."[33] Needless to say, if Aristotle would have opposed the Cartesian view, he would also have opposed the position of those who would reduce the whole human soul and all its activities to the condition of an epiphenomenon of the body, making the highest activity of human thought a mere efflorescence of the brain, though the direction of Aristotle's psychology, as it developed, would seem to have been towards a position suspiciously resembling an epiphenomenalist position, especially if one is right in supposing that the active intellect of man

was not, in Aristotle's eyes, an individualised principle, which persisted after death as the individual mind of, e.g. Socrates or Callias. The absence of a doctrine of historical organic evolution would, however, naturally preclude Aristotle from accepting epiphenomenalism in the modern sense.

12. The well-worn question arises, "What was Aristotle's precise doctrine as to the Active Intellect?" Aristotle's *precise* doctrine one cannot give: it is a matter of interpretation, and different interpretations have been advanced both in the ancient and in the modern world. What Aristotle says in the *De Anima* is as follows: "This Nous is separable and impassible and unmixed, being essentially an actuality. For the active is always of higher value than the passive, and the originative principle than the matter. Actual knowledge is identical with its object; potential knowledge is prior in time in the individual, but in general it is not temporally prior; but Nous does at one time function and at another not. When it has been separated it is that only which it is in essence, and this alone is immortal and eternal. We do not remember, however, because active reason is impassible, but the passive reason is perishable, and without the active reason nothing thinks." [34]

Of this much-disputed passage various interpretations have been given. Alexander of Aphrodisias (*flor. c.* A.D. 220) identified "reason," i.e. the Active Intellect, with God, being followed in this by Zabarella (end of sixteenth and early seventeenth century A.D.), who would make God's function in the soul to be the illumination of the potentially known, as the sun's light makes what is visible to be actually seen. Now, although, as Sir David Ross points out, [35] it would not be necessarily inconsistent on Aristotle's part to speak of God's immanence in the *De Anima,* while speaking of His transcendence in the *Metaphysics,* while on the other hand it might be possible for the two books to represent divergent views of God, the interpretation of Alexander of Aphrodisias and Zabarella, as Ross allows, is most unlikely. For it is probable that Aristotle, having described God as the Unmoved Mover Whose causal activity is one of attraction—as *Finis*—and as knowing only Himself, should go on, in another book, to depict God as immanent in man in such a way as actually to impart knowledge to him?

If the Active Intellect is not to be identified with God, is it to be regarded as individual and particular in each single man or as an identical principle in all men? Aristotle's words,

"We do not remember," when taken together with his assertion[36] that memory and loving and hating perish at death, as belonging to the whole man and not to Reason, which is "impassable," seem to indicate that the Active Intellect in its separate existence has no memory. Although this does not prove with certainty that the Active Intellect of each man is not individual in its state of separation, it does seem to raise a difficulty in accepting such an interpretation. Moreover, when Aristotle asserts that "potential knowledge is prior in time in the individual, but in general it is not temporally prior, but Nous does not at one time function and at another not," he seems to be drawing a distinction between the individual, who at one time knows and at another not, and the Active Intellect, which is an essentially active principle. Perhaps, then, Aristotle regarded the Active Intellect as a principle which is identical in all men, an Intelligence that has above it the hierarchy of the other separate Intelligence, that enters into man and functions within him, and that survives the death of the individual. If this were correct, then the conclusion would necessarily follow that the individualised human soul perishes with the matter it informed.[37] (Yet, even if one is inclined to such an interpretation, one must admit that there is very considerable difficulty in supposing that, in Aristotle's opinion, the active intellect of Plato was numerically the same as that of Socrates. All the same, if he believed in the individual character of the active intellect in each single man, what did he mean when he said that it came "from outside"? Was this simply a relic of Platonism?)

Chapter Thirty-One

ARISTOTLE'S ETHICS

1. The Ethics of Aristotle are frankly teleological. He is concerned with action, not as being right in itself irrespective of every other consideration, but with action as conducive to man's good. What conduces to the attainment of his good or end will be a "right" action on man's part: the action that is opposed to the attainment of his true good will be a "wrong" action.

"Every art and every inquiry, every action and choice, seems to aim at some good; whence the good has rightly been defined as that at which all things aim." [1] But there are different goods, corresponding to different arts or sciences. Thus the doctor's art aims at health, seamanship at a safe voyage, economy at wealth. Moreover, some ends are subordinate to other and more ultimate ends. The end of giving a certain medicine might be to produce sleep, but this immediate end is subordinate to the end of health. Similarly, the making of bits and reins for cavalry horses is the end of a certain craft, but it is subordinate to the wider and more comprehensive end of conducting warlike operations efficiently. These ends, therefore, have further ends or goods in view. But if there is an end which we desire for its own sake and for the sake of which we desire all other subordinate ends or goods, then this ultimate good will be the best good, in fact, *the* good. Aristotle sets himself to discover what this good is and what the science corresponding to it is.

As to the second question, Aristotle asserts that it is political or social science which studies the good for man.

The State and the individual have the same good, though this good as found in the State is greater and nobler.[2] (Here we see an echo of the *Republic*, that in the ideal State we see justice writ large.) Ethics, then, are regarded by Aristotle as a branch of political or social science: we might say that he treats first of individual ethical science and secondly of political ethical science, in the *Politics*.

As to the question what is the good of man, Aristotle points out that it cannot be answered with the exactitude with which a mathematical problem can be answered, and that owing to the nature of the subject-matter, for human action is the subject-matter of ethics, and human action cannot be determined with mathematical exactitude.[3] There is also this big difference between mathematics and ethics, that while the former starts from general principles and argues to conclusions, the latter starts with the conclusions. In other words, in ethics we start from the actual moral judgments of man, and by comparing, contrasting and sifting them, we come to the formulation of general principles.[4] This view presupposes that there are natural tendencies implanted in man, the following of which in a general attitude of consistent harmony and proportion, i.e. recognising relative importances and unimportances, is the ethical life for man. This view affords a basis for a natural as opposed to an arbitrary ethic, but considerable difficulties arise as to the theoretical establishment of moral *obligation*, especially in a system such as that of Aristotle, who cannot link up his ethic of human action with the Eternal Law of God, as Christian philosophers of the Middle Ages, who accepted so much from Aristotle, tried to do. However, in spite of such defects, Aristotle's ethic is eminently common-sense for the most part, founded as it is on the moral judgments of the man who was generally looked upon as a good and virtuous man. Aristotle intended his ethic to be a justification and supplementation of the natural judgments of such a man, who is, he says, best qualified to judge in matters of this kind.[5] It may be thought that the taste of the intellectual and professor comes out strongly in his picture of the ideal life, but one can scarcely accuse Aristotle of attempting a purely *a priori* and deductive ethic, or an *Ethica more geometrico demonstrata*. Moreover, although we can discern evidence of contemporary Greek taste in matters of human conduct, e.g. in Aristotle's account of the moral virtues, the philosopher certainly considered himself to be dealing with human nature as such, and to be founding his ethic on the universal characteristics of human nature—in spite of his opinion of the "barbarians." If he were alive today and had to answer, e.g. Friedrich Nietzsche, he would no doubt insist on the basic universality and constancy of human nature and the necessity of constant valuations, which are not merely relative but are founded in nature.

What do people generally view as the end of life? Happiness, says Aristotle, and he, like a true Greek, accepts this view. But obviously this does not take us very far by itself, for different people understand very different things by happiness. Some people identify it with pleasure, others with wealth, others again with honour, and so on. More than that, the same man may have different estimations of what happiness is at different times. Thus when he is ill he may regard health as happiness, and when he is in want he may regard wealth as happiness. But pleasure is rather an end for slaves than freemen, while honour cannot be the end of life, for it depends on the giver and is not really our own. Honour, moreover, seems to be aimed at assuring us of our virtue (hence, perhaps, the Victorian attachment to "respectability"); so perhaps moral virtue is the end of life. No, says Aristotle, for moral virtue can go with inactivity and misery; and happiness, which is the end of life, that at which all aim, must be an activity and excludes misery.[6]

Now, if happiness is an activity and an activity of man, we must see what activity is peculiar to man. It cannot be the activity of growth or reproduction, nor yet of sensation, since these are shared by other beings below man: it must be the activity of that which is peculiar to man among natural beings, namely, the activity of reason or activity in accordance with reason. This is indeed an activity of virtue —for Aristotle distinguished, besides the moral virtues, the intellectual virtues—but it is not what people ordinarily mean when they say that happiness consists in being virtuous, since they are generally thinking of moral virtues, such as justice, temperance, etc. In any case, happiness, as the ethical end, could not consist simply in virtue as such: it consists rather in activity according to virtue or in virtuous activity, understanding by virtue both the intellectual and the moral virtues. Moreover, says Aristotle, it must, if it really deserves the name of happiness, be manifested over a whole life and not merely for brief periods.[7]

But if happiness is essentially activity in accordance with

virtue, Aristotle does not mean by this simply to exclude all the common notions about happiness. For instance, the activity to which virtue is the tendency is necessarily accompanied by pleasure, since pleasure is the natural accompaniment of an unimpeded and free activity. Again, without some external goods a man cannot well exercise that activity —an Aristotelian view to which the Cynics took exception, for the most part at least.[8] The character of happiness as an activity, and an activity peculiar to man, is therefore preserved without at the same time having to sacrifice or exclude pleasure and external prosperity. Once more Aristotle shows the common-sense character of his thought, and that he is not "over-transcendental" or hostile to this earth.

This being established, Aristotle goes on to consider, first the general nature of good character and good action, then the leading moral virtues, the virtues of that part of man which can follow the plan laid down by reason, then the virtues of the intellect. At the end of the *Nicomachean Ethics* he considers the ideal life, or the ideal life of activity in accordance with virtue, which life will be the truly happy life for man.

2. As to goodness of character in general, Aristotle says that we start by having a capacity for it, but that it has to be developed by practice. How is it developed? By doing virtuous acts. At first sight this looks like a vicious circle. Aristotle tells us that we become virtuous by doing virtuous acts, but how can we do virtuous acts unless we are already virtuous? Aristotle answers[9] that we begin by doing acts which are objectively virtuous, without having a reflex knowledge of the acts and a deliberate choice of the acts as good, a choice resulting from an habitual disposition. For instance, a child may be told by its parents not to lie. It obeys without realising perhaps the inherent goodness of telling the truth, and without having yet formed a habit of telling the truth; but the acts of truth-telling gradually form the habit, and as the process of education goes on, the child comes to realise that truth-telling is right in itself, and to choose to tell the truth for its own sake, as being the right thing to do. It is then virtuous in this respect. The accusation of the vicious circle is thus answered by the distinction between the acts which *create* the good disposition and the acts which *flow from* the good disposition once it has been created. Virtue itself is a disposition which has been developed out of a capacity by the proper exercise of that

capacity. (Further difficulties might arise, of course, concerning the relation between the development of moral
valuations and the influence of social environment, suggestion
of parents and teachers, etc., but with these Aristotle does
not deal.[10])

3. How does virtue stand to vice? It is a common characteristic of all good actions that they have a certain order
or proportion, and virtue, in Aristotle's eyes, is a mean
between two extremes, the extremes being vices, one being
a vice through excess, the other being a vice through defect.[11]
Through excess or defect of what? Either in regard to a
feeling or in regard to an action. Thus, in regard to the
feeling of confidence, the excess of this feeling constitutes
rashness—at least when the feeling issues in action, and it
is with human actions that ethics are concerned—while the
defect is cowardice. The mean, then, will be a mean between
rashness on the one hand and cowardice on the other hand:
this mean is courage and is the virtue in respect to the
feeling of confidence. Again, if we take the action of giving
of money, excess in regard to this action is prodigality—and
this is a vice—while defect in regard to this action is illiberal-
ity. The virtue, liberality, is the mean between the two vices,
that of excess and that of defect. Aristotle, therefore, describes or defines moral virtue as "a disposition to choose,
consisting essentially in a mean relatively to us determined
by a rule, i.e. the rule by which a practically wise man
would determine it." [12] Virtue, then, is a disposition, a disposition to choose according to a rule, namely, the rule
by which a truly virtuous man possessed of moral insight
would choose. Aristotle regarded the possession of practical
wisdom, the ability to see what is the right thing to do in
the circumstances, as essential to the truly virtuous man, and
he attaches much more value to the moral judgments of the
enlightened conscience than to any *a priori* and merely theoretical conclusions. This may seem somewhat naïve, but it
must be remembered that for Aristotle the prudent man will
be the man who sees what is truly good for a man in any
set of circumstances: he is not required to enter upon any
academic preserve, but to see what truly befits human
nature in those circumstances.

When Aristotle speaks of virtue as a mean, he is not thinking of a mean that has to be calculated arithmetically: that
is why he says in his definition "relatively to us." We cannot
determine what is excess, what mean and what defect by

hard-and-fast, mathematical rules: so much depends on the character of the feeling or action in question: in some cases it may be preferable to err on the side of excess rather than on that of defect, while in other cases the reverse may be true. Nor, of course, should the Aristotelian doctrine of the mean be taken as equivalent to an exaltation of mediocrity in the moral life, for as far as excellence is concerned virtue is an extreme: it is in respect of its essence and its definition that it is a mean. One may illustrate this important point by a diagram given in the *Ethica* of Professor Nicolai Hartmann of Berlin,[13] in which the horizontal line at the bottom of the figure represents the ontological dimension, and the vertical line the axiological dimension.

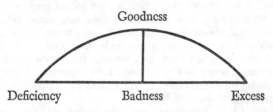

This diagram illustrates the important point that virtue (ἀρετή) has a double position. (i) As regards the onto-logical dimension, it is a mean (μεσότης); as regards the axiological dimension, it is an excellence or extreme (ἀκρότης). It is not as though virtue were a composition of vices from a valuational point of view, since, from this point of view, it stands in opposition to both vices; but it is nevertheless a mean from the ontological viewpoint, since it combines in itself both the good points which, run to excess, constitute vices. For example, courage is not boldness alone, nor is it cool foresight alone, but a synthesis of both—this character of a synthesis preventing courage from degenerating into the daring of the foolhardy man on the one hand or the prudence of the coward on the other hand. "What Aristotle so strongly felt in the lower moral values, without being able to formulate it, was just this, that all valuational elements, taken in isolation, have in them a point beyond which they are dangerous, that they are tyrannical, and that for the true fulfilment of their meaning in their real carrier there is always a counterweight. Because of this profoundly justified feeling, he assigned virtue to no one of these elements but to their synthesis. It is precisely in

their synthesis that the danger in values is diminished, their
tyranny in consciousness paralysed. In this matter Aristotle's
procedure is a model for every further treatment of the
problem of contrasts." [14]

One must, however, admit that Aristotle's treatment of the
virtues betrays the fact that he was under the influence
of the predominantly *aesthetic* attitude of the Greek towards
human conduct, a fact that appears in a clear light in his
treatment of the "great-souled" man. The notion of a cruci-
fied God would have been abhorrent to him: it would
most probably have seemed in his eyes at once unaesthetic
and irrational.

4. A presupposition of moral action is Freedom, since it
is only for voluntary actions that a man incurs responsibility,
i.e. voluntary in a wide sense. If a man acts under physical
external compulsion or in ignorance, he cannot be held responsible. Fear may lessen the voluntary character of an
action, but an action such as throwing the cargo overboard
in a storm, though not one that a sane man would perform
in ordinary circumstances, is yet voluntary, since it springs
from the agent himself. [15]

In regard to ignorance Aristotle certainly makes some
pertinent observations, as when he points out that while
a man who acts in rage or under the influence of drink may
be said to act *in* ignorance, he cannot be said to act *from*
ignorance, for that ignorance is itself due to rage or drink. [16]
However, his assertion that an action done through ignorance
is involuntary if it is subsequently regretted by the agent,
non-voluntary if not subsequently regretted, can scarcely be
accepted, for although the agent's subsequent attitude may
reveal his general character, i.e. whether he is on the whole
a good or bad man, it cannot serve to differentiate between
unwilling and merely involuntary acts. [17]

In regard to the Socratic position that no man acts against
knowledge, Aristotle does on occasion show that he is alive
to the reality of the moral struggle [18] (he was too good a
psychologist to disregard the point), but when he is treating
formally of the question, in reference to continence and
incontinence, [19] he tends to overlook this and to emphasise
the view that the man who does a wrong act does not know
at the moment of action that the act is wrong. This may
certainly happen sometimes, e.g. in the case of actions done
under the stress of passion, but Aristotle does not allow
sufficiently for the truth that a man may do deliberately

what he knows to be wrong, and, moreover, what he knows to be wrong at the moment that he does it. It might be remarked that, owing to what might be called the strictly human character of Aristotle's ethic, by which "right" is explained in terms of "good," he could answer that even the incontinent man acts *sub ratione boni*. This is true, but all the same the incontinent man may know well enough that the action he performs is morally wrong. In fact, Aristotle, while professedly rejecting the Socratic theory, was none the less dominated by it to a certain extent. He lacked a proper concept of duty, though in this he seems to have been at one with other Greek theorists before the rise of the Stoics, with certain reservations in the case of Plato. An action may be good or contributory to good without thereby being strictly obligatory, a duty, and Aristotle's ethical theory does not account for this distinction.

5. Aristotle, like Plato before him, had no really distinct concept of will, but his description or definition of choice as "desireful reason" or "reasonable desire" [20] or as "the deliberate desire of things in our power," [21] shows that he had some idea of will, for he does not identify preferential choice (προαίρεσις) with either desire by itself or with reason by itself. His description of it would seem to indicate that he regarded it as substantially *sui generis*. (Aristotle does indeed declare that προαίρεσις has to do with means and not with ends, but in his use of the word, both in the *Ethics* itself and also elsewhere, he is not consistent.[22])

Aristotle's analysis of the moral process is as follows. (i) The agent desires an end. (ii) The agent deliberates, seeing that B is the means to A (the end to be obtained), C the means to B, and so on, until (iii) he perceives that some particular means near to the end or remote from it, as the case may be, is something that he can do here and now. (iv) The agent chooses this means that presents itself to him as practicable *hic et nunc*, and (v) does the act in question. Thus a man might desire happiness (in fact, he always does, Aristotle thought). He then sees that health is a means to happiness, and that exercise is a means to health. He then perceives that to go for a walk is something that he can do here and now. He chooses this act and does it, i.e. takes the walk. This analysis may be a very good statement of the way in which we fix on actions in view of an end: the difficulty is to allow for any real moral obligation in Aristotle's system, at least if considered in itself and without any of the supplementary treatment that later philosophers have given it.

From the doctrine that virtuous activity is voluntary and in accordance with choice, it follows that virtue and vice are in our power, and that Socrates' doctrine is false. True, a man may have formed a bad habit of such strength that he cannot cease to perform the intrinsically bad actions that naturally flow from that habit, but he could have refrained from contracting that habit in the first place. A man may have so blinded his conscience that he fails now to discern the right, but he is himself responsible for his blindness and for bringing about his ignorance. This may be said to be the general thought of Aristotle, though, as we have seen, in his formal treatment of the Socratic position he does not do sufficient justice to moral weakness and to sheer wickedness.

6. Aristotle's treatment of the moral virtues is often enlightening and shows his common-sense moderation and clear judgment. For example, his characterisation of courage as a mean between rashness or foolhardiness and cowardice, seems, when developed, to set the true nature of courage in relief and to distinguish it from forms of pseudo-courage. Similarly, his description of the virtue of temperance as a mean between profligacy and "insensibility," serves to bring out the truth that temperance or self-control in regard to the pleasures of touch does not of itself involve a puritanical attitude towards sense and the pleasures of sense. Again, his insistence that the mean is a mean "relatively to us" and cannot be arithmetically determined, brings out his practical, empirical and common-sense outlook. As he pertinently remarks, "If ten pounds of food are too much for a man and two are too little, the trainer in gymnastics will not order six pounds, for this may be too much or too little for the special case: for a Milo it may be too little, but for one who is beginning to train it may be too much." [23]

It can hardly be denied, however (and who would expect anything else?) that his treatment of the virtues is, to a certain extent, determined by contemporary Greek taste. [24] Thus his view that the "great-souled" and self-respecting man will be ashamed of receiving benefits and so putting himself in the position of an inferior, while on the contrary he will always pay back benefits received with greater ones in order to make his friend his debtor, may be in accordance with Greek taste (or with those of Nietzsche), but will scarcely be acceptable in all quarters. Again, Aristotle's pictures of the "great-souled" man as slow in step, deep in voice and sedate in speech is largely a matter of aesthetic taste.[25]

7. In Book Five of the *Ethics* Aristotle treats of Justice. Under Justice he understands (*a*) what is lawful and (*b*) what is fair and equal. (τὸ μὲν δίκαιον ἄρα τὸ νόμιμον καὶ τὸ ἴσον, τὸ δ' ἄδικον τὸ παράνομον καὶ τὸ ἄνισον *E.N*, 1129 a 34). The first kind of justice, "universal" justice, is practically equivalent to obedience to law, but since Aristotle envisages the law of the State—ideally, at least—as extending over the whole of life and enforcing virtuous actions in the sense of materially virtuous actions (since of course law cannot enforce virtuous actions, formally or subjectively considered), universal justice is more or less coterminous with virtue, looked at in its social aspect at any rate. Aristotle, like Plato, is firmly convinced of the positive and educative function of the State. This is diametrically opposed to theories of the State, such as those of Herbert Spencer in England and Schopenhauer in Germany, who rejected the positive functions of the State and confined the functions of law to the defence of personal rights, above all the defence of private property.

"Particular" justice is divided into (*a*) Distributive Justice, whereby the State divides goods among its citizens according to geometrical proportions, i.e. according to merit (as Burnet says, the Greek citizen regarded himself as a shareholder in the State, rather than as a taxpayer), and (*b*) Remedial Justice. This latter is subdivided into two types, (i) that dealing with voluntary transactions (Civil Law), and (ii) that dealing with involuntary transactions (Criminal Law). Remedial Justice proceeds according to arithmetical proportion. Aristotle added to these two main divisions of particular justice Commercial or Commutative Justice.

According to Aristotle, Justice is a mean between acting unjustly and being unjustly treated.[26] But this is hardly acceptable and is obviously asserted merely in order to bring justice into line with the other virtues already discussed. For the business man, for instance, who is just in his dealings, is the man who chooses to give the other fellow his due and to take exactly his own share without further extortion, rather than to give the other man less than his due or to take for himself more than what is owing to him. To give the other fellow more than his share or to accept for himself less than his own due, is scarcely a vice—or even, necessarily, to be unjustly treated. However, Aristotle goes on to say, rather more happily, that justice is not really a mean as the other virtues are, but is a mean in the sense that it produces a state of affairs that stand midway between that in which A has too much and that in which B has too much.[27]

Finally[28] Aristotle draws the very valuable distinction between various types of action that are materially unjust, pointing out that to do an action which results in damage to another, when the damage was not foreseen or intended —and still more if the damage would not ordinarily result from that action—is very different from doing an action which would naturally result in damage to another, particularly if that damage was foreseen and intended. The distinctions drawn afford room for equity as a type of justice superior to legal justice, the latter being too general for application to all particular cases. καὶ ἔστιν αὕτη ἡ φύσις ἡ τοῦ ἐπιει-κοῦς, ἐπανόρθωμα νόμου, ἡ ἐλλείπει διὰ τὸ καθόλου.[29]

8. Discussing the intellectual virtues Aristotle divides them according to the two rational faculties, (i) the scientific faculty—τὸ ἐπιστημονικόν, by which we contemplate objects that are necessary and admit of no contingency, and (ii) the calculative faculty—τὸ λογιστικόν, or faculty of opinion, which is concerned with objects that are contingent. The intellectual virtues of the scientific faculty are ἐπιστήμη, "the disposition by virtue of which we demonstrate," [30] and which has regard to proof, and νοῦς or intuitive reason, whereby we grasp a universal truth after experience of a certain number of particular instances and then see this truth or principle to be self-evident.[31] The union of νοῦς and ἐπιστήμη is theoretical wisdom or σοφία, and it is directed to the highest objects—probably including not only the objects of Metaphysics, but also those of Mathematics and Natural Science. The contemplation of these objects belongs to the ideal life for man. "Wisdom or philosophy may be defined as the combination of intuitive reason and science, or as scientific knowledge of the most precious things, with the crown of perfection, so to speak, upon it." Knowledge is dignified by its object, and Aristotle remarks that it would be absurd to call political science the highest type of knowledge, unless indeed men were the highest of all beings—and that he did not believe.[32] "There are other things in the universe of a nature far more divine

than his, as, for example, the starry heavens of which the universe is built. From all of which it is clear that wisdom is a combination of science and the speculative reason, directed to the noblest objects in creation." [33]

The virtues of τὸ λογιστικόν are τέχνη or art, "the disposition by which we make things by the aid of a true rule," [34] and practical wisdom or φρόνησις, "a true disposition towards action, by the aid of a rule, with regard to things good or bad for men." [35] φρόνησις is subdivided according to the objects with which it is concerned. (1) As concerned with the individual's good, it is φρόνησις in the narrow sense. (ii) As concerned with the family, with household management, it is called Economics (οἰκονομία). (iii) As concerned with the State, it is called Political Science in the wider sense. This latter, Politics in a wide sense, is again subdivided into (a) the Architectonic or Legislative faculty, Politics in the narrower sense, and (b) the Subordinate or Administrative faculty. The last again subdivides into (a) Deliberative and (β) Judicial. (It is important to note that, in spite of these divisions, it is really the same virtue that is called practical wisdom in connection with the individual and Politics in connection with the good of the State.)

Practical wisdom, says Aristotle, is concerned with the practical syllogism, e.g. A is the end, B is the means, therefore B should be done. (If Aristotle were confronted with the difficulty that this only gives us an hypothetical imperative and not a categorical imperative, he might answer that in ethical matters the end is happiness, and as happiness is an end that all seek and cannot help seeking, that they seek by nature, the imperative that bears on our choice of means to this end is different from the imperatives that bear on the means to some freely-chosen end, and that while the latter are hypothetical, the former is a categorical imperative.) But Aristotle, with his customary good sense, expressly recognises that some people may have knowledge of the right action to do from their experience of life, although they have not got a clear idea of the general principles. Hence it is better to know the conclusion of the practical syllogism, without the major premiss, than to know the major premiss without knowing the conclusion. [30]

In reference to Socrates' view that all virtue is a form of prudence, Aristotle declares that Socrates was partly right and partly wrong. "He was wrong in holding that all virtue is a form of prudence, but right in holding that no virtue can exist without prudence." [37] Socrates held that all the virtues were forms of reason (as being forms of knowledge), but Aristotle declares that the truth is rather that they are all *reasonable*. "Virtue is not only the right and reasonable attitude, but the attitude which leads to right and reasonable choice, and right and reasonable choice in these matters is what we mean by prudence." [38] Prudence, therefore, is necessary for the truly virtuous man, (a) as being "the excellence of an essential part of our nature," and (b) inasmuch as "there can be no right choice without both prudence and virtue, seeing that the latter secures the choice of the right end, and the former the choice of the right means to its attainment." [39] But prudence or practical wisdom is not the same thing as cleverness (δεινότης). Cleverness is the faculty by which a man is enabled to find the right means to any particular end, and a rogue may be very clever in discovering the right means to attain his ignoble end. Mere cleverness is, then, different from prudence, which presupposes virtues and is equivalent to moral insight.[40] Prudence cannot exist without cleverness, but it cannot be reduced to cleverness, for it is a moral virtue. In other words, prudence is cleverness as dealing with the means that lead to the attainment, not of any sort of end, but of the true end of man, what is best for man, and it is moral virtue that enables us to choose the right end, so that prudence presupposes moral virtue. Aristotle is quite well aware that it is possible for a man to do what is right, what he ought to do, without being a good man. He is good only if his action proceeds from moral choice and is done because it is good.[41] For this prudence is necessary.

Aristotle admits that it is possible to have "natural" virtues in separation from one another (e.g. a child might be naturally courageous, without being at the same time gentle), but in order to have a moral virtue in the full sense, as a reasonable disposition, prudence is necessary. Moreover, "given the single virtues of prudence, all the virtues necessarily follow from it." [42] Socrates was then right in holding that no virtue can exist without prudence, though he was wrong in supposing that all virtues are forms of prudence. In the *Eudemian Ethics*[43] Aristotle remarks that for Socrates all the virtues were forms of knowledge, so that to know what justice is, for example, and to be just would come simultaneously, just as we are geometers from the moment we have learned geometry. In reply Aristotle says that it is necessary to distinguish between theoretical science and productive science. "We do not wish to know what bravery is but to be brave, nor what justice is but to be just." Similarly, he observes in the *Magna Moralia*[44] that "any one who knows the essence of justice is not forthwith just," while in the *Nicomachean Ethics* he compares those who think they will become good by mere theoretical knowledge, to patients who listen attentively to what the doctor says, but carry out none of his orders.[45]

9. Aristotle refuses to admit that pleasures as such are bad. Pleasure cannot indeed be *the* good, as Eudoxus thought, for pleasure is the natural accompaniment of an unimpeded activity (as a sort of colouring attached to the activity), and it is the activity that should be aimed at, not the accompanying pleasure. We ought to choose certain activities, even if no pleasure resulted from them.[46] Nor is it true to say that all pleasures are desirable, for the activities to which certain pleasures are attached are disgraceful.

But if pleasure is not *the* good, we must not fall into the opposite extreme and say that all pleasure is wrong because some pleasures are disgraceful. As a matter of fact, says Aristotle, we might really say that disgraceful pleasures are not really pleasant, just as what appears white to a man with bad eyes, may not be really white. This observation is perhaps not very convincing: more convincing is Aristotle's remark that the pleasures themselves may be desirable, but not when obtained in such a way: and still more convincing is his suggestion that pleasures differ specifically according to the activities from which they are derived.[47]

Aristotle will not allow that pleasure is simply a replenishment, i.e. that pain represents a falling-short in the natural state, and that pleasure is a replenishment of the deficiency. It is true, indeed, that where there is replenishment there is pleasure, and that where there is exhaustion there is pain, but we cannot say universally of pleasure that it is a replenishment after antecedent pain. "The pleasures of mathematics, among the pleasures of sense those of smell as well as many sights and sounds, lastly, hopes and memories, are instances of pleasure which involve no antecedent pain." [48]

Pleasure, then, is something positive, and its effect is to perfect the exercise of a faculty. Pleasures differ specifically according to the character of the activities to which they

are attached, and the good man must be our standard
as to what is truly pleasant and unpleasant. (Aristotle remarks on the importance of training children to delight in
and dislike the proper things, for which purpose the educator
uses pleasure and pain "as a species of rudder." [49]) Some
pleasures are pleasant only to those whose nature is corrupt:
the true pleasures for man are those that accompany the
activities that are proper to man. "All others, like the
activities which they accompany, are so only in a partial
and secondary sense." [50]

In all this discussion of Pleasure, Aristotle's good sense
and psychological insight are evident. He may be thought
by some to over-emphasise the pleasures of theoretical and
purely intellectual activity, but he sedulously avoids all extreme positions, refusing to agree with Eudoxus on the one
hand that pleasure is *the* good, or with Speusippus on the
other hand that all pleasures are bad.

10. Aristotle devotes Books Eight and Nine of the *Ethics*
to the subject of Friendship. Friendship, he says, "is one of
the virtues, or at any rate implies virtue. Moreover, it is one
of the prime necessities of life." [51] Aristotle tends to give a
somewhat self-centred picture of friendship. Thus he emphasises our need for friends at different periods of our life,
and suggests that in friendship a man is loving himself—at
first hearing a rather egoistic viewpoint. But he attempts
the reconciliation of egoism and altruism by pointing out
that it is necessary to distinguish the uses of the term
"self-loving." Some men seek to get as much as possible for
themselves of money, honour or the pleasures of the body,
and these we call self-loving by way of reproach: others, i.e.
good men, are anxious to excel in virtue and noble actions,
and these, though "self-loving," we do not blame as such.
The latter type of man "will give away money in order that
his friend may have more. For the money goes to the
friend, but the noble deed to himself, and in this way he
appropriates the greater good. Similarly with regard to
honours and offices." [52] The picture of a man relinquishing
money or office to his friend in order that he himself may
have the noble action to his credit, is not altogether pleasing; but Aristotle is doubtless right in observing that there
can be a good type of self-love as well as a bad type. (Indeed we are bound to love ourselves and to make ourselves
as good as possible.) A happier thought is Aristotle's saying
that a man's relations to his friend are the same as his

relations to himself, since the friend is a second self.[53] In other words, the concept of the self is capable of extension and may grow to include friends, whose happiness or misery, success or failure, become as our own. Moreover, incidental observations, such as "friendship consists in loving rather than in being loved," [54] or that "men wish well to their friends for their sake," [55] show that his view of friendship was not so egoistic as his words would sometimes lead one to suppose.

That Aristotle's concept of friendship was a very wide one can be seen from the divisions that he makes between different types of friendship. (i) On the lowest level are friendships of utility, in which men do not love their friends for what they are in themselves, but only for the advantage which they receive from them.[56] Such friendships are necessary to man, since man is not economically self-sufficient. A business friendship would be of this type. (ii) Friendships of pleasure. These are founded on the natural delight that men take in the society of their fellow-men, and are characteristic of the young, for "young people live by feeling, and have a main eye to their own pleasure and to the present moment." [57] But both these types of friendship are unstable, for when the motive of the friendship—utility or pleasure—is gone, the friendship also is destroyed. (iii) Friendships of the good. This type of friendship is perfect friendship and endures as long as both retain their character —"and virtue," says Aristotle, "is a lasting thing."

As we would expect, Aristotle makes not a few observations on the subject of friendship, which, if not profound, are shrewd and to the point, and which are applicable not only to natural friendship, but also to supernatural friendship with Christ Our Lord. For example, he observes that friendship differs from affection in that the latter is a feeling, the former a trained habit of mind,[58] and that "the wish for friendship is of rapid growth, but friendship itself is not." [59]

11. "If happiness is activity in accordance with virtue, it is reasonable that it should be in accordance with the highest virtue, and this will be that of the best thing in us." [60] The faculty, the exercise of which constitutes perfect happiness, is, according to Aristotle, the contemplative faculty, by which he means the faculty of intellectual or philosophic activity, thus showing the intellectualist standpoint which he shared with Plato. The precise relation of moral action to the highest

type of human happiness is left obscure, but of course Aristotle makes it quite clear in the *Ethics* that without moral virtue true happiness is impossible.

Aristotle gives several reasons for saying that man's highest happiness consists in τὸ θεωρῆσαι.[61] (i) Reason is the highest faculty of man, and theoretic contemplation is the highest activity of reason. (ii) We can keep up this form of activity longer than any other, e.g. than bodily exercise. (iii) Pleasure is one of the elements of happiness, and "philosophy is admittedly the pleasantest of the activities in which human excellence manifests itself." (The last remark may have seemed a trifle unusual even to Aristotle himself, for he adds, "the pleasures of philosophy at least appear to be wonderfully pure and reliable, nor indeed is it surprising if the life of him who knows is pleasanter than that of the learner.") (iv) The philosopher is more self-sufficient than any other man. He cannot indeed dispense with the necessaries of life any more than others can (and Aristotle considered that the philosopher needs external goods in moderation and friends); but all the same "the thinker is able to pursue his studies in solitude, and the more of a thinker he is, the more capable he is of doing so." The co-operation of others is a great assistance to him, but if it be wanting, the thinker is better able than other men to get along without it. (v) Philosophy is loved for its own sake and not for the sake of any results that accrue from it. In the field of practical activity, it is not the action itself that is desirable, but some result to be attained by means of the activity. Philosophy is no mere means to a further end. (vi) Happiness would seem to imply leisure. Now, "the practical virtues find the field of their exercise in war or politics, which cannot be said to be leisurely employments, least of all war."

It is in the exercise of reason, then, and in the exercise of that reason concerning the noblest objects, that man's complete happiness is found, provided that it is extended over "a complete term of years." Such a life expresses the divine element in man, but we shall refuse to listen to those who advise us, being human and mortal, to mind things that are human and mortal. On the contrary, as far as possible, we ought to try to put off our mortality and do all we can to live the life to which the highest element in us points. For though it be but a small part of us, yet in power and value it far surpasses all the others. Moreover, it would seem to be the real self in each of us, since it is sovereign over all and better than all. And accordingly it would be strange if we were not to choose the life of our own true selves, but of something other than ourselves.[62]

What objects does Aristotle include among the objects of theoretic contemplation? He certainly includes the invariable objects of metaphysics and mathematics, but does he include the objects of natural science? Probably only so far as they are non-contingent, since the highest activity of man is, as we have already seen, concerned with objects that are not contingent. In the *Metaphysics*[63] Aristotle makes physics a branch of theoretic wisdom, though in another place in the *Metaphysics*[64] he implies that it is also the study of contingent events. Physics therefore can belong to "contemplation" only in so far as it studies the invariable or necessary element in the contingent events that constitute the object of physics.

The highest object of metaphysics is God, but in the *Nicomachean Ethics* Aristotle does not expressly include the religious attitude expressed in the definition of the ideal life contained in the *Eudemian Ethics,* namely, "the worship and contemplation of God." [65] Whether Aristotle meant this attitude of religious adoration to be understood in the picture of the ideal life given in the *Nicomachean Ethics,* or had come to lose sight of this earlier religious attitude, we cannot well decide. In any case his treatment of contemplation exercised a great influence on posterity, not least on Christian philosophers, who naturally found it well adapted to their purpose. The intellectualist attitude of Aristotle finds its echo in the teaching of St. Thomas Aquinas, that the essence of the Beatific Vision consists in the act of the intellect rather than in the will's act, on the ground that the intellect is the faculty by which we *possess*, the will the faculty by which we enjoy the object already possessed by the intellect.[66]

Chapter Thirty-Two

POLITICS

1. The State (and by State Aristotle is thinking of the Greek City-State), like every other community, exists for an end. In the case of the State this end is the supreme good of man, his moral and intellectual life. The family is the primitive community that exists for the sake of life, for the supply of men's everyday wants,[1] and when several families join together and something more than the mere supply of daily needs is aimed at, the village comes into existence. When, however, several villages are joined together to form a larger community that is "nearly or quite self-sufficing," [2] there comes into existence the State. The State comes into existence for the bare ends of life, but it continues in existence for the sake of the good life, and Aristotle insists that the State differs from family and village, not merely quantitatively but qualitatively and specifically.[3] It is only in the State that man can live the good life in any full sense, and since the good life is man's natural end, the State must be called a natural society. (The Sophists were therefore wrong in thinking that the State is simply the creation of convention.) "It is evident that the State is a creature of nature, and that man is by nature a political animal. And he who by nature and not by mere accident is without a State, is either above humanity or below it." [4] Man's gift of speech shows clearly that nature destined him for social life, and social life in its specifically complete form is, in Aristotle's view, that of the State. The State is prior to the family and to the individual in the sense that, while the State is a self-sufficing whole, neither the individual nor the

family are self-sufficient. "He who is unable to live in society, or who has no need because he is sufficient for himself, must be either a beast or a god." [5]

The Platonic-Aristotelian view of the State as exercising the positive function of serving the end of man, the leading of the good life or the acquisition of happiness, and as being *natura prior* (to be distinguished from *tempore prior*) to the individual and the family, has been of great influence in subsequent philosophy. Among Christian mediaeval philosophers it was naturally tempered by the importance they rightly attached to individual and family, and by the fact that they accepted another "perfect society," the Church, whose end is higher than that of the State (also by the fact that the nation-State was comparatively undeveloped in the Middle Ages); but we have only to think of Hegel in Germany and of Bradley and Bosanquet in England, to realise that the Greek conception of the State did not perish along with Greek freedom. Moreover, though it is a conception that can be, and has been, exaggerated (especially where Christian truth has been absent and so unable to act as a corrective to one-sided exaggeration), it is a richer and truer conception of the State than that of, e.g. Herbert Spencer. For the State exists for the temporal well-being of its citizens, i.e. for a positive and not merely for a negative end, and this positive conception of the State can quite well be maintained without contaminating it with the exaggerations of Totalitarian State mysticism. Aristotle's horizon was more or less bounded by the confines of the Greek City-State (in spite of his contacts with Alexander), and he had little idea of nations and empires; but all the same his mind penetrated to the essence and function of the State better than did the *laissez-faire* theorists and the British School from Locke to Spencer.

2. In the *Politics*, as we have it, Aristotle's treatment of the family is practically confined to discussion of the master-slave relationship and to the acquisition of wealth. Slavery (the slave, according to Aristotle, is a living instrument of action, i.e. aid to his master's life) is founded on nature. "From the hour of their birth, some are marked out for subjection, others for rule." [6] "It is clear that some men are by nature free, and others slaves, and that for these slavery is both expedient and right." [7] This view may well seem to us monstrous, but it must be remembered that the essence of Aristotle's doctrine is that men differ in

intellectual and physical capacities and are thereby fitted
for different positions in society. We regret that Aristotle
canonised the contemporary institution of slavery, but this
canonisation is largely an historical accident. Stripped of its
historic and contemporary accidentals, what is censurable in
it is not so much the recognition that men differ in ability
and in adaptability (the truth of this is too obvious to need
elaboration), but the over-rigid dichotomy drawn between
two types of men and the tendency to regard the "slave-
nature" as something almost less than human. However,
Aristotle tempered his acceptance and rationalisation of
slavery by insisting that the master should not abuse his
authority, since the interests of master and slave are the
same,[8] and by saying that all slaves should have the hope of
emancipation.[9] Moreover, he admitted that the child of a
natural slave need not himself be a natural slave, and rejected slavery by right of conquest on the ground that
superior power and superior excellence are not equivalent,
while on the other hand the war may not be a just war.[10]
Nevertheless, regarded in itself, this rationalisation of slavery
is regrettable and betrays a limited outlook on the part of
the philosopher. In fact, Aristotle rejected the legitimacy of
the historical origin of slavery (conquest), and then pro-
ceeded to give a philosophic rationalisation and justification
of slavery!

3. There are, in general, two distinct modes of acquiring
wealth, and an intermediate mode.[11]

(i) The "natural" mode consists in the accumulation of
things needed for life by, e.g. grazing, hunting, agriculture.
Man's needs set a natural limit to such accumulation.

(ii) The intermediate mode is that of barter. In barter
a thing is used apart from its "proper use," but in so far
as it is employed for the acquisition of the needs of life,
barter may be called a natural mode of acquiring wealth.

(iii) The second, and "unnatural," mode of acquiring
wealth is the use of money as a means of exchange for goods.
It seems very odd to us that Aristotle should condemn
retail trade, but his prejudice is largely determined by the
ordinary Greek attitude towards commerce, which was
regarded as illiberal and unfit for the free man. Of importance is Aristotle's condemnation of "usury," the breeding
of money out of money, as he calls it. "Money was intended
to be used in exchange, but not to increase at interest."
This, literally taken, would condemn all taking of interest

on money, but Aristotle was probably thinking of the practice of money-lenders, or usurers in our sense, who make victims of the needy, credulous and ignorant: though he certainly found a rationalisation of his attitude in his doctrine about the "natural" purpose of money. Cows and sheep have a natural increase, as have fruit-trees, but money has no such natural increase: it is meant to be a means of exchange and nothing else. To serve as a means of exchange is its natural purpose, and if it is used to get more wealth merely by a process of lending it, without any exchange of goods for money and without any labour on the part of the lender, then it is being used in an unnatural way. Needless to say, Aristotle did not envisage modern finance. If he were alive to-day, we cannot say how he would react to our financial system, and whether he would reject, modify or find a way round his former views.

4. Aristotle, as one might expect, refused to allow himself to be carried away by Plato's picture of the ideal State. He did not think that such radical changes as Plato proposed were necessary; nor did he think that they would all, if feasible, be desirable. For instance, he rejected the Platonic notion of the crèche for the children of the Guardian-class, on the ground that he who is a child of all is a child of none. Better to be a real cousin than a Platonic son![12] Similarly, he criticised the nation of communism, on the ground that this would lead to disputes, inefficiency, etc. The enjoyment of property is a source of pleasure, and it is of no use for Plato to say that the State would be made happy if the Guardians were deprived of this source of happiness, for happiness is either enjoyed by individuals or it is not enjoyed at all.[13] In general, Plato aimed at excessive unification. Aristotle had no sympathy for the accumulation of wealth as such; but he saw that there is a need, not so much of equalising all property as of training citizens not to desire excessive wealth and, if any are incapable of being trained, then of preventing them acquiring it.

5. The qualifications of citizenship are taken by Aristotle from the practice of the Athenian democracy, which was not the same as the modern democracy with its representative system. In his view all the citizens should take their share in ruling and being ruled by turn,[14] and the minimum of citizen-rights is the right to participate in the Assembly and in the administration of justice. A citizen, therefore, is he ᾧ ἐξουσία κοινωνεῖν ἀρχῆς βουλευτικῆς καὶ κριτικῆς.[15]

The fact that Aristotle considered it essential for the citizen to sit in the Assembly and in the Law Courts, led him to exclude the class of mechanics and artisans from the citizenship, for they had not got the necessary leisure. Another reason is that manual toil deliberalises the soul and makes it unfit for true virtue.[16]

6. Discussing various types of Constitution Aristotle divides governments into those which aim at the common interest and those which aim at their own private interest.[17] Each of these broad divisions has three subdivisions, so that there are three good types of Constitution and three wrong or deviation-types of Constitution. To the right form Kingship corresponds the deviation-form Tyranny, to Aristocracy Oligarchy, and to Polity Democracy, and in his treatment of the comparative merits of the various Constitutions appears Aristotle's political sense. For him the ideal is that one man should so transcend all the other citizens individually and in the mass in respect of excellence that he would be the natural monarch and ruler. But in point of fact the perfect man does not appear, and, in general, pre-eminent heroes are found only among primitive peoples. This being so, Aristocracy, i.e. the rule of many good men, is better than monarchy. Aristocracy is the best form of government for a body of people who can be ruled as freemen by men whose excellence makes them capable of political command. However, Aristotle recognises that even Aristocracy is perhaps too high an ideal for the contemporary State, and so he advocates "Polity," in which "there naturally exists a warlike multitude able to obey and to rule in turn by a law which gives office to the well-to-do according to their desert."[18] This is practically equivalent to rule by the middle-class, and is more or less a half-way house between Oligarchy and Democracy, since in a Polity it is indeed a multitude that rules—in distinction from Oligarchy—yet it is not a propertyless mob, as in Democracy, for ability to serve as a warrior, i.e. as a heavily-armed hoplite, presupposes a certain amount of property. Aristotle is probably thinking—though he does not refer to it—of the Constitution at Athens in 411 B.C., when power rested with the Five Thousand who possessed heavy armour and the system of payment for attendance at meetings had been abolished. This was the Constitution of Theramenes.[19] Aristotle admired this type of Constitution, but his contention that the middle-class is the most stable, since both rich and poor are more likely to

trust the middle-class than one another (so that the middle-class need fear no coalition against it) may not sound so convincing to us as it did to him, though there is doubtless some truth in the view.[20]

7. Aristotle treats acutely of the various kinds and degrees of revolution which tend to occur under different Constitutions, of their causes and the means of preventing them; and, owing to his great historical knowledge, he was able to give apt historical illustrations of the points he wished to make.[21] He points out, for instance, that the revolutionary state of mind is largely brought about by one-sided notions of justice—democrats thinking that men who are equally free should be equal in everything, oligarchs thinking that because men are unequal in wealth they should be unequal in everything. He emphasises the fact that rulers should have no opportunity of making money for themselves out of the offices they hold, and stresses the requisites for high office in the State, namely, loyalty to the Constitution, capacity for administrative work and integrity of character. Whatever be the type of Constitution, it must be careful not to go to extremes; for if either democracy or oligarchy is pushed to extremes the ensuing rise of malcontent parties will be sure to lead in the end to revolution.

8. In Books Seven and Eight of the *Politics* Aristotle discusses his positive views of what a State should be.

(i) The State must be large enough to be self-sufficing (of course Aristotle's notion of what a self-sufficing community actually is would be altogether inadequate for modern times), but not so large that order and good government are rendered impracticable. In other words, it must be large enough to fulfil the end of the State and not so large that it can no longer do so. The number of citizens requisite for this purpose cannot of course be arithmetically determined *a priori*.[22]

(ii) Similarly with the territorial extent of the State. This should not be so small that a leisured life is impossible (i.e. that culture is impracticable) nor yet so large that luxury is encouraged. The city should not aim at mere wealth, but at importing her needs and exporting her surplus.[23]

(iii) Citizens. Agricultural labourers and artisans are necessary, but they will not enjoy citizen rights. Only the third class, that of the warriors, will be citizens in the full sense. These will be warriors in youth, rulers or magistrates in

middle-age and priests in old age. Each citizen will possess
a plot of land near the city and another near the frontier
(so that all may have an interest in the defence of the
State). This land will be worked by the non-citizen
labourers.[24]

(iv) Education. Aristotle, like Plato, attached great importance to education and, again like Plato, he considered
it to be the work of the State. Education must begin with
the body, since the body and its appetites develop earlier
than the soul and its faculties; but the body is to be trained
for the sake of the soul and the appetites for the sake of
the reason. Education is therefore, first and foremost, a moral
education—the more so because the citizen will never have to
earn his living by work as husbandman or artisan, but will
be trained to be, first a good soldier, and then a good
ruler and magistrate.[25] This emphasis on moral education
shows itself in Aristotle's views concerning pre-natal care
and the games of the children. The Directors of Education
will take all these matters very seriously, and will not consider
the games of the children and the stories that are told them
as things too insignificant for them to attend to. (In
regard to musical education Aristotle makes the amusing remark, that "The rattle is a toy suited to the infant mind,
and musical education is a rattle or toy for children of a
larger growth." [26])

As the *Politics* is unfortunately incomplete—the sections
dealing with education in science and philosophy being missing—we cannot say what precise directions Aristotle would
have given in regard to the higher education of the citizens.
One thing, however, is obvious, that both Plato and Aristotle had a lofty and noble conception of education and of the
ideal of the citizens. They would have but scant sympathy
with any scheme of education that laid the emphasis on
technical and utilitarian training, since such a scheme
leaves the higher faculties of the soul untended and so fails
to fit man to attain his proper end, which is the purpose of
education. For although it may sometimes look as though
Aristotle wanted to educate men merely to be cogs in the
State machine, this is really not the case: in his eyes the end
of the State and the end of the individual coincide, not in
the sense that the individual should be entirely absorbed
in the State but in the sense that the State will prosper
when the individual citizens are good, when they attain
their own proper end. The only real guarantee of the

stability and prosperity of the State is the moral goodness and integrity of the citizens, while conversely, unless the State is good and the system of its education is rational, moral and healthy, the citizens will not become good. The individual attains his proper development and perfection through his concrete life, which is a life in Society, i.e. in the State, while Society attains its proper end through the perfection of its members. That Aristotle did not consider the State to be a great Leviathan beyond good and evil is clear from the criticism he passes on the Lacedaemonians. It is a great mistake, he says, to suppose that war and domination are the be-all and end-all of the State. The State exists for the good life, and it is subject to the same code of morality as the individual. As he puts it, "the same things are best for individuals and states." [27] Reason and history both show that the legislator should direct all his military and other measures to the establishment of peace. Military States are safe only in wartime: once they have acquired their empire, they rust away like iron and fall. Both Plato and Aristotle, in their preoccupation with the fostering of a truly cultural political life, set their faces against imperialist dreams of military aggrandisement.

Chapter Thirty-Three

AESTHETICS OF ARISTOTLE

1. Beauty

1. Aristotle distinguishes the beautiful from the merely pleasant. For example, in the *Problemata*[1] he contrasts sexual preference with aesthetic selection, thus distinguishing real objective beauty from "beauty" that has reference only to desire. Again in the *Metaphysics*[2] he says that the mathematical sciences are not unrelated to the beautiful. The beautiful, therefore, for him cannot be the merely pleasant, that which pleasantly stimulates the senses.

2. Does Aristotle distinguish beauty from the good? He would seem not to have been very clear on this point.

    (a) In the *Rhetoric*[3] he states that "the beautiful is that good which is pleasant because it is good," a definition which would not seem to admit of any real distinction between the beautiful and the moral. (Professor W. Rhys Roberts translates τὸ καλόν as Noble, cf. *Oxford Trans.*, Vol. XI.)

    (b) In the *Metaphysics*, however, he expressly states that "the good and the beautiful are different (for the former always implies conduct as its subject, while the beautiful is found also in motionless things)." [4] This statement seems to differentiate between the beautiful and the moral at least, and may be taken to imply that the beautiful as such is not simply the object of desire. This should allow of a doctrine of aesthetic contemplation and of the *disinterested* character of such contemplation—as stated by e.g. Kant and Schopenhauer.

3. A further definition or description—and a more satis-

factory one—is found in the *Metaphysics*[5] where Aristotle says that "the chief forms of beauty are order and symmetry and definiteness." It is the possession of these three properties that confers on mathematics a certain diagnostic value in regard to beautiful objects. (Aristotle seems to have been conscious of his obscurity, for he goes on to promise a more intelligible treatment, though, if the promise was ever fulfilled, its fulfilment is not extant.)

Similarly in the *Poetics*[6] Aristotle says that "beauty is a matter of size and order" or consists in size and order. Thus he declares that a living creature, in order to be beautiful, must present a certain order in its arrangement of parts and also possess a certain definite magnitude, neither too great nor too small. This would tally more or less with the definition in the *Metaphysics* and would imply that the beautiful is the object of contemplation and not of desire.

4. It is interesting to note that Aristotle in the *Poetics*[7] makes the subject-matter of Comedy to be the ridiculous, "which is a species of the ugly." (The ridiculous is "a mistake or deformity not productive of pain or harm to others.") This would imply that the ugly may be employed in a work of art, subordinated to the total effect. Aristotle does not, however, treat expressly of the relation of the ugly to the beautiful nor of the question, how far the "ugly" may become a constitutive element of the beautiful.[8]

2. Fine Art in General

1. Morality aims at conduct itself (πράττειν), Art at producing something, not at activity itself. But Art in general (τέχνη) must be subdivided[9] into:

(a) Art that aims at completing the work of nature, e.g. producing tools, since nature has provided man only with his hands.

(b) Art that aims at *imitating* nature. This is Fine Art, the essence of which Aristotle, like Plato, finds in imitation. In other words, in art an imaginary world is created which is an imitation of the real world.

2. But "imitation" has not, for Aristotle, the rather contemptuous colouring that it has for Plato. Not believing in Transcendental Concepts, Aristotle would naturally not make art a copy of a copy, at the third remove from truth. In fact, Aristotle inclines to the opinion that the artist goes rather to the ideal or the universal element in things, trans-

lating it into the medium of whatever art is in question. He says[10] that Tragedy makes its personages better, Comedy worse, than the "men of the present day." According to Aristotle, Homer's personages are better than we are. (Homer, it will be remembered, came in for some very hard knocks at the hands of Plato.)

3. Imitation, Aristotle insists, is natural to man, and it is also natural for man to delight in works of imitation. He points out that we may delight to view artistic representations of what is, in reality, painful to us to see.[11] (Cf. Kant, in passage already quoted in footnote.) But the explanation of this fact he seems to find in the purely intellectual pleasure of recognising that this man in the picture, for example, is someone we know, e.g. Socrates. This pleasure in recognition is no doubt a fact, but it hardly goes far towards constructing a theory of art: in fact, it is really irrelevant.

4. Aristotle expressly states that poetry "is something more philosophic and of graver import than history, since its statements are of the nature rather of universals, whereas those of history are singulars." [12] He goes on to explain that by a singular statement he means what e.g. Alcibiades did or had done to him, and by an universal statement "what such or such a kind of man will probably or necessarily say or do." The poet's function is, therefore, "to describe, not the thing that has happened, but a kind of thing that might happen, i.e. what is possible as being probable or necessary." It is in this that Aristotle finds the distinction between poet and historian, not in the one writing verse and the other prose. As he remarks: "you might put the work of Herodotus into verse, and it would still be a species of history."

On this theory, then, the artist deals rather with *types*, which are akin to the universal and ideal. An historian might write the life of Napoleon, telling what the historic figure Napoleon said and did and suffered: the poet, however, though he called the hero of his epic Napoleon, would rather portray universal truth or "probability." Adherence to historic fact is of minor importance in poetry. The poet may indeed take a subject from real history, but if what he describes is in—to use Aristotle's words—"the probable and possible order of things," he is none the less a poet. Aristotle even says that it is much better for the poet to describe what is probable but impossible than what is possible but improbable. This is simply a way of emphasising the universal character of poetry.

5. It is to be noted that Aristotle says that the statements of poetry are of the nature *rather* of universals. In other words, poetry is not concerned with the abstract universal: poetry is not philosophy. Aristotle accordingly censures didactic poetry, for to give a system of philosophy in verse is to write versified philosophy; it is not to produce poetry.

6. In the *Poetics* Aristotle confines himself to a consideration of Epic, Tragedy and Comedy, particularly Tragedy: painting and sculpture and music are only mentioned incidentally, as when he tells us[13] that the painter Polygnotus portrayed personages "better than we are," Pauson worse, and Dionysius "just like ourselves." But what he does have to say on the subject of the other arts is important for his theory of imitation.

Thus *Music* (which is treated more or less as an accompaniment to the drama) was declared by Aristotle to be the most imitative of all the arts. Pictorial art only indicates mental or moral moods through external factors such as gesture or complexion, whereas musical tunes contain *in themselves* imitations of moral moods. And in the *Problemata*[14] he asks, "Why does what is heard alone of the objects of sense possess emotional import?" Aristotle would seem to be thinking of the direct stimulative effect of music which, though a fact, is hardly an aesthetic fact; yet the theory that music is the most imitative of the arts would none the less seem to extend the concept of imitation so far as to include *symbolism,* and to open the way to the romantic conception of music as a direct embodiment of spiritual emotion. (In the *Poetics* Aristotle remarks that "rhythm alone, without harmony, is the means in the dancer's imitations; for even he, by the rhythms of his attitudes, may represent men's characters, as well as what they do and suffer." [15])

7. In the *Politics*[16] Aristotle observes that drawing is useful in the education of the young, to acquire a "more correct judgment of the works of artists," and he argues also[17] that "music has a power of forming the character, and should therefore be introduced into the education of the young." It might seem, then, that Aristotle's interest in Fine Art is mainly educational and moral; but, as Bosanquet remarks, "to introduce aesthetic interest into education is not the same as to introduce educational interest into aesthetic." [18] Aristotle certainly regarded both music and the drama as having as one of their functions that of moral education; but it does not necessarily follow that a person who recog-

nises this function thereby makes the moral effect of an art a characteristic of its essence.

But though Aristotle dwells on the educational and moral aspect of art, that does not mean that he was blind to its recreative nature or effect.[19] If by allowing to music and the drama a recreative function he had referred merely to sense-pleasure or a tickling of the fancy, this would have been irrelevant to aesthetic; but higher recreation might well mean something more.

3. Tragedy

1. Aristotle's famous definition of tragedy is as follows:[20] "A tragedy—is the imitation of an action that is serious (σπουδαίας) and also, as having magnitude, complete in itself; in language with pleasurable accessories, each kind brought in separately in the parts of the work; in a dramatic, not in a narrative form; with incidents arousing pity and fear, wherewith to accomplish its catharsis (κάθαρσις) of such emotions."

I may add in explanation one or two points:

(i) "Serious," "noble," "good," indicate the character of the content of tragedy. This it shares with Epic poetry, and by it both are distinguished from Comedy and Satire, which deal with the inferior or ugly or ridiculous.

(ii) "Complete in itself," i.e. having beginning, middle and—being an organic whole. This *unity of plot* or organic unity of structure is the only unity strictly demanded by Aristotle.

In the *Poetics*[21] Aristotle does indeed observe that tragedy, in distinction from epic poetry, "endeavours to keep as far as possible within a single circuit of the sun or something near that"; but this is simply a statement of fact and he does not expressly state a demand for Unity of Time. As for Unity of Place, it is not mentioned. It is incorrect, therefore, to say that Aristotle demanded the three Unities in drama.

(iii) "Language with pleasurable accessories." Aristotle tells us himself that he means "with rhythm and harmony or song superadded."

(iv) "Each kind brought in separately," i.e. "some portions are worked out with verse only, and others in turn with song." Aristotle is naturally thinking of

Greek tragedy with its alternations of spoken verse and choral songs.

(v) "In a dramatic, not in a narrative form." This distinguishes tragedy from epic poetry.

(vi) Catharsis. This states the psychological end or aim of tragedy, and I shall return to it presently.

2. Aristotle enumerates six formative elements of tragedy ... fable or plot, characters, diction, thought, spectacle and melody.[22]

(i) The most important of these elements, in Aristotle's opinion, is the Plot, which is "the end and purpose of the tragedy." It is more important than Character, for "in a play—they do not act in order to portray the characters; they include the characters for the sake of action." Aristotle gives his reason for this somewhat strangely sounding dictum. "Tragedy is essentially an imitation not of persons but of action and life, of happiness and misery. All human happiness or misery takes the form of action; the end for which we live is a certain kind of activity, not a quality. Character gives us qualities, but it is in our actions—what we do—that we are happy or the reverse—a tragedy is impossible without action, but there may be one without Character." [23] (It is true perhaps that we can enjoy a good story in which the character-drawing is defective better than one in which the character-drawing is good but the plot is ridiculous.)

(ii) Aristotle, however, does not mean to belittle the importance of character-delineation in the drama: he admits that a tragedy without it is a defective tragedy and esteems it the most important element after the Plot.

(iii) "Thirdly comes the element of Thought, i.e. the power of saying whatever can be said, or what is appropriate to the occasion." Aristotle is thinking here, not of speech as revealing character directly but of speech "on a purely indifferent subject," i.e. Thought shown "in all they say when proving or disproving some particular point, or enunciating some universal proposition." Euripides certainly used tragedy as an opportunity for discussions on various topics; but we may well feel that the drama is scarcely the place for Socratic disquisitions.

(iv) Diction, i.e. the verse and prose. This is important, but, as Aristotle wisely remarks, "one may string together a series of characteristic speeches of the utmost finish as regards Diction and Thought, and yet fail to produce the true tragic effect."

(v) Melody is "the greatest of the pleasurable accessories of Tragedy."

(vi) The Spectacle is indeed an attraction; but it is "the least of all the parts, and has least to do with the art of poetry." The getting-up of the *mise en scène* is "more a matter for the costumier than for the poet." It is a pity that Aristotle's words on this matter have not been heeded in later times. Elaborate scenery and spectacular effect are poor substitutes for plot and character-drawing.

3. Aristotle demands, as we have seen, unity of plot, in the sense of organic, structural unity. The plot must be neither so vast that it cannot be taken in at once by the memory nor so short that it is small and insignificant. But he points out that unity of plot "does not consist, as some suppose, in its having one man as its subject," nor in describing everything that happens to the hero. The ideal is that the several incidents of the plot should be so connected "that the transposal or withdrawal of any one of them will disjoin and dislocate the whole. For that which makes no perceptible difference by its presence or absence is no real part of the whole." The incidents must follow one another, not "episodically" but with probability or necessity. As Aristotle observes, "there is a great difference between a thing happening *propter hoc* and *post hoc*" (διὰ τάδε ἢ μετὰ τάδε).

4. Aristotle thought of Tragedy (complex, at least) as involving Peripety or Discovery, or both: (i) Περιπέτεια is the change from one state of things to the opposite, e.g. when the Messenger reveals the secret of Oedipus' birth, the whole state of affairs is changed within the play, for Oedipus realises that he has, unwittingly committed incest, (ii) Ἀναγνώρισις is "a change from ignorance to knowledge, and thus to either love or hate, in the personages marked for good or evil fortune." [24] In the case of Oedipus the Discovery is of course attended by Peripety, and this is, according to Aristotle, the finest form of Discovery. Thus is attained the tragic effect, the arousing of pity and fear.

5. Since tragedy is an imitation of actions arousing pity

and fear, there are three forms of plot that must be avoided:

(i) A good man must not be seen passing from happiness to misery, as this is, in Aristotle's opinion, simply odious and will distract our minds by such disgust and horror that the tragic effect will not be realised.

(ii) A bad man must not be seen passing from misery to happiness. This is quite "untragic," appealing neither to our pity nor to our fear.

(iii) An extremely bad man must not be seen falling from happiness to misery. This may arouse human feeling but neither pity nor fear, for pity is occasioned by undeserved misfortune and fear by the misfortune of one like ourselves.

It remains, then, that tragedy should portray an "intermediate" type of person passing through misfortune, brought about by some error of judgment and not by vice or depravity. Aristotle accordingly refuses to agree with critics who censured Euripides for giving an unhappy ending to many of his plays, for this is the proper thing for tragedy, though not for Comedy. (Though there were occasional comic interludes in Greek tragedies, the tendency was to have unmixed tragedy or unmixed comedy, and Aristotle's views rather reflect this tendency.)

6. Tragic pity and fear should be aroused by the plot itself, and not by extraneous elements, e.g. by the portrayal of a brutal murder on the stage. (Aristotle would of course thoroughly approve of the way in which the murder of Agamemnon took place behind the scenes. Presumably he would censure the murder of Desdemona on the stage.)

7. We come now to the consideration of the psychological aim of tragedy, the arousing of pity and fear for the κάθαρσις of these emotions. The exact meaning to be attached to this famous doctrine of the κάθαρσις has been a subject of constant discussion: as Professor Ross says, "a whole library has been written on this famous doctrine." [25] The solution of the difficulty is rendered all the harder by the fact that the second book of the *Poetics* is missing—in which, it is conjectured, Aristotle explained what he meant by *catharsis* (and probably also treated of Comedy).

Two main lines of explanation have been defended. (i) The catharsis in question is a *purification* of the emotions of pity and fear, the metaphor being drawn from ceremonial purification (the view of Lessing); (ii) the catharsis is a *temporary elimination* of the emotions of pity and fear, the metaphor being drawn from medicine (the view of Bernays). This latter view is the one that is most acceptable, i.e. from the exegetic standpoint, and now generally holds the field. According to this view the proximate object of tragedy, in Aristotle's eyes, is to arouse the emotions of pity and fear, i.e. pity for the past and actual sufferings of the hero, fear for those which loom before him. The ulterior object of tragedy then would be to relieve or purge the soul of these emotions through the harmless and pleasurable outlet afforded by the medium of art. The implication is that these emotions are undesirable, or rather that they are undesirable when in excess, but that all men, or at any rate most men, are subject to them, some in an excessive degree, so that it is a healthy and beneficial practice for all—necessary in the case of some—to give them a periodic opportunity of excitation and outlet through the medium of art, the process being at the same time a pleasurable one. This would be Aristotle's answer to Plato's criticism of tragedy in the *Republic:* tragedy has not a demoralising effect but is a harmless pleasure. How far Aristotle recognised an intellectual element in this recreation, is a question we cannot answer with only a truncated *Poetics* before us.

That Aristotle had in mind a purgative effect and not a moral purificative effect seems to be borne out by the *Politics*.

(i) According to Aristotle the flute has an exciting, and not an ethical effect, and should be left to professionals and kept for times when the hearing of music is a κάθαρσις rather than a form of education.[26] The inference is that catharsis is connected, not with ethical effect but with emotional effect.

(ii) Aristotle admits the "enthusiastic" harmonies in a well-ordered State, because they restore those who are subject to fits of enthusiasm to the normal condition. He then goes on to enumerate three purposes for which music should be studied: (*a*) "education," (*b*) "purification" ("the word 'purification' we use at present without explanation, but when hereafter we speak of poetry, we will treat the subject with more precision"), (*c*) "for intellectual enjoyment, for relaxation and for recreation after exertion." From this enumeration alone one might suppose, applying what is said to tragedy, that the tragic effect might be ethical and purgative at the same time.

But Aristotle proceeds to make a distinction. "In education ethical melodies are to be performed, but we may listen to the melodies of action and passion when they are performed by others. For feelings such as pity and fear, or again, enthusiasm, exist very strongly in some souls, and have more or less influence over all. Some persons fall into a religious frenzy whom we see disenthralled by the use of mystic melodies, which bring healing and purification to the soul. Those who are influenced by pity or fear and every emotional nature have a like experience, others in their degree are stirred by something which specially affects them, and all are in a manner purified and their souls lightened and delighted. The melodies of purification likewise give an innocent pleasure to mankind." [27] From this it would appear that the catharsis of pity and fear, though an "innocent pleasure," is not looked upon by Aristotle as ethical in character; and if it is not ethical in character, then "purification" should not be interpreted as purification in an ethical sense, but in a non-ethical sense, i.e. as a metaphor from medicine.

This interpretation is not acceptable to all. Thus Professor Stace declares that "The theory of certain scholars, based upon etymological grounds, that it means that the soul is purged, not *through*, but *of* pity and terror, that by means of a diarrhoea of these unpleasant emotions we get rid of them and are left happy, is the thought of men whose scholarship may be great, but whose understanding of art is limited. Such a theory would reduce Aristotle's great and illuminating criticism to the meaningless babble of a philistine." [28] The question, however, is not what is the *right* view of tragedy, but what was *Aristotle's* view. In any case, even the upholders of the "diarrhoea" theory could agree with Stace's own interpretation of Aristotle's meaning ("the representation of truly great and tragic sufferings arouses in the beholder pity and terror which purge his spirit, and render it serene and pure"), provided that "pure" is not understood as the term of an educational process.

4. Origins of Tragedy and Comedy

1. According to Aristotle,[29] tragedy began with "improvisation" on the part of the leader of the Dithyramb, no doubt between the two halves of the chorus. In origin, therefore, it would be connected with the worship of Dionysus, just as the renaissance of the drama in Europe was connected with the mediaeval mystery plays.

2. Comedy began in a parallel manner, from the phallic songs, "which still survive as institutions in many of our cities." He thought no doubt of the leader coming to improvise some scurrilous piece.

3. The most significant thing in the development of the drama is for Aristotle the increasing importance of the actor. Aeschylus first increased the number of actors to two, curtailing the business of the Chorus. Sophocles added a third actor and scenery.

4. When spoken parts were introduced, the iambic metre was brought in as "the most speakable of metres." ("The reason for their original use of the trochaic tetrameter was that their poetry was satyric and more connected with dancing than it now is.")

Discussion of the highly problematic question of the origins of tragedy and comedy scarcely belongs to the history of philosophy; so I will content myself with the foregoing brief indication of the view of Aristotle, which bristles with difficulties (i) as to interpretation, (ii) as to its correctness.

Note on the Older Peripatetics

The old Academy continued the mathematical speculation of Plato: the older Peripatetics continued Aristotle's empirical trend, while adhering closely to the general philosophical position of their Master, though they made slight modifications and developments, e.g. in the field of logic. Thus both Theophrastus and Eudemus of Rhodes adhered pretty faithfully to the metaphysical and ethical tenets of Aristotle, this being especially true of Eudemus who was termed by Simplicius the γνησιώτατος of Aristotle's disciples.[30] Theophrastus ardently defended the Aristotelian doctrine of the eternity of the world against Zeno the Stoic.

Theophrastus of Eresus in Lesbos succeeded Aristotle as head of the Peripatetic School in 322/1 and continued in that office until his death in 288/7 or 287/6.[31] He is chiefly remarkable for his continuation of Aristotle's work in the field of empirical science. Applying himself particularly to Botany, he left works on that subject which made him the botanical authority up to the end of the Middle Ages, while through his zoological studies he seemed to have grasped the fact that changes of colour in the animal world are partly due to "adaptation to environment." A scholar of wide interests, like Aristotle himself, Theophrastus also composed a history of philosophy (the famous φυσικῶν δόξαι) and works on the history and nature of religion, Περὶ θεῶν, Περὶ εὐσεβείας and Περὶ τὸ θεῖον ἱστορία. Of these works only part of the history of philosophy has come down to us, while Porphyry has preserved some of the Περὶ εὐσεβείας[32] Believing that all living beings are akin, Theophrastus rejected animal-sacrifices and the eating of flesh-meat and declared that *all* men are related to one another and not merely the fellow-members of a nation. One may also mention his celebrated work, the *Characters,* a study of thirty types of character.

Aristoxenus of Tarentum brought with him into the Peripatetic School certain of the later Pythagorean theories, e.g. the doctrine that the soul is the harmony of the body, a doctrine that led Aristoxenus to deny the soul's immortality.[33] He thus championed the view suggested by Simmias in the *Phaedo* of Plato. But he followed in the footsteps of Aristotle by his empirical work on the nature and history of music.

Aristoxenus' theory of the soul was shared by Dicaearchus of Messene,[34] who composed a βίος Ἑλλάδος, in which he traced the civilisation of Greece through the stages of primitive savagery, nomadic life and agriculture. He differed from Aristotle in that he accorded the practical life the preference over the theoretical.[35] In his Τριπολιτικός he declared that the best constitution is a mixture of the three types of government, monarchy, aristocracy and democracy, and considered that this type of mixed constitution was realised at Sparta.

Demetrius of Phaleron, a pupil of Theophrastus, and a prolific writer[36] is remarkable for his political activity (he was head of the government at Athens from 317 until 307) and for having urged Ptolemy Soter to found the library and School of Alexandria (whither Demetrius betook himself about 297). As this project was realised by Ptolemy Philadelphus, the successor of Ptolemy Soter, shortly after 285,

Demetrius furnished the link between the work of the Peripatos at Athens and the scientific and research work of the Greeks at Alexandria, the city which was to become a celebrated centre of scholarship and learning.

Chapter Thirty-Four

PLATO AND ARISTOTLE

Plato and Aristotle are, without a shadow of doubt, not only the two greatest Greek philosophers, but also two of the greatest philosophers the world has seen. They had much in common with one another (how should it not be so, when Aristotle was for many years a pupil of Plato and began from the Platonic standpoint?); but there is also a marked difference of outlook between them, which, if one prescinds from the very considerable common element, enables one to characterise their respective philosophies as standing to one another in the relation of thesis (Platonism) to antithesis (Aristotelianism), a thesis and an antithesis which need to be reconciled in a higher synthesis, in the sense that the valuable and true elements in both need to be harmoniously developed in a more complete and adequate system than the single system of either philosopher taken in isolation. Platonism may be characterised by reference to the idea of Being, in the sense of abiding and steadfast reality, Aristotelianism by reference to the idea of Becoming; but, if unchanging being is real, so also are change and becoming real, and to both aspects of reality must justice be done by any adequate system of philosophy.

To characterise the philosophy of Plato by reference to the idea of Being and that of Aristotle by reference to the idea of Becoming, is to be guilty of a generalisation, a generalisation which does not, of course, represent the whole truth. Did not Plato treat of Becoming, did he not propound a theory of teleology, it may be asked with justice; did he not recognise the material world as the sphere of change and did he not even explicitly admit that change or movement

113

(so far as this is involved by the nature of life or soul) must belong to the sphere of the real? On the other hand, did not Aristotle find a place, and a very important place, for unchanging being, did he not, even in the changing, material world, discover an element of stability, of fixity, did he not declare that the sublimest occupation of man is the contemplation of unchanging objects? One cannot but give an affirmative answer to these questions; yet the truth of the generalisation is not disposed of, since it refers to what is peculiarly characteristic in each system, to its general tone or flavour, to the general orientation of the philosopher's thought. I will attempt briefly to justify this generalisation, or at least to indicate the lines along which I should attempt to justify it in detail, did space permit.

Plato, like Socrates, assumed the validity of ethical judgments; like Socrates again, he attempted to reach a clear apprehension of ethical values dialectically, to enshrine their nature in definition, to crystallise the ethical idea. He came to see, however, that if ethical concepts and ethical judgments are objective and universally valid, these concepts must possess some objective foundation. Obviously enough moral values are ideals, in the sense that they are not concrete things like sheep or dogs: they are what ought to be realised in the concrete world, or what it is desirable to realise in the concrete world, through human conduct: hence the objectivity attaching to values cannot be the same kind of objectivity that attaches to sheep or dogs, but must be an ideal objectivity or an objectivity in the ideal order. Moreover, material things in this world change and perish, whereas moral values, Plato was convinced, are unchanging. He concluded, therefore, that moral values are ideal, yet objective, essences, apprehended intuitively at the end of a process of dialectic. These moral values, however, have a common share in goodness or perfection, so that they are rightly said to participate in, to derive their goodness or perfection from, the supreme ideal essence, absolute goodness or perfection, the Idea of the Good, the "sun" of the ideal world.

In this way Plato elaborated a metaphysic on the basis of the Socratic ethic, and, being based on the thought of Socrates, it could, without undue propriety, be put into the mouth of Socrates. But, in the course of time, Plato came to apply his dialectic, not only to moral and aesthetic values, but to the common concept in general, maintaining that, just as good things participate in goodness, so individual substances participate in the specific essence. This new viewpoint cannot be said to constitute a radical break in Plato's thought, inasmuch as the theory of values itself rested to a certain extent on a logical foundation (that the common name must have an objective reference), it is rather an extension of the theory; but the new viewpoint forced Plato to consider more closely, not only the relation between the Ideas themselves, but also between sensible objects and the Ideas or exemplary essences. He thus developed his theory of the hierarchic noetic structure and the "communion" between the Ideas and explained participation as imitation, with the result that, in place of pure values on the one hand and bearers of values on the other, there was substituted the dichotomy between true essential Reality, the objective noetic structure and sensible particulars, between the original and the mirrored or "copy." This division came to have the force of a division between Being on the one hand and Becoming on the other, and there can be no question on which side of the dividing line Plato's chief interest lay.

It may be objected that Plato regarded the specific essence of e.g. man as an ideal and that the true meaning of Becoming is to be sought in the gradual approximation to and realisation of the ideal in the material world, in human personality and society, a realisation which is the task of God and of God's human co-operators. This is perfectly true, and I have not the slightest wish to belittle the importance of teleology in the Platonic philosophy; but none the less, the emphasis was most decidedly placed by Plato on the sphere of Being, of true Reality. Through his doctrine of teleology he certainly admitted some relation between the changing world and the unchanging world of Being; but becoming as such and particularity as such were to him the irrational, the factor that must be dismissed into the sphere of the indeterminate. How could it be otherwise for a thinker to whom logic and ontology are one, or at least parallel? Thought is concerned with the universal and thought apprehends Being: the universal, then, is Being and the particular as such is not Being. The universal is unchanging, so that Being is unchanging, the particular changes, becomes, perishes, and in so far as it changes, becomes, perishes, it is not Being. Philosophical activity or dialectic is an activity of thought and is thus concerned with Being primarily and only secondarily with Becoming, in so far as it "imitates" Being, so that Plato, as philosopher, was primarily interested in essential and unchanging Being. He was also interested, it is true, in the moulding of the world according to the pattern of Being; but the emphasis is placed unmistakably on Being rather than on Becoming.

It might seem that much of what I have said in regard to Plato would apply equally well, perhaps even better, to Aristotle, who asserted that the metaphysician is concerned with being as being, who referred change and becoming to the final causality of the unmoved First Mover, who taught that man's highest activity is the theoretic contemplation of unchanging objects, of those beings which are *par excellence* being, actuality, form. Nevertheless, this very real side of the Aristotelian philosophy represents rather the Platonic legacy, even if elaborated and developed by Aristotle himself. I do not intend for a moment to question the fact that Aristotle attributed great importance to this aspect of his philosophy or the fact that Aristotle accomplished a great deal in this line of speculation, e.g. by bringing out clearly the intellectual and immaterial nature of pure form and so making a contribution of tremendous value to natural theology; but I wish to inquire into the character of Aristotle's peculiar contribution to philosophy in so far as he deviated from Platonism, to ask what was the antithesis that Aristotle set over against the Platonic thesis.

What was Aristotle's chief objection against the Platonic theory of Ideas? That it left an unbridged chasm between sensible objects and the Ideas. As the sensible objects were said to imitate or participate in the Ideas, one would expect to find Plato admitting some internal essential principle, some formal cause within the object itself, placing it in its class, constituting it in its essence, whereas in point of fact Plato did not allow for an interior formal principle of this sort, but left a dualism of pure universal and pure particular, a dualism which resulted in depriving the sensible world of most of its reality and meaning. What was Aristotle's answer to this objection? While admitting the general Platonic position that the universal element, or essential form, is the object of science, of rational knowledge, he identified this universal element with the immanent essential form of the sensible object, which, together with its matter, constitutes the object and which is the intelligible principle in the object. This formal principle realises itself in the activity of the object, e.g. the formal principle in an organism, its entelechy, expresses itself in organic functions, unfolds itself in matter, organises, moulds and shapes matter, tends towards an end, which is the adequate manifestation of the essence, of the "idea," in the phenomenon. All nature is conceived as a hierarchy of species, in each of which the essence tends towards its full actualisation in a series of phenomena, drawn, in some rather mysterious way, by the ultimate final causality of the supreme Unmoved Mover, which is itself complete actuality, pure immaterial Being or Thought, self-subsistent and self-contained. Nature is thus a dynamical process of self-perfection or self-development, and the series of phenomena has meaning and value.

From this brief statement of Aristotle's position it should be quite clear that his philosophy is not simply a philosophy of Becoming. Being may truly be predicated of something in so far as it is actual, and that which is *par excellence* Being is also *par excellence* Actuality, unmixed with potency; the world of becoming, being a world of realisation, of reduction of potency to act, is a world in which actuality or being is being constantly realised in matter, in phenomena, under the final attraction of ultimate Actuality or Being; so that the explanation of Becoming is to be found in Being, for Becoming is for the sake of Being, which is always logically, even when it is not temporally, prior. If I say, then, that Aristotle was possessed by the concept of Becoming, that his philosophy, as peculiarly his, may justly be characterised by reference to his doctrine of Becoming, I do not mean to deny that Being was, for him as for Plato, of supreme importance or that he gave a metaphysic of Being which was, in some respects, greatly superior to that of Plato: what I mean is, that Aristotle, through his theory of the entelechy, the immanent substantial form, which tends to its realisation in the processes of nature, was enabled to attach a meaning and reality to the sensible world which are missing in the philosophy of Plato and that this particular contribution to philosophy gives a characteristic tone and flavour to Aristotelianism as distinct from Platonism. Aristotle said that the end of man is an activity, not a quality, whereas one has the impression that for Plato quality would take precedence of activity: Plato's "Absolute" was not the immanent activity of Aristotle's "self-thinking Thought" and Plato's "Absolute" was the supreme Exemplar. (That Aristotle's characterisation of matter tended to diminish the

reality and intelligibility of the material world is no objection against my main thesis, since his doctrine of matter
was very largely an effect of his Platonic education, and my
main thesis is concerned with Aristotle's *peculiar* contribution
to the philosophy of nature.)

Aristotle thus made a most important contribution to the
philosophy of nature and he certainly regarded himself as
having broken fresh ground. In the first place, he regarded
his doctrine of the *immanent* essence as an antithesis to, or
correction of, Plato's doctrine of the transcendental essence,
and, in the second place, his remarks concerning the emer-
gence of the idea of finality in philosophy, even if those
remarks are to some extent patently unjust to Plato, show
clearly that he regarded his theory of immanent teleology
as something new. But though Aristotle provided a needed
correction or antithesis to Platonism in this respect, he discarded much that was of value in the process of correcting
his predecessor. Not only was Plato's conception of Providence, of Divine Reason immanent in the world and operating in the world, discarded by Aristotle, but also Plato's
conception of exemplary causality. Plato may have failed to
work out a systematised view of Absolute Being as exemplary
Cause of essences, as Ground of value; he may have failed
to realise, as Aristotle realised, that the immaterial form is
intelligent, that supreme Actuality is supreme Intelligence;
he may have failed to bring together and identify the supreme
Efficient, Exemplary and Final Causes; but, in his opposition
to Plato's inadequate view of the concrete object of this
world, Aristotle allowed himself to miss and pass over the
profound truth in the Platonic theory. Each thinker, then,
has his high-points, each made an invaluable contribution
to philosophy, but neither thinker gave the complete truth,
even so far as that is attainable. One may be drawn towards
either Plato or Aristotle by temperamental affinity, but one
would not be justified in rejecting Aristotle for Plato or
Plato for Aristotle: the truths contained in their respective
philosophies have to be integrated and harmoniously combined in a complete synthesis, a synthesis which must incorporate and build upon that cardinal tenet, which was held in
common by both Plato and Aristotle, namely, the conviction
that the fully real is the fully intelligible and the fully good,
while utilising also the peculiar contributions of each
philosopher, in so far as these contributions are true and
so compatible.

In the pages devoted to Neo-Platonism we shall witness an attempt, successful or unsuccessful as the case may be, to accomplish such a synthesis, an attempt which has been repeated in the course of both mediaeval and modern philosophy; but it might be as well to point out that, if such a synthesis is possible, it is made possible largely through the Platonic elements which are contained in Aristotelianism. Let me give one example, to illustrate my meaning. If Aristotle, in correcting what he considered to be the excessively dualistic character of the Platonic anthropology (I refer to the soul-body relationship), had explicitly rejected the supersensible character of the rational principle in man and had reduced thought, for example, to matter in motion, he would indeed have posited an antithesis to the Platonic theory, but this antithesis would have been of such a character that it could not combine with the thesis in a higher synthesis. As it was, however, Aristotle never, as far as we know, rejected the presence of a supersensible principle in man—he affirms it in his *De Anima*—even though he insisted that the soul cannot inhabit *any* body but is the entelechy of a particular body. A synthesis was, therefore, rendered possible, which would include the Aristotelian idea of the soul as the form of the body, while allowing, with Plato, that the *individual* soul is more than the body and survives death in individual self-identity.

Again, it might appear perhaps at first sight that the Aristotelian God, the Thought of Thought, constitutes an incompatible antithesis to the Platonic Idea of the Good, which, though intelligible, is not depicted as intelligent. Yet, since pure form is not only the intelligible but also the intelligent, the Platonic Absolute Good cried out, as it were, to be identified with the Aristotelian God, an identification which was accomplished in the Christian synthesis at least, so that both Plato and Aristotle contributed different, though complementary, facets of theism.

(In the foregoing remarks I have spoken of a synthesis of Platonism and Aristotelianism; but one is entitled to speak of the necessity of a synthesis only when there is question of two "antithetical" theories, each of them being more or less true in what it affirms and false in what it denies. For example, Plato was correct in affirming exemplarism, wrong in neglecting immanent substantial form, while Aristotle was correct in asserting his theory of the immanent substantial form, wrong in neglecting exemplarism. But there are other aspects of their philosophies in regard to which one can hardly speak of the necessity for a synthesis, since Aristotle himself accomplished the synthesis. For instance, the Aristotelian logic, that marvellous creation of genius, does not need to be synthesised with the Platonic logic, owing to the simple fact that it was a tremendous advance on Plato's logic [or what we know of it, at least] and itself comprised what was valuable in the Platonic logic).

Part Five

POST-ARISTOTELIAN
PHILOSOPHY

Chapter Thirty-Five

INTRODUCTORY

1. With the reign of Alexander the Great the day of the free and independent Greek City-State had really passed away. During his reign and that of his successors, who fought with one another for political power, any freedom that the Greek cities possessed was but nominal—at least it depended on the goodwill of the paramount sovereign. After the death of the great Conqueror in 323 B.C. we must speak rather of Hellenistic (i.e. in opposition to National-Hellenic) than of Hellenic civilisation. To Alexander the sharp distinction between Greek and "Barbarian" was unreal: he thought in terms of Empire, not in terms of the City: and the result was, that while the East was opened up to the influence of the West, Greek culture on its side could not remain uninfluenced by the new state of affairs. Athens, Sparta, Corinth, etc.—these were no longer free and independent units, united in a common feeling of cultural superiority to the barbarian darkness round about them: they were merged in a larger whole, and the day was not far distant when Greece was to become but a Province of the Roman Empire.

The new political situation could not be without its reaction on philosophy. Both Plato and Aristotle had been men of the Greek City, and for them the individual was inconceivable apart from the City and the life of the City: it was in the City that the individual attained his end, lived the good life. But when the free City was merged in a greater cosmopolitan whole, it was but natural that not only cosmopolitanism, with its ideal of citizenship of the world, as we

see it in Stoicism, but also individualism should come to the
fore. In fact these two elements, cosmopolitanism and individualism, were closely bound together. For when the life
of the City-State, compact and all-embracing, as Plato and
Aristotle had conceived it, had broken down and citizens
were merged in a much greater whole, the individual was
inevitably cast adrift by himself, loosed from his moorings
in the City-State. It was but to be expected, then, that in
a cosmopolitan society philosophy should centre its interest in
the individual, endeavouring to meet his demand for guidance in life, which he had to live out in a great society
and no longer in a comparatively small City-family, and
so displaying a predominantly ethical and practical trend—
as in Stoicism and Epicureanism. Metaphysical and physical
speculation tend to drop into the background: they are of
interest not for their own sake but as providing a basis and
preparation for ethics. This concentration on the ethical
makes it easy to understand why the new Schools borrowed
their metaphysical notions from other thinkers, without attempting fresh speculation on their own. Indeed it is to
the pre-Socratics that they return in this respect, Stoicism
having recourse to the Physics of Heraclitus and Epicureanism to the Atomism of Democritus. More than that, the post-
Aristotelian Schools returned to the pre-Socratics, at least in
part, even for their ethical ideas or tendencies, the Stoics
borrowing from Cynic ethics and the Epicureans from the
Cyrenaics.

This ethical and practical interest is particularly marked
in the development of the post-Aristotelian Schools in the
Roman period, for the Romans were not, like the Greeks,
speculative and metaphysical thinkers; they were predominantly men of practice. The old Romans had insisted on
character—speculation was somewhat foreign to them—and in
the Roman Empire, when the former ideals and traditions of
the Republic had been swamped, it was precisely the philosopher's task to provide the individual with a code of conduct which would enable him to pilot his way through the
sea of life, maintaining a consistency of principle and action
based on a certain spiritual and moral independence. Hence
the phenomenon of philosopher-directors, who performed a
task somewhat analogous to that of the spiritual director as
known to the Christian world.

This concentration on the practical, the fact that philosophy
took as its office the provision of standards of life, naturally

led to a wide diffusion of philosophy among the cultured classes of the Hellenistic-Roman world and so to a kind of Popular Philosophy. Philosophy in the Roman period became more and more part of the regular course of education (a fact which demanded its presentation in an easily apprehended form), and it was in this way that philosophy became a rival to Christianity, when the new Religion began to lay claim to the allegiance of the Empire. Indeed one may say that philosophy, to a certain extent at least, offered to satisfy the religious needs and aspirations of man. Disbelief in the popular mythology was common, and where this disbelief reigned—among the educated classes—those who were not content to live without religion at all had either to attach themselves to one of the many cults that were introduced into the Empire from the East and which were definitely more calculated to satisfy man's spiritual aspirations than the official State religion with its businesslike attitude, or to turn to philosophy for the satisfaction of those needs. And so it is that we can discern religious elements in such a predominantly ethical system as Stoicism, while in Neo-Platonism, the last flower of Ancient Philosophy, the syncretism of religion and philosophy reaches its culmination. More than that, we may say that in Plotinian Neo-Platonism, in which the mystical flight of the spirit or ecstasy is made the final and highest point of intellectual activity, philosophy tends to pass over into religion.

Insistence on ethics alone leads to an ideal of spiritual independence and self-sufficiency such as we find in both Stoicism and Epicureanism, while insistence on religion tends rather to assert dependence on a Transcendental Principle and to ascribe the purification of the self to the action of the Divine, an attitude that we find in a mystery-cult like that of Mithras. It is to be noted, however, that both tendencies, the tendency to insist on the ethical, the self-sufficient perfection of the personality or the acquisition of a true moral personality, and the tendency to insist on the attitude of the worshipper towards the Divine or the need of the non-self-sufficient human being to unite himself with God, contributed to meet the same want, the want of the individual in the Greco-Roman world to find a sure basis for his individual life, since the religious attitude too brought with it a certain independence *vis-à-vis* the secular Empire. In practice, of course, the two attitudes tended to coalesce, the emphasis being placed sometimes on the ethical (as in

Stoicism), sometimes on the religious factor (as in the mystery-cults), while in Neo-Platonism there was an attempt at a comprehensive synthesis, the ethical being subordinated to the religious, but without losing its importance.

2. In the development of the Hellenistic-Roman philosophy it is usual to distinguish several phases:[1]

(i) The first phase or period extends from about the end of the fourth century B.C. to the middle of the first century B.C. This period is characterised by the founding of the Stoic and Epicurean philosophies, which place the emphasis on conduct and the attainment of personal happiness, while harking back to pre-Socratic thought for the cosmological bases of their systems. Over against these "dogmatic" systems stands the Scepticism of Pyrrho and his followers, to which must be added the sceptical vein in the Middle and New Academies. The interaction between these philosophies led to a certain Eclecticism, which showed itself in a tendency on the part of the Middle Stoa, the Peripatetic School and the Academy to eclectic assimilation of one another's doctrines.

(ii) Eclecticism on the one hand and Scepticism on the other hand continue into the second period (from about the middle of the first century B.C. to the middle of the third century A.D.), but this period is characterised by a return to philosophical "orthodoxy." Great interest is taken in the founders of the Schools, their lives, works and doctrines, and this tendency to philosophical "orthodoxy" is a counterpart to the continuing eclecticism. But the interest in the past was also fruitful in scientific investigation, e.g. in editing the works of the old philosophers, commenting on them and interpreting them. In such work the pre-eminence belongs to the Alexandrians.

This scientific interest is not, however, the sole characteristic of the second period. Over against the scientific interest we find the tendency to religious mysticism, which becomes ever stronger. It has been pointed out (e.g. Praechter, p. 36) that this tendency has a common root with the scientific tendency, namely, the disappearance of productive speculation. While the latter factor might lead to scepticism or to devotion to scientific pursuits, it might equally result in a tendency to religious mysticism. This tendency was of course favoured by the growing religious consciousness of the time and by acquaintance with religions of eastern origin. Western philosophers, e.g. the Neo-Pythagoreans, endeavoured to incorporate these religious-mystical elements into their speculative systems, while eastern thinkers, e.g. Philo of Alexandria, tried to systematise their religious conceptions in a philosophic framework. (Thinkers like Philo were, of course, also influenced by the desire to win over the Greeks for their un-Greek doctrines by presenting the latter in philosophic guise.)

(iii) The third period (from about the middle of the third century A.D. to the middle of the sixth century A.D.— or, in Alexandria, to the middle of the seventh century) is that of Neo-Platonism. This final speculative effort of Ancient Philosophy attempted to combine all the valuable elements in the philosophic and religious doctrines of East and West in one comprehensive system, practically absorbing all the philosophic Schools and dominating philosophical development for a number of centuries, so that it cannot justifiably be overlooked in a history of philosophy or be relegated to the dustbin of esoteric mysticism. Moreover, Neo-Platonism exercised a great influence on Christian speculation: we have only to think of names like those of St. Augustine and the Pseudo-Dionysius.

3. A feature of the Hellenistic world that must not be passed over is the increased cultivation of the special sciences. We have seen how philosophy and religion tended to become united: with regard to philosophy and the special sciences the opposite holds good. Not only had the domain of philosophy become more sharply delineated than it was in the early days of Greek thought, but the different sciences had themselves reached such a pitch of development that they required special treatment. Moreover, the improvement in the external conditions for research and study, though itself largely an outcome of specialisation, reacted in turn on the cultivation of the sciences, promoting an intensification of departmental work and research. The Lyceum had, of course, greatly contributed to the growth and development of the sciences, but in the Hellenistic age there arose scientific Institutes, Museums and Libraries in the great capital cities of Alexandria, Antioch, and Pergamon, with the result that philological and literary research, mathematical, medical and physical studies, were enabled to make great strides. Thus according to Tzetzes, the "outer" library at Alexandria contained 42,800 volumes, while the main library in the Palace contained some 400,000 "mixed" and some 90,000 "unmixed" or "simple" volumes, the latter

being probably small papyrus rolls while the former were bigger rolls. Later on the larger volumes, divided into books, were reduced to "simple" volumes. We are told that when Antony presented Cleopatra with the Pergamene library, he gave her 200,000 "simple" volumes.

It may be, of course, that the influence of philosophy on the special sciences was not always favourable to their advance, for speculative assumptions sometimes took a place which did not belong to them and led to hasty and precipitate conclusions, when experiment and exact observation should have exercised the decisive rôle. On the other hand, however, the special sciences were helped by being given a philosophical foundation, for they were thereby rescued from crude empiricism and from an exclusively practical and utilitarian orientation.

Chapter Thirty-Six

THE EARLY STOA

1. The founder of the Stoic School was Zeno, who was born about 336/5 B.C. at Citium in Cyprus and died about 264/3 at Athens. He seems to have at first followed his father in commercial activity.[1] Coming to Athens about 315-313 he read the *Memorabilia* of Xenophon and the *Apology* of Plato and was filled with admiration for Socrates' strength of character. Thinking that Crates the Cynic was the man who most resembled Socrates, he became his disciple. From the Cynics he seemed to have turned to Stilpo,[2] though Zeno is also reported to have listened to Xenocrates and, after Xenocrates' death, to Polemon. About the year 300 B.C. he founded his own philosophic School, which takes its name from the Στοὰ Ποικίλη, where he lectured. He is said to have taken his own life. Of his writings we possess only fragments.

Zeno was succeeded in the leadership of the School by Cleanthes of Assos (331/30-233/2 or 231) and Cleanthes by Chrysippus of Soloi in Cilicia (281/278-208/205), who was called the second founder of the School because of his systematisation of the Stoic doctrines. Εἰ μὴ γὰρ ἦ Χρύσιππος, οὐκ ἂν ἦν Στοά.[3] He is said to have written more than 705 books and was famed for his dialectic, though not for his style of composition.

Among Zeno's pupils were Ariston of Chios, Herillus of Carthage, Dionysius of Heracleia, Person of Citium. A pupil of Cleanthes was Sphairus of the Bosphorus. Chrysippus was succeeded by two pupils, Zeno of Tarsus and Diogenes of Seleucia. The latter came to Rome in 156/5

B.C., together with other philosophers, as ambassadors of Athens in an attempt to obtain remission of the fine. The philosophers gave lectures in Rome, which excited admiration among the youth of the City, though Cato thought that such philosophical interests were not consonant with the military virtues and he advised the Senate to get rid of the embassy as soon as possible.[4] Diogenes was succeeded by Antipater of Tarsus.

2. Logic of the Stoa

Logic was divided by the Stoics into Dialectic and Rhetoric, to which some added the Theory of Definitions and the Theory of the Criteria of Truth.[5] Something will be said here of the Stoic epistemology, omitting their account of formal logic, though we may note the fact that the Stoics reduced the ten Categories of Aristotle to four, namely, the substrate (τὸ ὑποκείμενον), the essential constitution (τὸ ποιὸν or τὸ ποιὸν ὑποκείμενον), the accidental constitution (τὸ πῶς ἔχον or τὸ πῶς ἔχον ποιὸν ὑποκείμενον) and the relative accidental constitution (τὸ πρός τι πῶς ἔχον, τὸ πρός τι πῶς ἔχον ποιὸν ὑποκείμενον). A further feature of the formal logic of the Stoa may also be mentioned. Propositions are simple if their terms are non-propositions, otherwise compound. The compound proposition, "if X, then Y" (τὸ συνημμένον), is declared to be (i) true, if X and Y are both true; (ii) false, if X is true and Y is false; (iii) true, if X is false and Y is true; (iv) true, if X and Y are both false. Thus our "material" implication is separated from our "formal" implication and our "strict" implication, and from entailment by ontological necessitation.[6]

The Stoics rejected not only the Platonic doctrine of the transcendental universal, but also Aristotle's doctrine of the concrete universal. Only the individual exists and our knowledge is knowledge of particular objects. These particulars make an impression on the soul (τύπωσις—Zeno and Cleanthes—or ἑτεροίωσις—Chrysippus), and knowledge is primarily knowledge of this impression. The Stoics adopted, therefore, the opposite position to that of Plato, for, while Plato depreciated sense-perception, the Stoics founded all knowledge on sense-perception. They would doubtless re-echo the words of Antisthenes, to the effect that he saw a horse but not "horseness." (Zeno, as we have seen, became a pupil of Crates the Cynic.) The soul is originally a *tabula rasa*, and, in order for it to know, there is need of perception. The Stoics did not of course deny that we have knowledge of our interior states and activities, but Chrysippus reduced this knowledge, too, to perception, which was rendered all the easier in that these states and activities were considered to consist of material processes. After the act of perception a memory (μνήμη) remains behind, when the actual object is no longer there, and experience arises from a plurality of similar recollections (ἐμπείρια).

The Stoics were therefore Empiricists, even "Sensualists"; but they also maintained a Rationalism which was scarcely consistent with a thoroughly empiricist and nominalist position. For although they asserted that reason (λόγος, νοῦς) is a product of development, in that it grows up gradually out of perceptions and is formed only about the fourteenth year, they also held, not only that there are deliberately-formed general ideas, but also that there are general ideas (κοιναὶ ἔννοιαι or προλήψεις), which are apparently antecedent to experience (ἔμφυτοι προλήψεις) in that we have a natural predisposition to form them—virtually innate ideas, we might call them. What is more, it is only through Reason that the system of Reality can be known.

The Stoics devoted a good deal of attention to the question of the criterion of truth. This they declared to be the φαντασία καταληπτική, the apprehensive perception or representation. The criterion of truth lies, therefore, in the perception itself, namely, in the perception that compels the assent of the soul, i.e. to all intents and purposes in clear perception. (This is scarcely consistent with the view that it is science alone that gives us certain knowledge of Reality.) However, the difficulty arose that the soul can withhold assent from what is objectively a true perception. Thus when the dead Alcestis appeared to Admetus from the underworld, her husband had a clear perception of her, yet he did not assent to this clear perception because of subjective hindrances, namely, the belief that dead people do not rise again, while on the other hand there may be deceptive apparitions of the dead. In view of this sort of objection the later Stoics, as Sextus Empiricus tells us, added to the criterion of truth, 'which has no hindrance." Objectively speaking, the perception of the dead Alcestis has the value of a criterion of truth—for it is objectively a καταληπτική φαντασία—but subjectively speaking, it cannot act as such, because of a belief which acts as a subjective hindrance.[7] This is all very well, but the difficulty still remains of ascertaining when there is such a hindrance and when there is not.

3. Cosmology of the Stoa

In their cosmology the Stoics had recourse to Heraclitus for the doctrine of the Logos and of Fire as the world-substance; but elements are also present which are borrowed from Plato and Aristotle. Thus the λόγοι σπερματικοί seem to be a transposition on to the material plane of the ideal theory.

According to the Stoics there are two principles in Reality, τὸ ποιοῦν and τὸ πάσχον. But this is not dualism as we find it in Plato, since the active principle, τὸ ποιοῦν, is not spiritual but material. In fact it is hardly dualism at all, since the two principles are both material and together form one Whole. The Stoic doctrine is therefore a monistic materialism, even if this position is not consistently maintained. It is uncertain what Zeno's view was, but Cleanthes and Chrysippus would seem to have regarded the two factors as ultimately one and the same.

> "All are but parts of one stupendous whole,
> Whose body Nature is and God the soul,"[8]

The passive principle is matter devoid of qualities, while the active principle is immanent Reason or God. Natural beauty or finality in Nature point to the existence of a principle of thought in the universe, God, Who, in His Providence, has arranged everything for the good of man. Moreover, since the highest phenomenon of nature, man, is possessed of consciousness, we cannot suppose that the whole world is devoid of consciousness, for the whole cannot be less perfect than the part. God, therefore, is the Consciousness of the world. Nevertheless God, like the substrate on which He works, is material. "(Zeno) *Nullo modo arbitrabatur quidquam effici posse ab ea (natura) quae expers esset corporis—nec vero aut quod efficeret aut quod efficeretur, posse esse non corpus."*[9] ὄντα γὰρ μόνα τὰ σώματα καλοῦσιν.[10] Like Heraclitus the Stoics make Fire to be the stuff of all things. God is the active Fire (πῦρ τεχνικόν), which is immanent in the universe (πνεῦμα διῆκον δι' ὅλου τοῦ κόσμου), but He is at the same time the primal Source from which the crasser elements, that make the corporeal world, come forth. These crasser elements proceed from God and are at length resolved into Him again, so that all that exists is either the primal Fire—God in Himself— or God in His different states. When the world is in existence God stands to it as soul to body, being the soul of the world. He is not something entirely different from the stuff of the world, His Body, but is a finer stuff, the moving and forming principle—the crasser stuff, of which the world is formed, being itself motionless and unformed, though capable of receiving all sorts of movement and form.

"Zenoni et reliquis fere Stoicis aether videtur summus deus, mente praeditus, qua omnia reguntur." [11]

God therefore, ὁ Λόγος, is the Active Principle which contains within itself the active forms of all the things that are to be, these forms being the λόγοι σπερματικοί. These active forms—but material—are as it were "seeds," through the activity of which individual things come into being as the world develops; or rather they are seeds which unfold themselves in the forms of individual things. (The conception of λόγοι σπερματικοί is found in Neo-Platonism and in St. Augustine, under the name of *rationes seminales*.) In the actual development of the world part of the fiery vapour, of which God consists, is transformed into air and from air is formed water. From part of the water comes earth, while a second part remains water and a third part is transformed into air, which through rarefaction becomes the elementary fire. Thus does the "body" of God come into being.

Now Heraclitus, as we have seen, most probably never taught the doctrine of the universal conflagration, in which the whole world returns to the primeval fire, from which it was born. The Stoics, however, certainly added this doctrine of the ἐκπύρωσις, according to which God forms the world and then takes it back into Himself through a universal conflagration, so that there is an unending series of world-constructions and world-destructions. Moreover, each new world resembles its predecessor in all particulars, every individual man, for example, occurring in each successive world and performing the identical actions that he performed in his previous existence. (Cf. Nietzsche's idea of the "Eternal Recurrence.") Consistently with this belief the Stoics denied human freedom, or rather liberty for them meant doing consciously, with assent, what one will do in any case. (We are reminded somewhat of Spinoza.) This reign of necessity the Stoics expressed under the concept of Fate (Εἱμαρμένη), but Fate is not something different from God and universal reason, nor is it different from Providence (Πρόνοια) which orders all things for the best. Fate and Providence are but different aspects of God. But this cosmological determinism is modified by their insistence on interior freedom, in the sense that a man can alter his judgment on events and his attitude towards events, seeing them and welcoming them as the expression of "God's Will." In this sense man is free.

Since the Stoics held that God orders all things for the best, they had to explain the evil in the world or at least to bring it into harmony with their "optimism." Chrysippus especially undertook the perennial difficulty of formulating a theodicy, taking as his fundamental tenet the theory that the imperfection of individuals subserves the perfection of the whole. It would follow that there is really no evil when things are looked at *sub specie aeternitatis*. (If we are reminded here of Spinoza, we are reminded also of Leibniz, not only by Stoic optimism, but also by their doctrine that no two individual phenomena of Nature are completely alike.) Chrysippus, in his fourth book on Providence, argues that goods could not have existed without evils, on the ground that of a pair of contraries neither can exist without the other, so that if you take away the one, you take away both.[12] There is certainly a great deal of truth in this contention. For instance, the existence of a sensible creature capable of pleasure implies also the capacity for feeling pain —unless, of course, God determines otherwise; but we are now speaking of the natural state of affairs and not of preternatural Divine ordinances. Moreover, pain, though spoken of as an evil, would seem to be—in a certain aspect—a good. For example, given the possibility of our teeth decaying, toothache would seem to be a definite good or benefit. The privation of right order in the teeth is certainly an evil, but— given the possibility of decay—we should be worse off if toothache were impossible, since it serves as a danger-signal, warning us that it is time that we had our teeth examined by a dentist. Similarly, if we never felt hungry—a pain— we might ruin our health by insufficient nourishment. Chrysippus saw this clearly and argued that it is good for man to have his head of delicate construction, though the very fact of its delicate construction involves at the same time the possibility of danger from a comparatively slight blow.

But though physical evil is not so great a difficulty, what of moral evil? According to the Stoics no act is evil and reprehensible *in itself:* it is the intention, the moral condition of the agent from whom the act proceeds, that makes the act evil: the act as a physical entity is indifferent. (If this were taken to mean that a good intention justifies any act, then such an act is in the moral order and will be either good or bad—though if the agent performs a bad act with a sincerely good intention in a state of inculpable ignorance of the fact that the act is contrary to right reason, the action is only *materialiter* evil and the agent is not guilty of formal sin.[13] However, if the act be considered merely in itself, as a positive entity, apart from its character as a human act, then Chrysippus is right in saying that the act as such is not evil—in fact, it is good. That it cannot of itself be evil, can easily be shown by an example. The physical action, the positive element, is precisely the same when a man is murderously shot as when he is shot in battle during a just war: it is not the positive element in the murder, the action considered merely abstractly, that is the *moral* evil. Moral evil, considered precisely as such, cannot be a positive entity, since this would reflect on the goodness of the Creator, the Source of all being. Moral evil consists essentially in a privation of right order in the human will, which, in the human bad act, is out of harmony with right reason.) Now, if a man can have a right intention, he can also have a wrong intention; hence, in the moral sphere, no less than in the physical sphere, contraries involve one another. How, asked Chrysippus, can courage be understood apart from cowardice or justice apart from injustice? Just as the capacity of feeling pleasure implies the capacity of feeling pain, so the capacity of being just implies the capacity of being unjust.

In so far as Chrysippus simply meant that the capacity for virtue implies *de facto* the capacity for vice, he was enunciating a truth, since for man in his present state in this world, with his limited apprehension of the *Summum Bonum*, freedom to be virtuous implies also freedom to commit sin, so that, if the possession of moral freedom is a good thing for man and if it is better to be able to choose virtue freely (even though this implies the possibility of vice) than to have no freedom at all, no valid argument against Divine Providence can be drawn from the possibility, or even the existence, of moral evil in the world. But in so far as Chrysippus implies that the presence of virtue in the universe necessarily implies the presence of its contrary, on the ground that opposites always involve one another, he is implying what is false, since human moral freedom, while involving the *possibility* of vice in this life, does not necessarily involve its actuality. (The apology for moral evil, as also for physical evil, which consists in saying that the good is thrown into higher relief through the presence of the bad, might, if pressed, imply the same false view. Given this present order of the world, it is certainly better that man should be free, and so *able* to sin, than that he should be without freedom; but it is better that man should use his freedom to choose virtuous actions, and the best condition of the world would be that all men should always do what is right, however much the presence of vice may set the good in high relief.)

Chrysippus was not so happy when he speculated whether external misfortunes might not be due to oversight on the part of Providence, as when trifling accidents occur in a large household that is, in general, well administered, through neglect of some kind;[14] but he rightly saw that those physical evils that befall the good may be turned into a blessing, both through the individual (through his interior attitude towards them) or for mankind at large (e.g. by stimulating medical investigation and progress). Further, it is interesting to notice, that Chrysippus gives an argument which recurs later in, e.g. Neo-Platonism, St. Augustine, Berkeley and Leibniz, to the effect that evil in the universe throws the good into greater relief, just as the contrast of light and shadow is pleasing in a picture or, to use an actual example employed by Chrysippus, as "Comedies have in them ludicrous verses which, though bad in themselves, nevertheless lend a certain grace to the whole play." [15]

In inorganic objects the Universal Reason or πνεῦμα operates as a ἕξις or principle of cohesion, and this holds good also for plants—which have no soul—though in them the ἕξις has the power of movement and has risen to the rank of φύσις. In animals there is soul (ψυχή), which shows itself in the powers of φαντασία and ὁρμή, and in human beings there is reason. The soul of man is therefore the noblest of souls: indeed it is part of the divine Fire which descended into men at their creation and is then passed on at generation, for, like all else, it is material. τὸ ἡγεμονικόν the dominant part of the soul, has its seat in the heart according to Chrysippus, apparently on the ground that the voice, which is the expression of thought, proceeds from the heart. (Some other Stoics placed τὸ ἡγεμονικόν in the head.) Personal immortality was scarcely possible in the Stoic system, and the Stoics admitted that all souls return to the primeval Fire at the conflagration. The only dispute was on the subject of what souls persist after death until the conflagration; and while Cleanthes considered that this held good for all human souls, Chrysippus admitted it only in regard to the souls of the wise.

In a monistic system such as that of the Stoics we would hardly expect to find any attitude of personal devotion towards the Divine Principle; but in point of fact such a tendency is indubitably visible. This tendency is particularly observable in the celebrated hymn to Zeus by Cleanthes:

O God most glorious, called by many a name,
Nature's great King, through endless years the same;
Omnipotence, who by thy just decree
Controllest all, hail, Zeus, for unto thee
Behoves the creatures in all lands to call.
We are thy children, we alone, of all
On earth's broad ways that wander to and fro,
Bearing thy image wheresoe'er we go.
Wherefore with songs of praise thy power I will forth show.
Lo! yonder heaven, that round the earth is wheeled,
Follows thy guidance, still to thee doth yield
Glad homage; thine unconquerable hand
Such flaming minister, the levin-brand,
Wieldeth, a sword two-edged, whose deathless might
Pulsates through all that Nature brings to light;
Vehicle of the universal Word, that flows
Through all, and in the light celestial glows
Of stars both great and small. O King of Kings
Through ceaseless ages, God, whose purpose brings
To birth, whate'er on land or in the sea
Is wrought, or in high heaven's immensity;
Save what the sinner works infatuate.
Nay, but thou knowest to make the crooked straight:
Chaos to thee is order: in thine eyes
The unloved is lovely, who did'st harmonise
Things evil with things good, that there should be
One Word through all things everlastingly.
One Word—whose voice alas! the wicked spurn;
Insatiate for the good their spirits yearn:
Yet seeing see not, neither hearing hear
God's universal law, which those revere,
By reason guided, happiness who win.
The rest, unreasoning, diverse shapes of sin

Self-prompted follow: for an idle name
Vainly they wrestle in the lists of fame:
Others inordinately Riches woo,
Or dissolute, the joys of flesh pursue.
Now here, now there they wander, fruitless still,
For ever seeking good and finding ill.
Zeus the all-beautiful, whom darkness shrouds,
Whose lightning lightens in the thunder clouds;
Thy children save from error's deadly sway:
Turn thou the darkness from their souls away:
Vouchsafe that unto knowledge they attain;
For thou by knowledge art made strong to reign
O'er all, and all things rulest righteously.
So by thee honoured, we will honour thee,
Praising thy works continuously with songs,
As mortals should; nor higher meed belongs
E'en to the gods, than justly to adore
The universal law for evermore.[16]

But this attitude of personal devotion towards the Supreme Principle on the part of some of the Stoics does not mean that they rejected the popular religion; on the contrary, they took it under their protection. Zeno did indeed declare that prayers and sacrifices are of no avail, but polytheism was nevertheless justified by the Stoics on the ground that the one Principle or Zeus manifests itself in phenomena, e.g. the heavenly bodies, so that divine reverence is due to these manifestations—a reverence which is also to be extended to deified man or "heroes." Moreover, Stoicism found a place for divination and oracles. This fact need really cause no great surprise, if we reflect that the Stoics maintained a deterministic doctrine and held that all the parts and events of the universe are mutually interconnected.

4. The Stoic Ethic

The importance of the ethical part of philosophy for the Stoics may be exemplified by the description of philosophy given by Seneca. Seneca belongs, of course, to the later Stoa, yet the emphasis laid by him on philosophy as the science of conduct was common to the early Stoa as well. *Philosophia nihil aliud est quam recta vivendi ratio vel honeste vivendi scientia vel ars rectae vitae agendae. non errabimus, si diximus philosophiam esse legem bene honesteque vivendi, et qui dixerit illam regulam vitae, suum illi nomen reddidit.*[17] Philosophy, therefore, is primarily concerned with conduct.

Now the end of life, happiness, εὐδαιμονία, consists in Virtue (in the Stoic sense of the term), i.e. in the natural life or life according to nature (ὁμολογουμένως τῇ φύσει ζῆν), the agreement of human action with the law of nature, or of the human will with the divine Will. Hence the famous Stoic maxim, "Live according to nature." For man to conform himself to the laws of the universe in the wide sense, and for man to conform his conduct to his own essential nature, reason, is the same thing, since the universe is governed by the law of nature. While earlier Stoics thought of "Nature," the Φύσις which man should follow, rather as the nature of the universe, later Stoics—from Chrysippus—tended to conceive nature from a more anthropological point of view.

The Stoic conception of life according to nature differs therefore from the old Cynic conception, as exemplified in the conduct and teaching of Diogenes. For the Cynics "nature" meant rather the primitive and instinctive, and so life according to nature implied a deliberate flouting of the conventions and traditions of civilised society, a flouting that externalised itself in conduct that was eccentric and not infrequently indecent. For the Stoics on the other hand, life according to nature meant life according to the principle that is active in nature, λόγος, the principle shared in by the human soul. The ethical end, therefore, according to the Stoics, consists essentially in submission to the divinely appointed order of the world, and Plutarch informs us that it was a general principle of Chrysippus to begin all ethical inquiries with a consideration of the order and arrangement of the universe.[18]

The fundamental instinct implanted in the animal by nature is the instinct of self-preservation, which means for the Stoics pretty well what we would call self-perfection or self-development. Now, man is endowed with reason, the faculty which gives him his superiority over the brute: therefore for man "life in accordance with nature is rightly understood to mean life in accordance with reason. Hence Zeno's definition of the end is to live in conformity with nature, which means to live a life of virtue, since it is to virtue that nature leads. On the other hand, a virtuous life is a life which conforms to our experience of the course of nature, our human natures being but parts of universal nature. Thus the end is a life which follows nature, whereby is meant not only our own nature, but the nature of the universe, a life wherein we do nothing that is forbidden by the universal, i.e. by right reason, which pervades all things and is identical with Zeus, the guide and governor of the universe." [19] Diogenes Laërtius' account of the ethical teaching of the Stoics thus declares that virtue is a life in accordance with nature, while a life in conformity with nature is, i.e. for man, life in accordance with right reason. (As has been pointed out by others, this does not tell us very much, since the statements that it is reasonable to live in accordance with nature and natural to live in accordance with reason do not give much help to determining the content of virtue.)

Since the Stoics held that everything necessarily obeys the laws of nature, the objection was bound to be raised: "What is the good in telling man to obey the laws of nature, if he cannot help doing so in any case?" The Stoics answered that man is rational and so, though he will follow the laws of nature in any case, he has the privilege of knowing these laws and of assenting to them consciously. Hence there is a purpose in moral exhortation: man is free to change his interior attitude. (This involves, of course, a modification of the deterministic position, to say the least of it—but then no determinists are or can be really consistent, and the Stoics are no exception to the rule.) The consequence is that, strictly speaking, no action is in itself right or wrong, for determinism leaves no place for voluntary action and moral responsibility, while in a monistic system evil is really only evil when seen from some particular standpoint—*sub specie aeternitatis* all is right and good. The Stoics seem to have accepted—theoretically at least—the notion that no actions are wrong in themselves, as when Zeno admitted that not even cannibalism, incest or homosexuality are wrong in themselves. [20] Zeno did not, of course, mean to commend such actions: he meant that the physical act is indifferent, moral evil pertaining to the human will and intention. [21] Cleanthes declared that the human being necessarily follows the path of Destiny: "—if, to evil prone, my will rebelled, I needs must follow still." [22] And the same thought occurs in the celebrated dictum of Seneca, *Ducunt volentem fata, nolentem trahunt*. [23] However, the determinism of the Stoics was greatly modified in practice, since the doctrine that the wise man is he who *consciously* follows the path of Destiny (a doctrine brought out in the dictum of Seneca just quoted), when coupled with their exhortatory ethic, implies liberty to a certain extent, as we have already remarked—a man is free to change his inner attitude and to adopt one of submission and resig-

nation rather than of rebellion. Moreover, they admitted a
scale of values, as we shall see, and it is at least tacitly implied that the wise man is free to choose the higher values
and eschew the lower. But no deterministic system can be
consistent in practice, a fact which need cause no surprise,
since freedom is an actuality of which we are conscious, and
even if it be theoretically denied, it creeps in again through
the back door.

According to the Stoics virtue alone is a good in the full
sense of the word; everything which is neither virtue nor vice
is also neither good nor evil but indifferent (ἀδιάφορον).
"Virtue is a disposition conformable to reason, desirable in and
for itself and not because of any hope or fear or any external
motive." [24] It was in accord with this view of the self-
sufficiency and self-desirability of virtue that the Platonic
myths concerning rewards and punishments in the next life
were ridiculed by Chrysippus. (We may compare therewith
the doctrine of Kant.) However, in regard to this middle
realm of the indifferent the Stoics admitted that some things
are preferable (προηγμένα) and others to be rejected
(ἀποπροηγμένα), while others again are indifferent in a
narrower sense. This was a concession to practice, perhaps
at the expense of theory, but it was doubtless demanded by
the Stoic doctrine, that virtue consists in conformity to
nature. Hence among the morally indifferent things the
Stoics introduced a division into (i) those things which are
in accordance with nature and to which a value may therefore be ascribed (τὰ προηγμένα); (ii) those things which
are contrary to nature and so valueless (τὰ ἀποπροηγμένα);
and (iii) those things which possess neither value nor "dis-
value" (τὰ ἀπαξία). In this way they constructed a scale of
values. Pleasure is a result or accompaniment of activity and
may never be made into an end. On this all the Stoics were
agreed, though they did not all go so far as Cleanthes, who
held that pleasure is not according to nature.

The Cardinal Virtues are Moral Insight (φρόνησις),
Courage, Self-control or Temperance, and Justice. These virtues stand or fall together, in the sense that he who possesses one possesses all. Zeno found the common source of
all virtues in φρόνησις, while for Cleanthes it was self-
mastery, φρόνησις being replaced by ἐγκράτεια. In spite
of differences, however, the Stoics in general adhered to
the principle that the Virtues are indissolubly connected as
expressions of one and the same character, so that the

presence of one virtue implies the presence of all. Conversely, they thought that when one vice is present, all the vices must be present. Character, then, is the chief point stressed and truly virtuous conduct—which is fulfilment of duty (τὸ καθῆκον, a term apparently invented by Zeno, but denoting rather what is suitable than duty in our sense) in the right spirit—is performed only by the wise man. The wise man is without passions, and in respect of his interior worth he takes second place to none, not even to Zeus. Moreover, he is lord over his own life, and may commit suicide.

If all the virtues are so bound up with one another that he who possesses the one must possess the others, it is an easy step to supposing that there are no degrees in virtue. Either a man is virtuous, i.e. completely virtuous, or he is not virtuous at all. And this would seem to have been the position of the early Stoics. Thus, according to Chrysippus, a man who has *almost* completed the path of moral progress is not yet virtuous, has not yet that virtue which is true happiness. A consequence of this doctrine is that very few attain to virtue and then only late in life. "Man walks in wickedness all his life, or, at any rate, for the greater part of it. If he ever attains to virtue, it is late and at the very sunset of his days." [25] But while this strict moral idealism is characteristic of the earlier Stoicism, later Stoics emphasised much more the conception of progress, devoting their attention to encouraging man to begin and continue in the path of virtue. Admitting that no individual actually corresponds to the ideal of the wise man, they divided mankind into fools and those who are progressing towards virtue or wisdom.

Characteristic of the Stoic ethic is their doctrine in regard to the passions and affections. These—pleasure (ἡδονή), sorrow or depression (λύπη), desire (ἐπιθυμία) and fear (φόβος) are irrational and unnatural; and so it is not so much a question of moderating and regulating them as of getting rid of them and inducing a state of Apathy. At least when the passions or affections become habits (νόσοι ψυχῆς) they have to be eliminated. Hence the Stoic ethic is in practice largely a fight against the "affections," an endeavour to attain to a state of moral freedom and sovereignty. (The Stoics tended, however, to moderate somewhat this extreme position, and we find some admitting rational emotions—εὐπάθειαι—in the wise man.) A quotation from Seneca well illustrates the Stoic attitude in regard to self-conquest.

"Quid praecipuum in rebus humanis est ? non classibus maria complesse nec in rubri maris litore signa fixisse nec deficiente ad iniurias terra errasse in oceano ignota quaerentem, sed animo omnia vidisse et, qua maior nulla victoria est, vitia domuisse. Innumerabiles sunt, qui populos, qui urbes habuerunt in potestate, paucissimi qui se. quid est praecipuum ? erigere animum supra minas et promissa fortunae, nihil dignam illam habere putare, quod speres: quid enim habet dignum, quod concupiscas ? qui a divinorum conversatione, quotiens ad humana recideris, non aliter caligabis, quam quorum oculi in densam umbram ex claro sole redierunt. quid est praecipuum ? posse laeto animo tolerare adversa. yuidquid acciderit, sic ferre, quasi volueris tibi accidere. debuisses enim velle, si scires omnia ex decreto dei fieri: flere, queri, gemere desciscere est. quid est praecipuum ? in primis labris animam habere. haec res efficit non e iure Quirium liberum, sed e iure naturae. liber enim est, qui servitutem effugit. haec est assidua et ineluctabilis et per diem et per noctem aequaliter premens. sine intervallo, sine commeatu. sibi servire gravissima est servitus: quam discutere facile est, si desieris multa te posceris, si desieris tibi referre mercedem, si ante oculos et naturam tuam et aetatem posueris, licet prima sit, actibi ipsi dixeris: quid insanio ? quid anhelo ? quid sudo ? Quid terram, quid forum verso ? nec multo opus est, nec diu." [26]

This side of the Stoic ethic—namely the endeavour to acquire complete independence of all externals—represents its Cynic heritage; but it has another side, whereby it passes beyond Cynicism and that is its Cosmopolitanism. Every man is naturally a social being, and to live in society is a dictate of reason. But reason is the common essential nature of all men: hence there is but one Law for all men and one Fatherland. The division of mankind into warring States is absurd: the wise man is a citizen, not of this or that particular State, but of the World. From this foundation it follows that all men have a claim to our goodwill, even slaves having their rights and even enemies having a right to our mercy and forgiveness. Now, this transcendence of narrow social limits was obviously favoured by the monism of the Stoic system, but an ethical basis for the Stoic Cosmopolitanism was found in the fundamental instinct or tendency of self-preservation or self-love (οἰκείωσις). In the first place, of course, this instinctive tendency to self-preservation shows itself in the form of self-love, i.e. the individual's self-love. But it extends beyond self-love in the narrow sense to embrace all that belongs to the individual, family, friends, fellow-citizens and, finally, the whole of humanity. It is naturally stronger in regard to what stands closer to the individual, and grows weaker in proportion as the object is more remote, so that the individual's task, from the ethical viewpoint, is to raise the οἰκείωσις to the same pitch of intensity in regard to the remote objects as it manifests in regard to the nearer objects. In other words, the ethical ideal is attained when we love all men as we love ourselves or when our self-love embraces all that is connected with the self, including humanity at large, with an equal intensity.

Chapter Thirty-Seven

EPICUREANISM

1. The founder of the Epicurean School, Epicurus, was born at Samos in 342/1 B.C. At Samos he listened to Pamphilus, a Platonist,[1] and then at Teos to Nausiphanes, a follower of Democritus, who exercised considerable influence upon him, in spite of Epicurus' later contentions.[2] When eighteen, Epicurus came to Athens for his military service, and then seems to have given himself to study at Colophon. In 310 he taught at Mitylene—though he afterwards transferred to Lampsacus—and in 307/6 he moved to Athens and there opened his School.[3] This School was instituted in Epicurus' own garden, and we learn from Diogenes Laërtius that the philosopher in his will bequeathed the house and garden to his disciples. From the situation of the School the Epicureans got the name of οἱ ἀπὸ τῶν κήπων. Almost divine honours were paid to Epicurus even in his lifetime, and this cult of the founder is no doubt responsible for the fact that philosophic orthodoxy was maintained among the Epicureans more than in any other School. The chief doctrines were given the pupils to learn by heart.[4]

Epicurus was a voluminous writer (according to Diog. Laërt. he wrote about 300 works), but most of his writings are lost. However, Diogenes Laërtius has given us three didactic letters, of which the letters to Herodotus and Menoeceus are considered authentic while that to Pythocles is considered to be an extract from Epicurus' writing made by a pupil. Fragments have also been preserved of his chief work, Περὶ Φύσεως, from the library of the Epicurean Piso (thought to be L. Piso, Consul in 58 B.C.).

Epicurus was succeeded as Scholarch by Hermarchus of Mitylene, who was in turn succeeded by Polystratus. An immediate disciple of Epicurus, together with Hermarchus and Polyaenus, was Metrodorus of Lampsacus. Cicero heard Phaedrus (Scholarch at Athens about 78-70) at Rome about 90 B.C. But the best-known disciple of the School is the Latin poet, T. Lucretius Carus (91-51 B.C.), who expressed the Epicurean philosophy in his poem *De Rerum Natura*, having as his chief aim the liberation of men from the fear of the gods and of death and the leading of them to peace of soul.

2. The Canonic

Epicurus was not interested in dialectic or logic as such, and the only part of logic to which he paid any attention was that dealing with the criterion of truth. That is to say, he was interested in dialectic only in so far as it directly subserved Physics. But Physics again interested him only in so far as it subserved Ethics. Epicurus therefore concentrated on Ethics even more than did the Stoics, depreciating all purely scientific pursuits and declaring mathematics useless, since it has no connection with the conduct of life. (Metrodorus declared that "It need not trouble any one, if he had never read a line of Homer and did not know whether Hector was a Trojan or a Greek.")[5] One of Epicurus' reasons for objecting to mathematics was that it is not substantiated by sense-knowledge, since in the real world the geometer's points, lines and surfaces are nowhere to be found. Now, sense-knowledge is the fundamental basis of all knowledge. "If you fight against all your sensations, you will have no standard to which to refer and thus no means of judging even those sensations which you pronounce false."[6] Lucretius asks what can be accounted of higher certainty than sense. Reason, by which we judge of sense-data, is itself wholly founded on the senses, and if the senses are untrue, then all reason as well is rendered false.[7] Moreover, the Epicureans pointed out that in astronomical questions, for instance, we cannot attain certainty, as we can argue for this position just as well as for that position, e.g. "For the heavenly phenomena may depend for their production on many different causes."[8] (It must be remembered that the Greeks lacked our modern scientific appliances, and that their opinions on scientific subjects were, very largely, of the nature of guesses, unsubstantiated by exact observation.)

Epicurus' Logic or Canonic deals with the norms or canons of knowledge and the criteria of truth. The fundamental criterion of truth is Perception (ἡ αἴσθησις), in which we attain what is clear (ἡ ἐνάργεια). Perception takes place when images (εἴδωλα) of objects penetrate the sense-organs (cf. Democritus and Empedocles), and is always true. It is to be noted that the Epicureans included under perception imaginative representations (φανταστικαὶ ἐπιβολαὶ τῆς διανοίας), *all* perception taking place through the reception of εἴδωλα. When these images stream continuously from the same object and enter by the sense-organs, we have perception in the narrower sense: when, however, individual images enter through the pores of the body they become, as it were, mixed up and imaginative pictures arise, e.g. of a centaur. In either case we have "perception," and, as both sorts of images arise from objective causes, both types of perception are true. How then does error arise? Only through *judgment*. If, for instance, we judge that an image corresponds exactly to an external object, when in point of fact it does not so correspond, we are in error. (The difficulty, of course, is to know when the image corresponds to an external object and when it does not, and when it corresponds perfectly or imperfectly; and on this point the Epicureans give us no help.)

The first criterion is therefore Perception. A second criterion is afforded by Concepts (προλήψεις). The concept, according to the Epicureans, is simply a memory image (μνήμη τοῦ πολλάκις ἔξωθεν φανέντος).[9] After we have had perception of an object, e.g. of a man, the memory image or general image of man arises when we hear the word "man." These προλήψεις are always true, and it is only when we proceed to form opinions or judgments that the question of truth or falsity arises. If the opinion or judgment (ὑπόληψις) has reference to the future, then it must be confirmed by experience, while if it has reference to hidden and unperceived causes (e.g. the atoms) it must at least not contradict experience.

There is yet a third criterion, namely feelings or πάθη, which are criteria for conduct. Thus the feeling of pleasure is the criterion of what we should choose, while the feeling of pain shows us what we should avoid. Hence Epicurus could say that "the criteria of truth are the senses, and the preconceptions, and the passions."[10]

3. The Physics

Epicurus' choice of a physical theory was determined by a practical end, that of freeing man from the fear of the gods and of the afterworld and so giving them peace of soul. While not denying the existence of the gods he wished to show that they do not interfere in human affairs and that man need not therefore occupy himself with propitiation and petition and "superstition" in general. Moreover, by rejecting immortality he hoped to free man from fear of death—for what reason is there to fear death when it is mere extinction, absence of all consciousness and feeling, when there is no judgment and when no punishment awaits one in the afterworld? "Death is nothing to us; for that which is dissolved is devoid of sensation, and that which is devoid of sensation is nothing to us." [11] Moved by these considerations Epicurus chose the system of Democritus (which he adopted with but slight modifications), since this system seemed best calculated to serve his end. Did it not explain all phenomena by the mechanical motions of atoms, thus rendering any recourse to divine intervention superfluous and did it not afford an easy handle for the rejection of immortality—the soul, as well as the body, being composed of atoms? This practical aim of the Epicurean Physics appears in a marked manner in Lucretius' *De Rerum Natura*, clothed in the splendid language and imagery of the poet.

Nothing proceeds from nothing, nothing passes into nothingness, declared Epicurus, re-echoing the thought of the old Cosmologists. "And, first of all, we must admit that nothing can come out of that which does not exist; for, were the fact otherwise, everything would be produced from everything and there would be no need of any seed. And if that which disappeared were so absolutely destroyed as to become non-existent, then everything would soon perish, as the things with which they would be dissolved would have no existence." [12] We may compare the lines of Lucretius, *Nunc age, res quoniam docui non posse creari de nilo neque item genitas ad nil revocari.*[13] The bodies of our experience are composed of pre-existing material entities—atoms—and their perishing is but a resolution into the entities of which they are composed. The ultimate constituents of the universe are therefore atoms, Atoms and the Void. "Now the universal whole is a body; for our senses bear us witness in every case that bodies have a real existence; and

the evidence of the senses, as I have said before, ought to
be the rule of our reasonings about everything which is
not directly perceived. Otherwise, if that which we call
the vacuum, or space, or intangible nature, had not a real
existence, there would be nothing in which the bodies could
be contained, or across which they could move, as we see
that they really do move. Let us add to this reflection that
one cannot conceive, either in virtue of perception, or of
any analogy founded on perception, any general quality
peculiar to all beings which is not either an attribute, or
an accident of the body, or of the vacuum." [14] These atoms
vary in size, form and weight (the Epicureans certainly
attributed weight to the atoms, whatever the earlier atomists
may have done) and are indivisible and infinite in number.
In the beginning they rained down through the void or empty
space, though Lucretius compares their motion to that of
motes in a sunbeam, and it may be that the Epicureans did
not think of the atoms as ever in actuality raining down in
parallel straight lines—a conception which would make the
"collision" very much of a *deus ex machina*.

In order to account for the origin of the world, Epicurus
had to allow for a collision of atoms: moreover he wished
at the same time to afford some explanation of human freedom (which the School maintained). He postulated, therefore, a spontaneous oblique movement or declination from
the straight line of descent on the part of individual atoms.
Thus occurred the first collision of atoms, and from the collision and the entanglements consequent on the deviation
the rotary movements were set up which led to the formation
of innumerable worlds, separated from one another by empty
spaces (the μετακόσμια or *intermundia*). The human
soul is also composed of atoms, smooth and round, but in
distinction to the animals it possesses a rational part which
is seated in the breast, as is shown by the emotions of
fear and joy. The irrational part, the principle of life, is
spread throughout the whole body. At death the atoms of
the soul are separated, and there can be no more perception: death is the privation of perception (στέρησις
αἰσθήσεως).

The world is, therefore, due to mechanical causes and
there is no need to postulate teleology. On the contrary, the
Epicureans entirely rejected the anthropocentric teleology
of the Stoics and would have nothing to do with the
Stoic theodicy. The evil with which human life is afflicted

is irreconcilable with any idea of divine guidance in the universe. The gods dwell in the *intermundia*, beautiful and happy and without thought of human affairs, eating and drinking and speaking Greek!

> *Apparet divinum numen sedesque quietae*
> *Quas neque concutiunt venti nec nubila nimbis*
> *Aspergunt neque nix acri concreta pruina*
> *Cana cadens violat semperque innubilus aether*
> *Integit, et largo diffuso lumine rident.*[15]

The gods are anthropomorphically conceived, for they too are composed of atoms—even if of the finest atoms and possessing only ethereal or quasi-bodies—and are divided sexually: they are like to mankind in appearance and breathe and eat as we do. Epicurus not only needed the gods in order to present them as an embodiment of his ethical ideal of calm tranquillity, but he also considered that the universality of belief in the gods can only be explained on the hypothesis of their objective existence. εἴδωλα come to us from the gods, especially in sleep, but perception presents us only with the existence and anthropomorphic character of the gods: knowledge of their happy condition is attained by reason or λόγος. Men may honour the gods for their excellence and may even take part in the customary ceremonial worship, but all fear of them is out of place and also all attempts to win their favour by sacrifices. True piety consists in right thought.

> *nec pietas ullast velatum saepe videri*
> *vertier ad lapidem atque omnis accedere ad aras*
> *nec procumbere humi prostratum et pandere palmas*
> *ante deum delubra nec aras sanguine multo*
> *spargere quadrupedum nec votis nectere vota,*
> *sed mage pacata posse omnia mente tueri.*[16]

The wise man, therefore, does not fear death—for death is mere extinction—nor the gods—for they are unconcerned with human affairs and exact no retribution. We may recall the celebrated lines of Virgil:

> *felix qui potuit rerum cognoscere causas:*
> *atque metus omnes et inexorabile fatum*
> *subiecit pedibus strepitumque Acherontis avari.*[17]

4. The Epicurean Ethic

Like the Cyrenaics Epicurus made *pleasure* the end of life.
Every being strives after pleasure, and it is in pleasure that
happiness consists. "... we affirm that pleasure is the beginning and end of living happily; for we have recognised
this as the first good, being connate with us; and it is with
reference to it that we begin every choice and avoidance; and
to this we come as if we judged of all good by passion
as the standard ..." [18] The question then arises what Epicurus understands by pleasure, when he makes it the end of
life. Two facts are to be noted: first, that Epicurus meant,
not the pleasures of the moment, individual sensations, but
the pleasure which endures throughout a lifetime; and secondly, that pleasure for Epicurus consisted rather in the
absence of pain than in positive satisfaction. This pleasure
is to be found pre-eminently in serenity of soul (ἡ τῆς
ψυχῆς ἀταραξία). With this serenity of soul Epicurus
conjoined also health of body, but the emphasis is rather
on intellectual pleasure, for, while very severe bodily pains
are of short duration, less severe pains may be overcome
or rendered endurable by intellectual pleasures. "... a correct
theory ... can refer all choice and avoidance to the health
of the body and the freedom from disquietude of the soul."
"... at times we pass over many pleasures when any difficulty is likely to ensue from them; and we think many pains
better than pleasures when a greater pleasure follows them,
if we endure the pain for a time." [19] When Epicurus speaks
of choice among pleasures and rejects certain pleasures, it is
to the permanence of pleasure that he is looking, and to
the presence or absence of subsequent pain, for there is
really no room in his ethic for a discrimination between
pleasures that is based on a difference of moral value.
(Though we may well discern a differentiation of pleasures
on grounds of moral value creeping in unawares—as it is
bound to do in any hedonistic ethic, unless the hedonist
is prepared to admit that the "basest" pleasures are on the
same level as the more refined pleasures. And what serious
moral philosopher has ever been prepared to admit that,
without introducing qualifications that suggest another criterion beside pleasure?) "Every pleasure is therefore a good
on account of its own nature, but it does not follow that
every pleasure is worthy of being chosen; just as every pain
is an evil, and yet every pain must not be avoided." "When,

therefore, we say that pleasure is a chief good, we are not speaking of the pleasures of the debauched man, or those which lie in sensual enjoyment, as some think who are ignorant, and who do not entertain our opinions, or else interpret them perversely; but we mean the freedom of the body from pain and of the soul from confusion. For it is not continued drinkings and revels ... that make life pleasant, but sober contemplations, which examine into the reasons for all choice and avoidance, and which put to flight the vain opinions from which the greater part of the confusion arises which troubles the soul." [20] "No pleasure is intrinsically bad: but the efficient causes of some pleasures bring with them a great many perturbations of pleasure." [21]

In practice we have to consider whether any individual pleasure may not be productive of greater pain and any individual pain may not be productive of greater pleasure. For instance, an individual pleasure might be very intense for the moment but might lead to ill-health or to enslavement to a habit; in which case it would be productive of greater pain. Conversely, a pain might be intense for the moment—as in an operation—and yet be productive of a greater good, health. Therefore, although every pain, abstractly considered, is an evil, and every pleasure is a good, we must in practice look to the future and endeavour to attain the maximum of durable pleasure—in Epicurus' opinion, health of body and tranquillity of soul. Epicurean hedonism would not then result in libertinism and excess, but in a calm and tranquil life; for a man is unhappy either from fear or from unlimited and vain desires, and if he but bridle these he may secure for himself the blessings of reason. The wise man will not multiply his needs, since that is to multiply sources of pain: he will rather reduce his needs to a minimum. (The Epicureans even went so far as to say that the wise man can be perfectly happy even when undergoing bodily torture. Thus Epicurus declared that, "Though he is being tortured on the rack, the wise man is still happy." [22] An extreme statement of this position is found in the saying: "If the wise man is being burned, if he is being tortured—nay, within the very bull of Phalaris, he will say: 'How delightful this is! How little I care for it'!" [23]) Hence the Epicurean ethic leads to a moderate asceticism, self-control and independence. "To accustom one's self, therefore, to simple and inexpensive habits is a great ingredient in the perfecting of health, and makes a man free from hesitation with respect to the necessary uses of life." [24]

Virtue is a condition of ἀταραξία or tranquillity of soul, though of course its value is estimated by Epicurus according to its power of producing pleasure. Virtues such as simplicity, moderation, temperance, cheerfulness, are much more conducive to pleasure and happiness than are unbridled luxury, feverish ambition and so on. "It is not possible to live pleasantly without living prudently, and honourably, and justly; nor to live prudently, and honourably, and justly, without living pleasantly. But he to whom it does not happen to live prudently, honourably, and justly, cannot possibly live pleasantly." "The just man is the freest of all men from disquietude; but the unjust man is a perpetual prey to it." "Injustice is not intrinsically bad; it has this character only because there is joined with it a fear of not escaping those who are appointed to punish actions marked with that character." "When, without any fresh circumstances arising, a thing which has been declared just in practice does not agree with the impressions of reason, that is a proof that the thing was not really just. In the same way, when in consequence of new circumstances, a thing which has been pronounced just does not any longer appear to agree with utility, the thing which was just, inasmuch as it was useful to the social relations and intercourse of mankind, ceases to be just at the moment when it ceases to be useful." [25] Moreover, in spite of the fact that the ethic of the Epicureans is fundamentally selfish or egocentric, in that it is based on the individual's pleasure, it was not in practice so selfish as it might sound. Thus the Epicureans thought that it is really pleasanter to do a kindness than to receive one, and the founder himself was commended for his contented and kind character. "He who desires to live tranquilly without having anything to fear from other men, ought to make himself friends; those whom he cannot make friends of, he should, at least, avoid rendering enemies; and if that is not in his power, he should, as far as possible, avoid all intercourse with them, and keep them aloof, as far as it is for his interest to do so." "The happiest men are they who have arrived at the point of having nothing to fear from those who surround them. Such men live with one another most agreeably, having the firmest grounds of confidence in one another, enjoying the advantages of friendship in all their fullness, and not lamenting, as a pitiable circumstance, the premature death of their friends." [26] It is probably true to say that Epicurus' practical moral judgment was sounder than the theoretical foundations of his ethic, an ethic which could obviously give little account of moral obligation.

Owing to the fact that man should not pursue heedlessly the first pleasure that offers itself, there is need of an art of calculation or mensuration in the conduct of life. We must therefore practise συμμέτρησις, and it is in the right mensuration of pleasures and pains, in the ability to take into account and balance one against another present or future happiness and unhappiness, that the essence of insight or φρόνησις, the highest virtue, consists. If a man is to live a truly happy, pleasurable and contented life, he must possess this insight, he must be φρόνιμος. "Now, the beginning and the greatest good of all these things is prudence, on which account prudence is something more valuable than even philosophy, inasmuch as all the other virtues spring from it, teaching us that it is not possible to live pleasantly unless one also lives prudently, and honourably, and justly; and that one cannot live prudently, and honourably, and justly, without living pleasantly; for the virtues are connate with living agreeably, and living agreeably is inseparable from the virtues." [27] When a man is φρόνιμος, he is virtuous, for the virtuous man is not so much the person who is actually enjoying pleasure at any given moment as the man who knows how to conduct himself in the search for pleasure. Once virtue has been thus defined, it is obvious that it is an absolutely necessary condition for lasting happiness.

Epicurus laid great stress on *Friendship*. "Of all the things which wisdom provides for the happiness of the whole life, by far the most important is the acquisition of friendship." [28] This may seem strange in a fundamentally egoistic ethic, but the emphasis on friendship is itself based on egoistic considerations, namely that without friendship a man cannot live a secure and tranquil life, while on the other hand friendship gives pleasure. Friendship rests, therefore, on an egoistic basis, the thought of personal advantage. This egoism was, however, modified through the Epicurean doctrine that an unselfish affection arises in the course of the friendship and that in a friendship a wise man loves the friend as he does himself. Nevertheless it remains true that the social theory of the Epicureans is egoistic in character, a fact that comes out clearly in their teaching that the wise man will not mix himself up in politics, as this disturbs tranquillity of soul. There are, however, two exceptions: the first, that of the man who needs to take part in politics in order to ensure his own personal security, the second, that of a man who has such an urge towards a political career that ἀταραξία would be quite impossible for him, were he to remain in retirement.

Pleasure and personal advantage are again decisive for the Epicurean theory of law. It is pleasanter to live in a society where law reigns and "rights" are respected than in a condition of *bellum omnium contra omnes*. The latter condition would be by no means favourable to tranquillity of soul or to ἀταραξία.

The Epicureans, as we have seen, went back to the School of Leucippus and Democritus for their Physics, as the Stoa went back to the Cosmology of Heraclitus. The Epicurean ethics, on the other hand, are more or less in agreement with that of the Cyrenaics. Both Aristippus and Epicurus make pleasure the end of life, and in both Schools attention is paid to the future, to calculation, to the "measuring" of pleasures and pains. There are, however, differences between the Epicureans and the Cyrenaics. For while the latter —in general, that is to say—considered *positive* pleasure (the smooth movement or λεία κίνησις) to be the end, the Epicureans stressed more the negative side, calm and tranquillity, ἡ καταστηματικὴ ἡδονή. Again, while the Cyrenaics considered bodily suffering worse than mental suffering, the Epicureans accounted mental suffering worse than bodily suffering, on the ground that the body suffers only from present evil whereas the soul can suffer also from the recollection of past evil and the expectation or fear of future evil. All the same it can be truly said that Cyrenaicism was absorbed in Epicureanism. Did not Epicurus agree with the Cyrenaic Hegesias in laying the emphasis on absence of suffering and with Anniceris in recommending to the wise the cultivation of friendship?

The Epicurean philosophy is, therefore, not a philosophy of heroes, nor has it the moral grandeur of the Stoic creed. Yet it is neither so selfish nor so "immoral" as its fundamental tenet might at first sight imply, and its attraction for certain types of men is easily understandable. It is certainly not a heroic creed or philosophy: but it was not meant by its author to be an incentive to base living, whatever its tenets might lead to in popular application to practice.

Note on Cynicism in the
First Period of the Hellenistic Epoch

Cynicism in this period tended to lose its serious character of emphasis on independence, suppression of desire and physical endurance, and to give itself rather to mockery of convention and tradition and prevailing beliefs and modes of behaviour. Not of course that this tendency was absent from the earlier Cynicism—we have only to think of Diogenes—but it showed itself in this period through the new literary genre of the satire or σπουδογέλοιον. In the first half of the third century B.C., *Bion of Borysthenes*, influenced by Cyrenaicism (he had listened to the Cyrenaic Theodorus at Athens), propagated the so-called "hedonistic Cynicism" in his "diatribes," dwelling on the happiness and pleasurable character of the simple Cynic life. *Teles*, who taught at Megara about 240 B.C., followed Bion in the composition of such "diatribes"—popular and anecdotal pieces—dealing with appearance and reality, poverty and riches, cynical "apathy," etc.

Menippus of Gadara (about 250 B.C.) created the Satire, in which he combined poetry with prose, criticised under various forms—e.g. journey to Hades, letters to the gods—natural philosophy and specialist learning, and mocked at the idolatrous honour paid to Epicurus by his followers. He was imitated by Varro, Seneca in his *Apocolocyntosis*, and Lucian.

Cercides of Megalopolis, composer of meliambs, displayed the same satyric tone, declaring, for example, that he would leave to the μετεωροσκόποι the solution of the ticklish question, why Cronus showed himself a father to some people and a stepfather to others.

Chapter Thirty-Eight

THE OLDER SCEPTICS, THE MIDDLE AND NEW ACADEMIES

1. *The Older Sceptics*

Just as in the Stoa and in the Garden of Epicurus theory was subordinated to practice, so in the School of Pyrrho, the founder of Scepticism, though there is of course this big difference, that whereas the Stoics and Epicureans looked to science or positive knowledge as a means to peace of soul, the Sceptics sought to attain the same end by the disavowal of knowledge, i.e. by scepticism, the opposite of science.

Pyrrho of Elis (*c.* 360-*c.* 270), who is said to have accompanied Alexander on his march to India,[1] was apparently influenced by the Democritean theory of the sense-qualities, the relativism of the Sophists and the Cyrenaic epistemology. He taught that the human reason cannot penetrate to the inner substance of things (things are ἀκατάληπτα in our regard):[2] we can only know how things appear to us. The same things appear differently to different people, and we cannot know which is right: to any assertion we could oppose the contradictory assertion with equally good grounds (ἰσοθένεια τῶν λόγων). We cannot, therefore, be certain of anything and the wise man will withhold his judgment (ἐπέχειν). Rather than say, "This is so," we should say, "So it appears to me" or "It may be so."

The same scepticism and consequent suspension of judgment is extended to the practical sphere. Nothing is in itself ugly or beautiful, right or wrong, or at least we cannot be sure of it: all external things in our lives are indifferent and the wise man will aim simply at tranquillity of soul and endeavour to preserve his soul in that condition. It is true that even the wise man cannot avoid acting and taking part in practical life, but he will follow in practice probable opinion, custom and law, conscious that absolute truth is unattainable.

Diogenes Laërtius informs us that Pyrrho expressed his philosophical views only by word of mouth,[3] but his views are known through those of his pupil *Timon of Phlius* (c. 320-230 B.C.), who is called by Sextus Empiricus ὁ προφήτης τῶν Πύρρωνος λόγων.[4] Timon composed Σίλλοι or mocking verses, in which he parodied Homer and Hesiod and made fun of the Greek philosophers, with the exception of Xenophanes and Pyrrho himself. According to Timon we can trust neither sense-perception nor reason. We must accordingly suspend all judgment, not allowing ourselves to be caught in any theoretical assertion, and then we shall attain to true ἀταραξία or tranquillity of soul.

(Cicero apparently did not know of Pyrrho as a Sceptic, but considered him rather as a moralist who preached and practised indifference towards external things. It may be, then, that Pyrrho did not personally develop the Sceptic position. But as he left no writings, we can hardly attain certainty on this point.)

2. *The Middle Academy*

Plato had held that the objects of sense-perception are not the objects of true knowledge, but he was very far from being a Sceptic, the whole point of his Dialectic being the attainment of true and certain knowledge of the eternal and abiding. A sceptical current of thought manifests itself, however, in what is known as the Second or Middle Academy, a scepticism directed principally against the Stoic dogmatism but also expressed in universal terms. Thus *Arcesilaus* (315/14-241/40), the founder of the Middle Academy, is reputed to have said that he was certain of nothing—not even of the fact that he was certain of nothing,[5] thus going further than Socrates, who knew that he knew nothing. He practised therefore a similar suspension of judgment or ἐποχή to that of the Pyrrhonists.[6] While trying to support his position by the example and practice of Socrates, Arcesilaus made the Stoic epistemology a special object of attack. No representation is given that might not be false: none of our sense-perceptions or presentations possess the guarantee of their own objective validity, for we may feel an equally intense subjective certainty even when the presentation is objectively false. We can therefore never be certain.

3. The New Academy

1. The founder of the Third or New Academy was *Carneades of Cyrene* (214/12-129/8 B.C.), who accompanied the Stoic Diogenes on the embassy to Rome in 156/5. Following the scepticism of Arcesilaus, Carneades taught that knowledge is impossible and that there is no criterion of truth. Against the Stoics he maintained that there is no sense-presentation by the side of which we could not place a false presentation that is indistinguishable from the true, appealing to the influence upon us of presentations in e.g. dreams, presentations which are, however, unreal, and to the facts of hallucination and delusion. Impressions of sense are, therefore, not infallible, and the Stoics cannot look to reason as a remedy, since they themselves admit that concepts are founded on experience.[7]

We are unable to prove anything, since any proof rests on assumptions which must themselves be proved. But this latter proof will itself rest on assumptions, and so on indefinitely. All dogmatic philosophy is accordingly out of the question: for either side in a question equally good—or equally bad—reasons can be adduced. Carneades attacked the Stoic theology, trying to show that their proofs for God's existence are not conclusive and that their doctrine as to God's Nature contained antinomies.[8] For example, the Stoics appealed to the *consensus gentium* as an argument for the divine existence. Now, if they can prove this *consensus gentium*, then they have proved a universal *belief* in the divine existence, but that does not prove that there are gods. And on what grounds do the Stoics assert that the Universe is wise and rational? It must first be proved to be *animate*, and this they have not proved. If they argue that there must be a universal Reason, from which man's reason proceeds, they have first to prove that the human mind cannot be the spontaneous product of nature. Again, the argument from design is not conclusive. If the universe is a designed product, then there must be a Designer; but the whole point at issue is, whether the universe is a designed product or not. Might it not be the undesigned product of natural forces?

The Stoic God is animate and so must be possessed of feeling. But if he can feel and receive impressions, then he can suffer from impressions and is ultimately liable to disintegration. Moreover, if God is rational and perfect, as the Stoics suppose Him to be, He cannot be "virtuous," as the Stoics also suppose Him to be. How, for example, can God be brave or courageous? What dangers or pains or labours affect Him, in respect of which He can show courage?

The Stoics maintain a doctrine of Divine Providence. But if this be so, how can they explain the presence of e.g. poisonous snakes? The Stoics say that God's Providence is manifested in His gift of reason to man. Now, the great majority of men use this reason to degrade themselves, so that to such men the possession of reason is an injury and not a benefit. If God really exercised Providence over all men, He should have made all men good and given all *right* reason. Moreover, it is useless for Chrysippus to speak of "neglect" on the part of God—i.e. in regard to "little" matters. In the first place what Providence has neglected to provide for, is not a little matter: in the second place, the neglect could not be intentional in God (for intentional neglect is a fault even in an earthly ruler); while in the third place unintentional neglect is inconceivable in respect of the Infinite Reason.

These and other criticisms of Carneades are directed against the Stoic doctrines, and so they are, in part, of but academic interest. By maintaining a materialistic doctrine of God the Stoics involved themselves in insurmountable difficulties, for if God were material He could disintegrate, and if He were the Soul of the world—possessed of a body—He could feel pleasure and pain. Criticisms against such a conception of the Deity can have for us no more than academic interest. Moreover, we would not dream of ascribing virtues to God in the anthropomorphic manner that the line of criticism adopted by Carneades presupposes. Nor would we undertake to prove in philosophy that everything is created for the good of man. Yet some of the difficulties raised by Carneades are of lasting interest, and an attempt must be made to meet them in every Theodicy, e.g. the presence of physical suffering and of moral evil in the world. I have already made some remarks on this subject when treating of the Stoic theodicy, and I hope to show later on, how other philosophers, mediaeval and modern, tried to answer these questions; but it must always be remembered that, even if the human reason is unable to answer fully and with complete satisfaction all the difficulties that can be raised against a position, that does not compel us to abandon that position, if it rests on valid argument.

Carneades saw that complete suspension of judgment is impossible, and so he elaborated a theory of Probability (πιθανότης). Probability has various grades and is both necessary and sufficient for action. He showed, for example, how we may approximate to the truth—even if we can never attain certainty—by the accumulation of reasons for accepting some position. If I merely saw the shape of someone I knew, it might be an hallucination, but if I hear the person speak, if I touch him, if he eats, I may for all practical purposes accept the presentation as true. It enjoys a very high degree of probability, especially if it is also intrinsically probable that the person should be in that place at that time. If a man leaves his wife in England and goes to India on business, he might well doubt the objective validity of the presentation, if he seems to see his wife on the quay when he disembarks at Bombay. But if, on returning to England, he finds his wife waiting for him on the landing-stage, the validity of the presentation bears its own inherent probability.

2. The Academy returned to dogmatism under *Antiochus* of Ascalon (d. *c.* 68 B.C.), who apparently started as an agnostic but later came to abandon this position,[9] and whose lectures were heard by Cicero in the winter of 79/8. He pointed out the contradiction involved in asserting that nothing is knowable or that all is doubtful; for, in asserting that all is doubtful, I am at any rate asserting my knowledge that all is doubtful. His own criterion of truth he apparently found in the agreement of eminent philosophers and endeavoured to show that the Academic, Peripatetic and Stoic systems were in essential agreement with each other. In fact he openly taught Stoic doctrines, shamelessly asserting that Zeno had borrowed them from the old Academy. He thus tried to deprive the Sceptics of one of their principal arguments, namely, the contradiction between the various philosophic systems. He shows himself at the same time to be an Eclectic.

This eclectic tendency comes out in his moral teaching. For, while holding with the Stoics that virtue is sufficient for happiness, he also taught with Aristotle that for happiness in its highest degree external goods and health of the body

are also necessary. In spite of the fact, then, that Cicero
declares him to have been more of a Stoic than an Aacd-
emician,[10] Antiochus was undoubtedly an Eclectic.

3. A Roman Eclectic was *M. Terentius Varro* (116-27
B.C.), scholar and philosopher. The only true theology in
Varro's opinion is that which recognises *one* God, Who is the
Soul of the world, which He governs according to reason.
The mythical theology of the poets is to be rejected on the
ground that it attributed unworthy characteristics and actions
to the gods, while the physical theologies of the natural
philosophers contradict one another. We must not, however,
neglect the official cult of the State, since this has a practical
and popular value. Varro even suggested that the popular
religion was the work of earlier statesmen, and that if the
work had to be done over again, it might be done better in
the light of philosophy.[11]

Varro seems to have been greatly influenced by Poseidonius. From the latter he accepted many theories concerning the origin and development of culture, geography,
hydrology, etc., and by his exposition of these theories he
influenced later Romans such as Vitruvius and Pliny.
Varro's tendency to Pythagorean "number-mysticism" also
derives from the thought of Poseidonius and thereby he
influenced later writers like Gellius, Macrobius and Martianus Capella. Cynic influence is visible in Varro's *Saturae
Menippeae,* of which we possess only fragments. Therein
he opposed Cynic simplicity to the luxury of the rich, whose
gluttony he subjected to mockery, and he made fun of the
philosophers' squabbles.

4. The most celebrated of all Roman eclectics is *M. Tullius
Cicero,* the great orator (Jan. 3rd 106-Dec. 7, 43 B.C.).
In his youth Cicero was a pupil of Phaedrus the Epicurean,
Philon the Academician, Diodotus the Stoic, Antiochus of
Ascalon, and Zeno the Epicurean. In Rhodes he listened to
the teaching of Poseidonius the Stoic. To the philosophic
studies of his youth at Athens and Rhodes there succeeded
years spent in public life and official activity, but in the last
three years of his life Cicero returned to philosophy. The
majority of his philosophic writings date from these later
years (e.g. the *Paradoxa,* the *Consolatio,* the *Hortensius,* the
Academica, the *De Finibus,* the *Tusculana,* the *De Natura
Deorum,* the *De Senectute,* the *De Divinatione,* the *De Fato,*
the *De Amicitia,* the *De Virtutibus*). The *De Republica*
(54 B.C. seq.) and the *De Legibus* (c. 52 seq.) are earlier

compositions. The writings of Cicero are scarcely to be called
original in content, as Cicero himself openly admits—
"ἀπόγραφα sunt, minore labore fiunt, verba tantum affero,
quibus abundo." [12] He had, however, the gift of presenting
the doctrine of the Greeks to Roman readers in a clear style.

While Cicero was unable to effect a scientific refutation
of Scepticism (he was inclined to the latter, owing to the
conflict of opposing philosophical Schools and doctrines),
he found a refuge in the intuitions of the moral consciousness,
which are immediate and certain. Realising the danger of
Scepticism for morality, he sought to place the moral judgment beyond its corroding influence and speaks of notiones
innatae, natura nobis insitae. These moral concepts proceed
therefore from our nature, and they are confirmed by general
agreement—consensus gentium.

In his ethical doctrine Cicero was inclined to agree with
the Stoics that virtue is sufficient for happiness, but he
could not bring himself to reject altogether the Peripatetic
teaching, which attributed value to external goods as well,
though he seems to have hesitated somewhat in his opinion
on this matter. [13] He agreed with the Stoics that the wise
man should be without πάθη [14] and combated the Peripatetic
teaching that virtue is a mean between opposite πάθη.
(But it is to be noted that Cicero's notion of πάθος or per-
turbatio is that of aversa a recta ratione contra naturam
animi commotio. [15]) For Cicero again, as for the Stoics,
practical, and not speculative, virtue is the higher. [16]

In the sphere of natural philosophy Cicero was inclined
to scepticism, though he by no means despised this province
of human thought. [17] He was particularly interested in the
proof of God's existence from nature and rejected the doctrine of atheistic atomism. "Hoc (i.e. the formation of the
world from the chance collision of atoms) qui existimat fieri
potuisse non intelligo cur non idem putet, si innumerabiles
unius et viginti formae litterarum vel aureae vel qualesilibet
aliquo coiciantur, posse ex iis in terram excussis annales
Enni ut deinceps legi possint, effici." [18]

Cicero considered that the popular religion should be
preserved in the interests of the community at large, while
at the same time it should be purified from gross superstition and the practice of attributing immorality to the gods
(e.g. the story of the rape of Ganymede). [19] Especially
should we preserve belief in Providence and the immortality
of the soul. [20]

Cicero stressed the ideal of human fellowship (cf. the Stoa), and appealed to the ninth letter of Plato. "—*ut profectus a caritate domesticorum ac suorum serpat longius et se implicet primum civium, deinde omnium mortalium societate atque, ut ad Archytam scripsit Plato, non sibi se solum natum meminerit sed patriae, sed suis, ut perexigua pars ipsi relinquatur.*" [21]

Chapter Thirty-Nine

THE MIDDLE STOA

In the second and third centuries before Christ the Stoic philosophers show a marked tendency to Eclecticism, admitting Platonic and Aristotelian elements into the School and departing from orthodox Stoicism. They were impelled to this course, not only by the attacks levelled against the Stoic dogmatism by the Academicians, but also by their contact with the Roman world, which was much more interested in the practical application of philosophic doctrines than in speculation. The dominant names of the Middle Stoa are those of Panaetius and Poseidonius.

1. *Panaetius of Rhodes* (*c.* 185-110/9 B.C.) lived for some time in Rome, where he interested the younger Scipio and Laelius in Greek philosophy and greatly influenced the Roman historian Q. Mucius Scaevola and the Greek historian Polybius. Cicero made use of his works, especially in the first two books of the *De Officiis.*[1] In 129 B.C. he succeeded Antipater of Tarsus as Scholarch at Athens.

While Panaetius modified certain Stoic doctrines on the one hand, he did not hesitate on the other hand to jettison altogether some of the cargo of Stoic orthodoxy. Thus he modified Stoic "puritanism" by allowing that the end of life in the case of ordinary men is simply the rational perfection of their individual nature. Stoicism thus became rather less "idealistic" in the hands of Panaetius, especially as he seems to have denied the existence of the truly wise man, the old Stoic ideal, and to have set the proficient (προκόπτων) to all intents and purposes in the first place. Moreover, he attached more value to external goods than did the early Stoa and rejected the ideal of "Apathy."

165

While thus modifying the Stoic ethic Panaetius cast overboard the Stoic theory of divination (which the early Stoics
maintained on a philosophical basis of determinism), rejected
astrology and jettisoned the doctrines of the world-conflagration and of the relative "immortality" of the soul.[2] He had
little sympathy with popular theology.[3] In his political teaching he appears to have been influenced by Plato and Aristotle, though he advocated a wider ideal, in accordance
with Stoic doctrine, than that of the two Greek philosophers.

It was apparently from Panaetius that Scaevola got his
threefold division of theology (cf. Varro). He distinguished
(i) the theology of the poets, which is anthropomorphic and
false, (ii) the theology of the philosophers, which is rational
and true, but unfitted for popular use, and (iii) the theology
of the statesmen, which maintains the traditional cult and is
indispensable for public education.[4]

2. The greatest of the disciples of Panaetius was *Poseidonius of Apamaea* (c. 135-51 B.C.). At first a pupil of
Panaetius at Athens, Poseidonius then made extensive jour-
neys, to Egypt, for example, and to Spain, after which he
opened a School at Rhodes in 97 B.C. It was here that Cicero
came to hear him in 78 B.C., and he was twice visited by
Pompey. His works have disappeared and it is only recently,
through the critical analysis of the literature that was indebted to his influence, that some idea has been obtained—
even if not in all points a very clear idea—of the greatness
of Poseidonius. Historian and geographer, rationalist and
mystic, he bound together various philosophic currents in a
framework of Stoic monism, tried to support his speculative
doctrines by a wealth of empirical knowledge, and infused
into the whole the warmth of religious inspiration. Indeed
Zeller does not hesitate to call him "the most universal mind
that Greece had seen since the time of Aristotle."[5] Proclus
(in *Eukleiden*) mentions Poseidonius and his School seven
times in connection with the philosophy of mathematics, e.g.
on parallels, on the distinction between theorems and problems, and on existence theorems.

Stoic monism is fundamental to the philosophy of Poseidonius, and he tries to display the articulated unity of Nature
in detail. The phenomenon of the tide's ebb and flow, as
caused by the moon, revealed to him the "sympathy" that
prevails between all parts of the cosmic system. The world
is a hierarchy of grades of being, from inorganic entities, as
in the mineral kingdom, through plants and animals up to

man, and so to the super-organic sphere of the Divine, the whole being bound together in one great system and every detail being arranged by Divine Providence. This universal harmony and structural ordering of the universe postulates Absolute Reason, God, at the summit of the hierarchy and as the all-pervading Rational Activity.[6] The world is permeated by a vital force (ζωτικὴ δύναμις) which proceeds from the sun, and God Himself is represented by Poseidonius, following in the footsteps of the orthodox Stoicism, as a rational, fiery breath. Moreover, in contradistinction to his teacher Panaetius, Poseidonius reaffirmed the Stoic doctrine of the conflagration or ἐκπύρωσις, a doctrine which emphasises the monistic character of the universe.

But, though his philosophy was monistic, Poseidonius admitted a dualism, apparently under the influence of Platonism. There are two divisions of the Cosmos, the supralunar world and the infralunar world. While the latter world is earthly and perishable, the former is heavenly and "imperishable" and sustains the lower world through the forces which it imparts. These two worlds are, however, bound together in man, who is the bond (δεσμός) between them.[7] Composed of body and spirit, he stands on the borderline between the perishable and the imperishable or the earthly and the heavenly; and as man is the ontological bond, so is knowledge of man the epistemological bond, binding together in itself all knowledge, knowledge of the heavenly and knowledge of the earthly. Moreover, just as man from the *corporeal* viewpoint is the *highest* grade, so, conversely, from the *spiritual* viewpoint he is the *lowest* grade. In other words, between man and the Supreme Godhead there exist "demons" or higher spiritual beings, who form an intermediate gradation between man and God. The hierarchical character of the universe is thus uninterrupted, though the dualism remains. This dualism is emphasised in the psychology of Poseidonius, for, although with the older Stoics he makes the soul a fiery πνεῦμα—and so material like the body—he then proceeds to emphasise the dualism of soul and body in a manner reminiscent of Plato. Thus the body is a hindrance to the soul, impeding the free development of its knowledge.[8] Further than that, Poseidonius readopted the Platonic theory of the pre-existence of the soul, which naturally underlined the dualism, and also admitted—against Panaetius—the immortality of the soul. This immortality, however, could be no more than a relative immortality (i.e. relative to the body) in the philosophy of Poseidonius, since he had reaffirmed the Stoic world-conflagration. His teaching on "immortality" thus followed that of the older Stoics.

In spite of this dualism in his psychology of man Poseidonius' influenced by Plato and Aristotle, emphasised the gradation-aspect in his general psychology. Thus the plants, which in the earlier Stoic view possess only φύσις and not ψυχή, enjoy τὸ ἐπιθυμητικόν, and also the θρεπτική and αὐξητικὴ δυνάμεις, while the animals possess in addition τὸ θυμοειδές, ἡ αἴσθησις, τὸ ὀρεκτικόν, and τὸ κινητικὸν κατὰ τόπον. Man, higher than the animals, possesses τὸ λογιστικόν and so the capacity of λόγος, νοῦς and διάνοια.

Thus, although Poseidonius admits the Platonic dualism, he subordinates it to an ultimate monism, influenced by the Heraclitean theory of opposition in harmony or unity in difference. In this attempt at a synthesis of dualism and monism he marks a stage on the way to Neo-Platonism.

In contrast to Panaetius, Poseidonius reaffirmed the Stoic theory of divination. Because of the universal harmony of the Cosmos and the reign of Fate the future can be divined in the present: moreover, the Providence of God would not have withheld from men the means of divining future events.[9] In states like sleep and ecstasy the soul, free from the body's hindrance, may see the underlying connection of events and divine the future. We have already mentioned that Poseidonius admitted the existence of "demons": he believed too that man can enter into communication with them.

Poseidonius propounded a theory of history or of cultural development. In the primitive golden age the wise, i.e. the philosophers, ruled (corresponding in mankind to the natural leadership of the strongest beast in the herd within the animal kingdom), and it was they who made those inventions which raised man from his primitive way of life to more refined conditions of material civilisation. Thus the wise discovered metals and founded the art of making tools, etc.[10] In the moral sphere the primitive stage of innocence was followed by decadence, and the prevalence of violence necessitated the institution of laws. The philosophers accordingly, leaving to others the elaboration of technical appliances, set themselves to the task of raising the moral condition of mankind, first of all through practical and political activity and later by a self-dedication to the life of speculation or θεωρία. Yet all these activities, from the lowest to the highest, were but different grades of one and the same wisdom or σοφία.

Poseidonius also interested himself in ethnographical questions, stressing the influence of climate and natural conditions on the character and way of life of a people, his travels affording him material for observation on this matter. In addition, his empirical bent led him to extend his activity over a wide field in the domain of the special sciences, e.g. in mathematics, astronomy, history and literature. But his outstanding characteristic is his ability for reducing all this wealth of empirical knowledge to the unity of a philosophical system, discovering everywhere connections, interactions and harmonies, trying to penetrate and exhibit the rational structure of the universe and the rational development of history.

Note on the Peripatetic School
in the Hellenistic-Roman Period

1. *Strato of Lampsacus,* ὁ φυσικός, succeeded Theophrastus as head of the Peripatetic School at Athens and occupied that position from about 287-269 B.C. His philosophic teaching betrays the influence of Democritus, which impelled him towards a monistic view of the universe. The world consists of particles, between which there is empty space. These particles, however, are endlessly divisible, and appear to possess qualities, since Strato assumes ultimate characteristics or qualities, namely the Warm and the Cold. The world was formed by natural necessity or the laws of nature, and can be ascribed to God only so far as God is to be identified with the unconscious forces of Nature itself. Thus, although Strato does not follow Democritus in matters of detail, the inspiration of his materialistic monism and his denial of the Aristotelian dualism must be attributed to the influence of the Democritean philosophy. This transformation of the Peripatetic system in the hands of Strato is consonant with the latter's special interest in physical science—it was this that won him the title of ὁ φυσικός. He appears to have influenced the medicine, astronomy and mechanics of the Alexandrian period.

In Strato's eyes all psychical activities, such as thought and feeling, are reducible to *motion,* and they are activities of the one rational soul, which is situated between the eyebrows. We can have as objects of our thought only that which has been the cause of a previous sense-impression,[11] and, conversely, every perception involves intellectual activity.[12] This might seem at first sight to be but a repetition of Aristotelian epistemology, but Strato seems to have meant it in a sense which involves the denial of a rational principle in man, essentially distinct from the animal soul. His denial of immortality was, therefore, a logical conclusion, for, if all thinking is essentially dependent on sense, there can be no question of a principle of thought surviving independently of the body.

2. Under Strato's successors—Lycon of Troas, Ariston of Chios, Critolaus of Phaselis, Diodorus of Tyre and Erymneus —the Peripatetic School does not seem to have made any real contribution to philosophy. Moreover, an eclectic tendency made itself visible in the School. Thus although Critolaus defended Aristotle's doctrine of the eternity of the world against the Stoics, he accepted the Stoics' reduction of God and the human soul to matter (Aether) and adopted the Cynic attitude in regard to pleasure.

3. With *Andronicus of Rhodes* the School took a new turn. Andronicus was the tenth Scholarch at Athens (i.e. excluding Aristotle himself) and occupied the post from about 70 B.C. to 50 B.C. He published the "pedagogical" works of Aristotle, investigated their authenticity, and commented on many of the works, giving special attention to logic. The line of commentators culminated in *Alexander of Aphrodisias*, who lectured on the Peripatetic philosophy at Athens between A.D. 198 and 211. Alexander was the most celebrated of the commentators of Aristotle, but he did not hesitate to depart from the latter's teaching. For instance, he adopted a nominalist position in regard to universals and denied anthropocentric teleology. Moreover, he identified the νοῦς ποιητικὸς with τὸ πρῶτον αἴτιον. Man possesses at birth only the νοῦς φυσικός or ὑλικός and later acquires the νοῦς ἐπίκτητος under the influence of the νοῦς ποιητικός. A consequence of this is the denial of the human soul's immortality. While in denying the immortality of the human soul Alexander is probably at one with Aristotle, it must be admitted that the denial follows much more obviously from Alexander's teaching than it does from the somewhat ambiguous remarks of Aristotle.

4. Alexander's eloquent defence of the study of logic in his commentary on the *Prior Analytics* is worthy of mention. He there declares that logic is not less deserving of

our attention and study owing to the fact that it is an instrument of philosophy rather than an actual part of philosophy. For if man's greatest good is to become like to God, and if this likeness is attained through contemplation and knowledge of truth, and the knowledge of truth through demonstration, then we should hold demonstration in the greatest honour and esteem, and so syllogistic reasoning also, inasmuch as demonstration is a form of syllogistic reasoning.[13] Together with this scholarly tendency grew the tendency to eclecticism. Thus the famous physician *Galen* (A.D. 129 to about A.D. 199) and *Aristocles* of Messana (*c.* A.D. 180) inclined to Stoicism with their doctrine of the immanent and active Nous, that pervades all nature.

5. The Peripatetics of the latest period can indeed hardly be called Peripatetics—certainly not without qualification: to all intents and purposes the School was absorbed in Neo-Platonism, the last great effort of Greek philosophy, and the late Peripatetics either inclined to eclecticism or contented themselves with commenting on the works of Aristotle. Thus Anatolius of Alexandria, who became bishop of Laodicea about A.D. 268 and may be identical with the Anatolius who was the teacher of Iamblichus,[14] combined, in his treatise on the numbers one to ten, consideration of the real properties of numbers with Pythagorean "number-mysticism."

Themistius (*c.* A.D. 320-*c.* 390), who taught at Constantinople and other places in the East and never became a Christian, affirmed indeed that he had chosen Aristotle as his guide to wisdom, and either paraphrased or commented on some of Aristotle's works, but was in fact much influenced by Platonism. With the later Platonism he defined philosophy as ὁμοίωσις θεοῦ κατὰ τὸ δυνατὸν ἀνθρώπῳ. (Cf. Plat. *Theaet.* 176 b.)

Chapter Forty

THE LATER STOA

In the early Roman Empire the chief characteristic of the
Stoa is its insistence on the practical and moral principles
of the School, which take on a religious colouring, being
bound up with the doctrine of man's kinship with God and
his duty of love towards his fellow-men. The noble morality
of the Stoa is strikingly displayed in the teaching of the
great Stoics of the period, Seneca, Epictetus and the Emperor Marcus Aurelius. At the same time a certain tendency
to eclecticism is visible in the Stoa as in other Schools. Nor
was the contemporary scientific interest absent from the
Stoa: we may think, for example, of the geographer Strabo.
We are fortunate in possessing an extensive Stoic literature
from this period, which enables us to form a clear idea of
the teaching of the School and the characteristics of its
great personalities. Thus we are well provided in regard
to Seneca's writings and we have four of the eight books
in which Flavius Arrianus reported the lectures of Epictetus, while the Meditations of Marcus Aurelius show us
the Stoic philosopher on the Roman throne.

1. *L. Annaeus Seneca* of Córdoba was tutor and minister
to the Emperor Nero, and it was in obedience to the latter's
command that the philosopher opened his veins in A.D. 65.

As we would expect of a Roman, Seneca emphasises
the practical side of philosophy, ethics, and—within the
sphere of ethics—is more concerned with the practice of
virtue than with theoretical investigations into its nature.
He does not seek intellectual knowledge for its own sake, but
pursues philosophy as a means to the acquirement of virtue.

Philosophy is necessary, but it is to be pursued with a practical end in view. *Non delectent, verba nostra, sed prosint—non quaerit aeger medicum eloquentem.*[1] His words on this topic not infrequently recall those of Thomas à Kempis, e.g. *plus scire quam sit satis, intemperantiae genus est.*[2] To spend one's time in the so-called liberal studies without having a practical end in view is waste of time—*unum studium vere liberale est quod liberum facit.*[3] and he calls on Lucilius to abandon the literary game of reducing sublime themes to grammatical and dialectical jugglery.[4] Seneca is interested to a certain extent in physical theories, but he insists that it is the conquest of the passions that is the really important point and which makes man equal to God,[5] and he often uses physical subjects simply as an opportunity for moralising conclusions, as when he makes use of the earthquakes in Campania (A.D. 63) to furnish matter for a moral discourse.[6] However, he certainly praises the study of Nature (under the influence of Poseidonius) and even declares that knowledge of Nature is to be sought for its own sake,[7] but even here the practical and human interest is visible.

Seneca adheres theoretically to the old Stoic materialism,[8] but in practice he certainly tends to regard God as transcending matter. This tendency to metaphysical dualism was a natural consequence or accompaniment of his marked tendency to psychological dualism. True, he affirms the materiality of the soul, but he proceeds to speak in Platonic strain of the conflict between soul and body, between the aspirations of the higher man and the doctrines of the flesh. *Nam corpus hoc animi pondus ac poena est, premente illo urgetur, in vinculis est.*[9] True virtue and true worth rest within: external goods do not confer true happiness but are transitory gifts of Fortune in which it would be foolish to place our trust. *Brevissima ad divitias per contemptum divitiarum via est.*[10] Seneca, as courtier of Caligula and Claudius and the wealthy tutor and minister of the young Nero, has been accused of practical inconsistency and hypocrisy, but it must be remembered that his very experience of the contrast between great wealth and splendour on the one hand and the constant fear of death on the other would very much help a man of his temperament to realise the ephemeral character of wealth, position and power. Moreover, he had unrivalled opportunities of observing human degradation, lust and debauchery at close quarters. Some ancient writers accumulated gossip about Seneca's private life, calculated

to show that he did not live up to his own principles.[11]
But, even if, allowing for the exaggeration and gossip of op-
ponents, he did not pass through life without falls from his
moral ideal—as is indeed only too likely in a man of his position and connections, attached to a depraved Court[12]—
that does not mean that he was insincere in his teaching
and preaching. His knowledge of the force of temptation
and of the degradation to which avarice, ambition and lust
could lead—to a certain extent perhaps from personal experience, but far more from his observation of others—lent power
and force to his pen and to his moral exhortation. In spite of
all rhetoric Seneca knew what he was talking about.

Although theoretically adhering to the traditional Stoic
determinism, Seneca maintained that, as rational, every man
has the power to take the path of virtue if he will only
will to do so. *Satis natura dedit roboris si illo utamur.*[13]
Moreover, God will help those who strive to help themselves.
Non sunt di fastidiosi: adscendentibus manum porrigunt, and
O te miserum si contemnis hunc testem.[14] The man who
does help himself, conquer his passions and lead a life
in accordance with right reason, is better off than our
ancestors of the Golden Age, for, if they were innocent,
they were innocent from ignorance and absence of temptation. *Non fuere sapientes—ignorantia rerum innocentes
erant.*[15]

Since he aimed at encouraging men to set their feet upon
the path of virtue and to continue therein in spite of
temptation and fall, Seneca was naturally forced to temper
the strict moral idealism of the earlier Stoics. He knew
too much about the moral struggle to suppose that man
can become virtuous by sudden conversion. And so we find
him distinguishing three classes of *proficientes.* (i) Those
who have abandoned some of their sins, but not all; (ii)
those who have formed the resolution to renounce evil
passions in general, even if still liable to occasional relapse;
(iii) those who have got beyond possibility of relapse, but
still lack confidence in themselves and the consciousness of
their own wisdom. They *approximate,* therefore, to wisdom
and perfect virtue.[16] Moreover, Seneca admits that external
goods, e.g. wealth, may be used for good ends. The wise
man will be the master of his wealth and not its slave.
He gives practical counsel as to how to secure moral progress, e.g. by the use of the daily self-examination, which
he himself practised.[17] It is useless to retire into solitude,

if you do not attempt at the same time to change yourself: change of place does not necessarily mean change of heart, and wherever you go, you will still have to struggle with yourself. It is easy to understand, how the legend of Seneca's correspondence with St. Paul could grow up, when we read such phrases as *Nos quoque evincamus omnia, quorum praemium non corona nec palma est.*[18]

Seneca lays emphasis on the Stoic doctrine of the relationship that exists among all human beings, and instead of the self-sufficiency of the wise man—a self-sufficiency tinged with contempt for others—he calls on us to help our fellow-men and to forgive those who have injured us. *Alteri vivas oportet, si vis tibi vivere.*[19] He stresses the necessity of active benevolence. "Nature bids me to be of use to men whether they are slave or free, freedmen or free born. Wherever there is a human being there is room for benevolence."[20] "See that you are beloved by all while you live and regretted when you die."

Yet punishment of evil-doers is necessary. *Bonis nocet qui malis parcet.*[21] The most effective punishment, however, for the purpose of reformation is the mildest. Punishment should not be inflicted out of rage or the desire of revenge (cf. *De Ira* and *De Clementia*).

2. *Epictetus of Hierapolis* (*c.* A.D. 50-138) was at first a slave belonging to a member of Nero's bodyguard, and, when he became a freedman, continued to live in Rome until the expulsion of the philosophers by the Emperor Domitian (A.D. 89 or 93). He then founded a School at Nicopolis in Epirus and probably continued at its head until his death. It was at Nicopolis that his lectures were attended by Flavius Arrianus, who composed eight books of Διατριβαί on the basis of the lectures. Of these eight books we possess four. Arrian also published a small catechism or handbook of his master's doctrines, the Ἐγχειρίδιον.

Epictetus insists that all men have the capacity for virtue and that God has given to all men the means of becoming happy, of becoming men of steadfast character and self-control. "What then is a man's nature? To bite, to kick, to throw into prison, and to behead? No, but to do good, to co-operate with others, to wish them well."[22] All men have the sufficient initial moral intuitions on which they can build up the moral life. "Observe whom you yourself praise when you praise without partiality? Do you praise the just or the unjust, the moderate or the immoderate, the tem-

perate or the intemperate?" [23] "There are certain things
which men who are not altogether perverted see by the
common notions which all possess." [24]

Yet, though all men possess sufficient basis for the build-
ing-up of the moral life, philosophic instruction is necessary
for all, in order that they may be able to apply their primary
conceptions (προλήψεις) of good and evil to particular
circumstances. "Primary conceptions are common to all
men," [25] but a conflict or difficulty may arise in the application of these primary conceptions to particular facts. It
is this which explains the diversity of ethical notions, in
the sense of applied notions, among different peoples and between various individuals. [26] Education is, therefore, necessary and, inasmuch as the right application of principles
depends on reasoning and reasoning on logic, a knowledge
of logic is not to be despised. The important thing, however,
is not that a man should possess a knowledge of formal
dialectic, but that he should be able to apply his principles
to practice and, above all, that he should actually carry
them into practice in his conduct. There are two factors
in which education chiefly consists: (i) in learning to apply
the natural primary conceptions to particular circumstances
in accordance with "nature," and (ii) in learning to distinguish between things in our power and things not in our
power. [27] Epictetus, in common with the Stoic School in
general, makes a great deal of this latter distinction. To
acquire honours and wealth, to enjoy continual health, to
avoid physical maltreatment or the disfavour of the Emperor,
to ward off death or disaster from himself or his friends and
relatives, all this does not depend solely on the efforts of
any individual man: he must be careful, then, not to set
his heart on any of these things, but to accept all that
happens to himself or his relatives and friends as Fate, as
the will of God: he must accept all events of this kind
without rebellion or discontent, as being the expression of
the Divine Will. What, then, is in man's power? His judgments on events and his will: these he can control, and
his self-education consists in attaining true judgment and
a right will. "The essence of good and evil lies in an attitude of the will," [28] and this will lies within a man's power,
for "the will may conquer itself, but nothing else can conquer
it." [29] That which is really necessary for man is, therefore,
to *will* virtue, to *will* victory over sin. "Be well assured that
nothing is more tractable than the human soul. You must

exercise your will and the thing is done, it is set right; as on the other hand relax your vigilance and all is lost, for from within comes ruin and from within comes help." [30] Sins differ from the material standpoint, but from the moral standpoint they are equal in that they all involve a perverted will. To overcome and set right this perverted will is within the power of all. "Now will you not help yourself? And how much easier is this help? There is no need to kill or imprison any man or to treat him with contumely or to go into the law-courts. You must just talk to yourself. You will be most easily persuaded; no one has more power to persuade you than you yourself." [31]

As practical means to moral progress Epictetus advises the daily examination of conscience (the faithful use of which leads to the substitution of good habits for bad ones), avoidance of bad companions and occasions of sin, constant self-vigilance, etc. We must not be discouraged by falls but must persevere, setting before our eyes some ideal of virtue, e.g. Socrates or Zeno. Again, ". . . remember that Another looks from above on what is happening and that you must please Him rather than this man." [32] In the course of moral progress he distinguishes three stages:

(i) A man is taught to order his *desires* in accordance with right reason, freeing himself from morbid emotions and attaining to tranquillity of soul.

(ii) A man is trained to action, to performance of his duty (τὸ καθῆκον), coming to act as a true son, brother, citizen, etc.

(iii) The third stage relates to judgment and assent, and "its aim is to make the other two secure, so that even in sleep, intoxication, or hypochondria we may not let any presentation pass untested." [33] An unerring moral judgment is produced.

Duties towards oneself must begin with cleanliness of the body. "I indeed would rather that a young man, when first moved to philosophy, should come to me with his hair carefully trimmed, than with it dirty and rough." [34] That is to say, if a man has a feeling for natural cleanliness and beauty there is more hope of elevating him to the perception of moral beauty. Epictetus inculcates temperance, modesty, and chastity, censuring, for example, the adulterer. Simplicity is to be cultivated, though there is no harm in pursuing wealth, if this is done for good ends. "If I can acquire money, and also keep myself modest and faithful and magnanimous, point out the way and I will acquire it. But if you ask me to lose the things which are good and my own, in order that you may gain the things which are not good, see how unfair and silly you are." [35] (This to people who urge a friend to acquire money that they also may have some.) Like all the Stoics, Epictetus lauded veracity and loyalty.

True piety is to be encouraged. "Of religion towards the Gods, know that the chief element is to have right opinions concerning them, as existing and governing the whole in fair order and justice, and then to set thyself to obey them, and to yield to them in each event, and submit to it willingly, as accomplished under the highest counsels." [36] Atheism and denial of Divine Providence, both general and particular, are condemned. "Concerning the Gods, there are some who say that a Divine Being does not exist; and others, that it exists indeed, but is idle and uncaring, and hath no fore-thought for anything; and a third class say that there is such a Being, and he taketh forethought also, but only in respect of great and heavenly things, but of nothing that is on the earth; and a fourth class, that he taketh thought of things both in heaven and earth, but only in general, and not of each thing severally. And there is a fifth class, whereof are Odysseus and Socrates, who say, 'Nor can I move without thy knowledge.'" [37]

Marriage and the family are in accordance with right reason, though the "missionary" may remain celibate in order to be free for his work.[38] The child must always obey the father, unless the latter commands something immoral. Patriotism and active sharing in public life are encouraged—somewhat inconsistently—but war is condemned and the ruler should win the allegiance of his subjects by his ex-ample and by his self-sacrificing care for them.

Yet cosmopolitanism and the love of humanity transcend narrow patriotism. All men have God for their Father and are brothers by nature. "Will you not remember who you are and whom you rule? That they are kinsmen, that they are brethren by nature, that they are the offspring of Zeus?" [39] To all men we owe love and should not return evil for evil. "To suppose that we shall be easily despised by others un-less in every possible way we do injury to those who first show us hostility, is the work of very ignoble and foolish men, for this implies that inability to do injury is the reason why we are thought contemptible, whereas the really contemptible man is not he who cannot do injury but he who cannot do benefit." [40] Epictetus does not, however, reject punishment any more than the other Stoics. They insist that violation of law must be punished, but that this punishment must proceed from mature deliberation and not from hasty anger, and that it should be tempered with mercy, calculated to be, not merely a deterrent, but also a remedy for the offender.

In *Disc.* 3, 22, Epictetus devotes a chapter to Cynicism, in which the Cynic philosopher appears as the preacher of the truth concerning good and evil, as the ambassador of God. Without sharing the Cynic contempt for science, Epictetus seems to have admired the Cynic's indifference towards external goods. This is all the more natural in that for Epictetus happiness depends on that which alone is in our power and independent of external conditions—namely, our will, our ideas concerning things, and the use that we make of our ideas. If we seek our happiness in goods which do not depend entirely on ourselves for attainment or continued possession, we invite unhappiness: we must practise abstinence therefor—ἀνέχου καὶ ἀπέχου—and seek our happiness within.

(Dr. Praechter tells of the Director of a Swiss sanatorium, who was accustomed to hand to his neurasthenic and psychasthenic patients a copy of the Enchiridion in a German translation, and who found it to be a valuable aid in effecting a cure.[41])

3. *Marcus Aurelius,* Roman Emperor from A.D. 161 to 180, composed his *Meditations* (in the Greek language) in twelve books in aphoristic form. For Epictetus he had a lively admiration,[42] and he was at one with Epictetus and Seneca in giving a religious colouring to his philosophy. With Marcus Aurelius, too, we find stress laid on Divine Providence and a wise ordering of the universe, the close relationship between man and God, the duty of love towards one's fellow-men. Thus the Emperor teaches compassion for human infirmity. "When any one does you a wrong, set yourself at once to consider what was the point of view, good or bad, that led him wrong. As soon as you perceive it you will be sorry for him, not surprised or angry. For your own view of good is either the same as his or something like in kind, and you will make allowance. Or, supposing your own view of good and bad has altered, you will find charity for his mistake comes easier." [43] "It is man's

special gift to love even those who fall into blunders; this takes effect the moment we realise that men are our brothers, that sin is ignorance and unintentional, that in a little while we shall both be dead, that, above all, no injury is done us; our inner self is not made worse than it was before." [44] Active benevolence is stressed. "Does the eye demand a recompense for seeing, or the feet for walking? Just as this is the end for which they exist, and just as they find their reward in realising the law of their being, so, too, man is made for kindness, and whenever he does an act of kindness or otherwise helps forward the common good, he thereby fulfils the law of his being and comes by his own." [45] "Love mankind, follow God." [46]

Marcus Aurelius shows a decided tendency to break through the Stoic materialism. He adheres indeed to the Stoic monism, as in the following passage: "All harmonises with me which is in harmony with thee, O universe. Nothing for me is too early nor too late which is in due season for thee. For thee are all things, in thee are all things, to thee all things return. The poet says, Dear City of Cecrops; and wilt not thou say, Dear City of Zeus?" [47] Moreover, the Emperor was punctiliously observant of the forms of polytheistic worship, a fact which will partly explain the persecution of Christians during his reign, since he clearly looked upon the fulfilment of the requirements of State-worship as implied in good citizenship. But although Marcus Aurelius adheres to the Stoic monism, he tends to transcend materialism by his division of man into three parts—σῶμα, ψυχή and νοῦς, ψυχή being material but νοῦς being expressly distinguished from all four elements, and so—logically speaking at least—from matter. The human νοῦς or τὸ νοερόν comes from the νοερόν of the Universe, it is an ἀπόσπασμα of God,[48] it is τὸ ἡγεμονικόν.[49] The influence of Platonism is clear, but it is possible that the Emperor, who had Claudius Severus, a Peripatetic, as one of his teachers,[50] was influenced also by the doctrine of Aristotle.

The νοῦς is the δαίμων which God has given to every man to be his guide, and this δαίμων is an emanation of the Divinity. It follows, then, that whoever disobeys the commands of the δαίμων which are the commands of reason, acts not only irrationally but also impiously. Immorality is thus impiety.[51] "Live with the gods. And he lives with the gods whoever presents to them his soul accepting their dispensations and busied about the will of God, even that particle of Zeus which Zeus gives to every man for his controller and governor—to wit, his mind and reason." [52] Man has it in his power to avoid wickedness. "As for those things which are truly evil, as vice and wickedness, such things they (the gods) have put in a man's own power, that he might avoid them if he would." [53]

Marcus Aurelius, after the Stoic tradition, admits only limited immortality. Although he stresses, as Seneca did, the dualism between soul and body and depicts death as a liberation, [54] he allows not only the possibility of the soul's "reabsorption" at the world-conflagration, but also the possibility that the soul is reabsorbed in the Cosmic Reason in virtue of the constant change in nature—a theme dwelt upon by the Emperor, who compares the flow of phenomena to a river. [55] In any case the soul enjoys but a limited persistence after death. [56]

Chapter Forty-One

CYNICS, ECLECTICS, SCEPTICS

1. Cynics

The moral corruption in the Roman Empire not unnaturally prompted a revival of Cynicism, and the writing of letters under the names of ancient Cynics seems to have been calculated to forward this revival. Thus we have 51 letters under the name of Diogenes and 36 under that of Crates.

Roman Stoics of the type of Seneca addressed themselves mainly to members of the highest classes in society, to men who belonged to that circle which was naturally drawn into court-life, to men, above all, who possessed some hankering after virtue and tranquillity of soul, but who were at the same time bewildered by the luxurious and sensation-loving life of the aristocracy, who felt the power of the flesh and the attractions of sin and yet were also weary of self-indulgence and ready to grasp and hold the helping hand that might be held out to them. But beside the aristocracy and the men of wealth there were the masses, who may have benefited to a certain extent by the humanitarian ideals propagated among their masters by the Stoics, but who were not directly touched by men like Seneca. To meet the spiritual and moral needs of the masses there grew up a different type of "apostle," that of the Cynic preacher or missionary. These men led the life of itinerant preachers, poor and self-denying, aiming at the "conversion" of the masses who came to listen to them—as when the celebrated Apollonius of Tyana (who belongs rather to the story of Neo-Pythagoreanism), mystic and reported miracle-worker,

preached a rivalry of public spirit to the inhabitants of
Smyrna, who were torn apart by faction, or discoursed on
virtue to the crowd gathered at Olympia to witness the
games and races[1]—as when Musonius (who, in spite of his
affinity with Cynicism, actually belonged to the Stoic School
and was the teacher of Epictetus), harangued the troops of
Vespasian and Vitellius on the blessings of peace and the
horrors of civil war at the risk of his own life[2] or denounced
impiety and demanded virtue from men and women alike.
They were often men of undaunted courage, as may be seen
from the example of Musonius, just described, or from
Demetrius' defiance of Nero: "You threaten me with death,
but nature threatens you." [3] Demetrius, praised by Seneca
in his writings, consoled the last hours of Thrasea by dis-
coursing on the soul and its destiny.[4]

Lucian criticises the Cynic preachers unmercifully, particularly for their bad manners, their lack of culture, their
coarseness and buffoonery, their vulgarity and obscenity.
Lucian was a foe to all enthusiasm, and religious fervor and
"mystic" exaltation were repugnant to him, so that he often
doubtless does an injustice to the Cynics owing to his lack
of sympathy and understanding; but it must be remembered
that Lucian was not alone in his criticism, for Martial,
Petronius, Seneca, Epictetus, Dion Chrysostom and others
are agreed in condemning abuses which were undoubtedly
real. Some of the Cynics were certainly impostors and buffoons who brought the name of philosophy into contempt,
as Dion Chrysostom states plainly.[5] Moreover, some of
them betrayed a repulsive egoism and lack of good taste
and proper respect, as when that same Demetrius, who had
denounced Nero, took it upon himself to insult the Emperor Vespasian—who was no Nero—or as when Peregrinus
attacked the Emperor Antoninus Pius.[6] (Vespasian took
no notice of Demetrius, while Peregrinus was merely told
by the Prefect to leave the city. The Cynic who publicly
attacked Titus in the theatre for his intercourse with Berenice was scourged, however, while Heros, who repeated the
performance, was beheaded.[7]) Lucian is inclined to put the
worst interpretation on the conduct of the Cynics. Thus,
when Peregrinus—called Proteus—who had become a Christian
in Palestine, but who had subsequently joined the ranks
of the Cynics, publicly burnt himself to death at Olympia
in order to give an example of contempt for death, to imitate the Cynic patron Heracles and to unite himself with

the divine element, Lucian assumes that his action was
due simply to a love of notoriety–κενοδοξία.[8] The motive
of vainglory may very well have entered in, but it may
not have been the sole motive operative with Peregrinus.

Nevertheless, in spite of extravagance and in spite of the
existence of impostors and buffoons, Cynicism cannot be
condemned root and branch. *Demonax* (*c.* A.D. 50-150) was
universally honoured at Athens for his goodness,[9] and when
the Athenians proposed to institute gladiatorial shows in
the city he advised them first of all to demolish the altar
of Pity. Though simple and frugal in his ways he seems
to have avoided ostentatious singularity. Brought before
the Athenian courts on a charge of impiety, since he declined
to offer sacrifice and refused to seek initiation into the
Eleusinian Mysteries, he replied that God has no need of
sacrifices, while, as for the Mysteries, if they contained a
revelation of good tidings to man, he would have to publish
it, whereas, if they were of no value, he would feel bound
to warn the people against them.[10] *Oenomaus* of Gadara
dismissed the pagan anthropomorphic fables concerning the
gods and fiercely attacked the revival of belief in divination
and oracles. The oracles, he said, were mere deception, while
in any case man is possessed of free will and man alone is
responsible for his actions. Julian the Apostate, champion of
paganism, was aroused to indignation by the very memory
of such a man as Oenomaus, who had attacked the pagan
oracles.[11]

A celebrated and honourable Cynic preacher was *Dion
Chrysostom,* who was born about A.D. 40 and lived, at any
rate, well into the reign of the Emperor Trajan. He came
of an aristocratic family of Prusa (Bithynia) and was at
first a rhetorician and Sophist. Condemned to banishment
from Bithynia and Italy in A.D. 82 during the reign of the
Emperor Domitian, he led a wandering life of poverty.
During the period of exile he underwent a sort of "conversion" and became an itinerant Cynic preacher with a
mission to the submerged masses of the Empire. Dion retained his rhetorical manner and liked, in his Orations, to
clothe the moral truths he expressed in an attractive and ele-
gant form; but though true to the rhetorical tradition, he
insisted in his preaching on living in conformity with the
Divine Will, on the moral ideal, on the practice of true virtue
and, on the insufficiency of purely material civilisation. In
the 'Ευβοϊκός he depicts the life of the poor countryman

as being more natural, freer and happier than that of the rich town-dweller; but he occupies himself also with the question, how the poor in the cities can most satisfactorily live their lives without hankering after luxury or involving themselves in what is harmful to soul or body. He warned the people of Tarsus that they had a wrong sense of values. Happiness is to be found, not in stately buildings, wealth and delicate living, but in temperance, justice and true piety. The great materialistic civilisations of the past—Assyria, for example—have perished, while the great Empire of Alexander is gone and Pella is a heap of bricks.[12] He harangues the people of Alexandria on their vices and lust for sensation, on their lack of dignity and their trivial interests.[13]

Dion's social interests led him towards Stoicism and he made use of the Stoic doctrines of world-harmony and of cosmopolitanism. As God rules over the world, so should the Monarch rule over the State, and as the world is a harmony of many phenomena, so should individual States be preserved, but in such a way that they live in peace and harmony and free intercourse with one another. Besides the influence of Stoicism Dion seems to have undergone the influence of Poseidonius, taking from him, the division of a threefold theology, that of the philosophers, that of the poets and that of the official or State cult. He became, after the end of his period of banishment under Domitian, a favourite of Trajan, who used to invite the philosopher to his table and take him as a companion in his carriage, though he did not pretend to understand Dion's rhetoric. τὶ μὲν λέγεις, οὐκ οἶδα. φιλῶ δε σε ὡς ἐμαυτόν.[14] It was before the court of Trajan that Dion delivered some of his orations, contrasting the ideal monarch with the tyrant. The true monarch is the shepherd of his people, appointed by God for the good of his subjects. He must be a truly religious[15] and virtuous man, the father of his people, a hard worker, hostile to flatterers.

For Dion Chrysostom the idea of God is innate and universal among all men, brought into full consciousness by the contemplation of the design and providence in the universe. Yet God is hidden from us, and we are like little children stretching out their hands for father or mother.[16] Yet though God in Himself is veiled from us, we naturally try to imagine Him as best we can, and this is best accomplished by the poets. Artists, too, attempt the same task, though more inadequately, for no sculptor or painter can portray the Nature of God. All the same, in portraying God in human form they do not do wrong, since it is only natural to have recourse to the highest being of which we have direct experience as an image of the Divine.

Later we find evidence of a Christianised Cynicism, e.g. in the person of Maximus of Alexandria, who came to Constantinople in A.D. 379 or 380 and formed an intimate friendship with St. Gregory Nazianzen, though he afterwards had himself consecrated bishop behind St. Gregory's back. Maximus imitated the ways of the Stoics, though there does not seem to have been much consistency in his behaviour.[17]

2. Eclectics

A professedly Eclectic School was founded by *Potamon* of Alexandria in the time of the Emperor Augustus. According to Diogenes Laërtius the School was named Ἐκλεκτικὴ αἵρεσις [18] and it seems to have combined Stoic and Peripatetic elements, though Potamon also wrote a commentary on Plato's *Republic*.

Eclectic tendencies were also shown by the School of *Q. Sextius* (b. *c.* 70 B.C.). They adopted Stoic and Cynic principles, with which they combined Pythagorean and Platonico-Aristotelian elements. Thus Sextius adopted the Pythagorean customs of self-examination and abstinence from flesh-meat, while his disciple Sotion of Alexandria took over from the Pythagoreans the theory of metempsychosis. The School does not appear to have been of any great consequence, though Seneca was a disciple of Sotion.[19]

3. Sceptics

Although the Academy before the time of Antiochus of Ascalon had shown, as we have seen, a marked sceptical tendency, it was to the School of Pyrrho that the revived Scepticism looked as its ancestor rather than to the Academy. Thus the founder of the revived School, Aenesidemus of Knossos, wrote eight books Πυρρωνείων λόγων. The members of the School attempted to show the relative character of all judgments and opinions, embodying their arguments for this position in what they called Τρόποι. However, though they naturally opposed philosophic dogmatism, they did not fail to recognise the claims of practical life, and stated norms according to which man should act in practice. This was not alien to the spirit of Pyrrho who, in spite of his scepticism, declared that custom, tradition, State law, afforded a norm for practical life.

Aenesidemus of Knossos (who taught at Alexandria and probably composed his work round about 43 B.C.) gave ten Τρόποι or arguments for the sceptical position.[20] They were:

(1) Difference between types of living beings imply different—and so relative—"ideas" of same object.

(2) Differences between individual men imply the same.

(3) The different structure and presentation of our various senses (e.g. there is an eastern fruit that smells unpleasant but tastes delicious).

(4) The difference between our various states, e.g. waking or sleeping, youth or age. For example, a current of air may seem a pleasant breeze to a young man, while to an old man it is a detestable draught.

(5) Differences of perspective, e.g. the stick immersed in water appears bent, the square tower appears round from a distance.

(6) The objects of perception are never presented in their purity, but a medium is always involved, such as air. Hence the mixing or ἐπιμιξία. For example, grass appears green at noon, golden in the evening light. A lady's dress looks different in sunlight to what it looks in electric light.

(7) Differences in perception due to differences of quality, e.g. one grain of sand appears rough, while if sand is allowed to slip through the fingers it appears smooth and soft.

(8) Relativity in general, ὁ ἀπὸ τοῦ πρός τι.

(9) Difference in impression due to frequency or infrequency of perception, e.g. the comet, seldom seen, makes more impression than the sun.

(10) Different ways of life, moral codes, laws, myths, philosophic systems, etc. (cf. Sophists).

These ten Τρόποι of Aenesidemus were reduced to five by Agrippa.[21]

(1) The variation of views concerning the same objects.

(2) The infinite process involved in proving anything (i.e. the proof rests on assumptions that require to be proved, and so on indefinitely).

(3) The relativity involved in the fact that objects appear differently to people according to the temperament, etc., of the percipient and according to their relation with other objects.

(4) The arbitrary character of dogmatic assumptions, assumed as starting-points, in order to escape the *regressus in infinitum.*

(5) The vicious circle or the necessity of assuming in the proof of anything the very conclusion that has to be proved.

Other Sceptics meanwhile reduced the Τρόποι to two:[22]

(1) Nothing can be rendered certain through itself. Witness the variety of opinions, between which no choice can be made with certainty.

(2) Nothing can be rendered certain through anything else, since the attempt to do so involves either the *regressus in infinitum* or the vicious circle.

(It is clear that these arguments for relativism have, for the most part at least, to do with perception. But perception does not err, since perception does not judge, and error lies in the false judgment. Moreover, it is in the power of reason to prevent error by avoiding precipitate judgment, by considering the matter more closely, by suspending judgment in certain cases, etc.)

Sextus Empiricus (*c*. A.D. 250), who is our main source for the details of Sceptic doctrine, argued against the possibility of proving any conclusion syllogistically.[23] The major premiss—for instance, "All men are mortal"—can be proved only by a complete induction. But the complete induction involves a knowledge of the conclusion—"Socrates is a mortal." For we cannot say, that *all* men are mortal unless we already know that Socrates is mortal. The Syllogism is, therefore, an instance of a vicious circle. (We may note that this objection against the syllogism, which was revived by John Stuart Mill in the nineteenth century, would only be valid if the Aristotelian doctrine of the specific essence were rejected in favour of Nominalism. It is in virtue of our perception of the essence or universal nature of man that we are entitled to assert that all men are mortal and not because we lay claim to any perfect and complete enumeration of particulars through actual observation, which in the case in point would be out of the question. The major premiss is founded, therefore, on the nature of man, and does not require explicit knowledge of the conclusion of the syllogism. The conclusion is contained *implicitly* in the major premiss, and the syllogistic process renders this implicit knowledge clear and explicit. The nominalist standpoint demands, of course, a new logic, and this Mill attempted to supply.) The Sceptics also argued against the validity of the notion of Cause, but they do not seem to have anticipated the epistemological difficulties raised by David Hume.[24] Cause is essentially *relative*, but the relative is not objective but is attributed extrinsically by the mind. Again, the cause must be either simultaneous with the effect or prior or posterior. It cannot be simultaneous, since then B might just as well be called the cause of A as A of B. Nor could the cause be prior to the effect, since then it would first exist without relation to its effect, and cause is essentially relative to the effect. Nor could the cause be posterior to the effect—for obvious reasons.

The Sceptics also attempted to prove the existence of antinomies in theology. For instance, God must be either infinite or finite.[25] Not the former, for He would then be unmoved and so without life or soul: not the latter, as He would then be less perfect than the Whole, whereas God is *ex hypothesi* perfect. (This is an argument against the Stoics for whom God is material: it does not affect those for whom God is Infinite Spirit. Infinite Spirit cannot move, but is living, or rather is Infinite Life.) Again, the Stoic doctrine of Providence is necessarily involved in a dilemma. There is much evil and suffering in the world. Now, either God has the will and power to stop this evil and suffering or He has not. The latter supposition is incompatible with the notion of God (though J. S. Mill arrived at the strange notion of a finite God, with Whom we co-operate). He has, therefore, the will and power to stop the evil and suffering in the world. But this He obviously does not do. It follows that there is at least no *universal* Providence on the part of God. But we can give no explanation why Divine Providence should extend to this being and not to that. We are forced, therefore, to conclude that there is *no* Providence at all.[26]

In regard to practical life the Sceptics taught that we should follow the presentations of perception and thought, satisfy our natural instincts, adhere to law and tradition, and pursue science. We can never indeed attain to certainty in science, but we can go on *seeking*.[27]

Chapter Forty-Two

NEO-PYTHAGOREANISM

The old Pythagorean School seems to have become extinct in the fourth century B.C.: if it did continue, we have certainly no evidence of effective and vigorous life. But in the first century B.C. the School came to life again under the form of what is known as Neo-Pythagoreanism. It was related to the old School, not only by reverence for the Founder, but also by a certain interest in scientific pursuits and, above all, by its religious colouring. Much of the old Pythagorean asceticism was adopted by the new School, which naturally adhered to the soul-body dualism—a salient feature, as we have seen, of the Platonic philosophy—and to this it added mystical elements, which answered the contemporary demand for a purer and more personal religion. Direct intuition of the Deity was claimed, and revelation—so much so that the philosopher is sometimes depicted as prophet and wonder-worker, e.g. Apollonius of Tyana.[1] The new School was very far, however, from being a mere reproduction of the former Pythagorean system, for it followed the current tendency to Eclecticism, and we find the Neo-Pythagoreans drawing widely on the Platonic, Aristotelian and Stoic philosophies. These borrowed elements were not fused together into one synthesis, common to all the members of the School, for the various members constructed their different syntheses, in one of which Stoic themes might predominate, in another themes from the Platonic philosophy. Neo-Pythagoreanism is of some historical importance, however, not only because it stands in close relation to the religious life of the time (it seems to have originated in

Alexandria, the meeting point of Hellenistic philosophy, special science and Oriental religion), but also because it marks a step on the way to Neo-Platonism. Thus Numenius taught the doctrine of the Divine Hierarchy—the first god, the πρῶτος θεός, being the οὐσίας ἀρχή or πατήρ, the second god being the Demiurge and the third god being the World, τὸ ποίημα.

Sextus Empiricus tells us of various tendencies within Neo-Pythagoreanism. Thus in one form of Neo-Pythagoreanism everything is derived from the monad or point (ἐξ ἑνὸς σημείου). The point generates the line in its flow, while from lines are generated surfaces, and from surfaces three-dimensional bodies. Here we have a monistic system, though obviously influenced by older mathematical conceptions. In another form of Neo-Pythagoreanism, although everything is derived ultimately from the point or μονάς, the greatest emphasis is laid on the dualism of the μονάς, and the ἀόριστος δυάς. All "unities" participate in the μονάς and all dualities in the ἀόριστος δυάς.[2] There is nothing particularly original in these forms of Neo-Pythagoreanism, but the notion of "emanation" is clearly present, which was to play a leading rôle in Neo-Platonism.

One of the motives that prompted the Neo-Platonic theory of emanation and the assertion of beings intermediary between the corporeal world and the supreme God was the desire of mainting God's purity free from all contact with the things of sense. God's utter transcendence, His position "beyond being," is brought into sharp relief. Now, this theme of the transcendence of God is already discernible in Neo-Pythagoreanism. It may have been influenced by the Judaeo-Alexandrian philosophy and by Oriental tradition, though we may discern its latent germs within the thought of Plato himself. The noted wonder-worker Apollonius of Tyana (who flourished about the end of the first century A.D.), whose "life" was written by Philostratus, distinguished the first god from the other gods. To this first god men should not offer any material sacrifice, since all material things are tainted with impurity. We should sacrifice to the other gods, but not to the first god, to whom we should offer none but the service of our reason, without outward speech or offering.

An interesting figure is that of *Nicomachus of Gerasa* (in Arabia), who lived about A.D. 140, and was author of an ἀριθμητικὴ εἰσαγωγή. In his system the Ideas existed before the formation of the world (Plato), and the Ideas are numbers (Plato again). But the Number-Ideas did not exit in a transcendental world of their own: rather were they Ideas in the Divine Mind, and so patterns or archetypes according to which the things of this world were formed (cf. Philo the Jew, Middle Platonism and Neo-Platonism). The transposition of the Ideas into the Mind of God had, therefore, taken place before the rise of Neo-Platonism, from which it passed over into the Christian tradition.

A similar transposition is to be observed in the philosophy of *Numenius of Apamea* (Syria), who lived in the second half of the second century A.D. and seems to have been well acquainted with the Jewish philosophy of Alexandria. According to Clement he spoke of Plato as Μωϋσῆς ἀττικίζων.¹ In Numenius' philosophy the πρῶτος θεός is the Principle of Being οὐσίας ἀρχή) and the βασιλεύς.⁴ He is also the activity of Pure Thought (νοῦς), and has no direct share in the formation of the world. Moreover, He is the Good. Numenius thus seems to have identified the Platonic Form of the Good with the Aristotelian God or νόησις νοήσεως. The second god is the Demiurge (*Timaeus*), who is good by participation in the being of the First God and who, as γενέσεως ἀρχή, forms the world. He does this by working on matter and forming it on the pattern of the archetypal Ideas. The world itself, the production of the Demiurge, is the third god. These three gods are also characterised by Numenius as πατήρ, ποιητής and ποίημα respectively, or as πάππος, ἔγγονος and ἀπόγονος.⁵

Dualism is very apparent in the psychology of Numenius, since he postulates two souls in man, a rational soul and an irrational soul, and declares the entry of the soul into the body as something evil, as a "fall." He seems also to have taught the existence of a good and a bad world-soul.⁶

The philosophy of Numenius was thus a syncretism or harmonisation of elements taken from preceding thinkers, a philosophy which laid great emphasis on the divine transcendence and which, in general, asserted a sharp antithesis between "higher" and "lower," both in reality as a whole and in human nature in particular.

In connection with Neo-Pythagoreanism stand the so-called *Hermetic Literature* and the *Chaldaic Oracles*. The former is the name given to a type of "mystical" literature that arose in the first century A.D. and that may, or may not, owe a debt to previous Egyptian writings. The Greeks found in Hermes the Egyptian god Thoth, and their appellation "Hermes Trismegistos" is derived from the Egyptian "Great Thoth." But whatever be the truth concerning the supposed influence of Egyptian tradition on the Hermetic literature, the latter owes its main contents to earlier Greek philosophy, and seems to have been indebted particularly to Poseidonius. The fundamental notion expressed in this literature is that of *salvation through knowledge of God* —γνῶσις—a notion that played a great part in "Gnosticism." A similar doctrine of salvation formed the content of the Chaldaic Oracles, a poem that was composed about A.D. 200, and which, like the Hermetic literature, combines Orphic-Pythagorean, Platonic and Stoic elements.

In its close relation to the religious interest and needs of the time, and in the work of preparing the ground for Neo-Platonism, Neo-Pythagoreanism resembles Middle Platonism, to which we must now turn.

Note on Apollonius of Tyana

The rhetorician Philostratus undertook the composition of the life of Apollonius at the request of Julia Domna, second wife of Septimius Severus. The book was composed about A.D. 200. The story given by Philostratus about the Memoirs of Apollonius by his disciple Damis, an Assyrian, which are said to have been given to Julia Domna by a relative of Damis, is probably a literary fiction.[7] In any case the motive of Philostratus seems to have been that of representing Apollonius as a wise man, as a true servant of the gods and a miracle-worker, instead of the magician or conjurer depicted by Moeragenes in his *Memorabilia* of Apollonius.[8] There are indications that Philostratus knew and utilised the Gospels, Acts of the Apostles and Lives of the Saints, but it remains uncertain how far it was his conscious intention to substitute the ideal of a "Hellenistic Christ" for the Christian Christ: resemblances have been greatly exaggerated. If the intention of Philostratus remains obscure, so does the foundation of truth at the base of his narrative: it is practically impossible to say exactly what sort of a man the historic Apollonius actually was.

The work of Philostratus had a great success and led to a cult of Apollonius. Thus Caracalla raised a shrine to the wonder-worker,[9] while Alexander Severus included him in his *Lararium* along with his Penates, Abraham, Orpheus and Christ.[10] Aurelian spared the city of Tyana, which he had vowed to destroy, out of respect for the birthplace of Apollonius.[11] Eunapius honours him in his Lives of the Sophists,[12] while Ammianus Marcellinus, companion of the Emperor Julian, cites him along with Plotinus as one of the privileged mortals who were visited by the *familiares genii*.[13]

Whatever the intention of Philostratus himself may have been, it is certain that the pagan apologists made use of the figure of Apollonius in their fight against Christianity. Thus Hierocles, Governor of Lower Egypt under Diocletian and a ferocious enemy of Christianity, tried to lessen the importance of the miracles of Christ by citing the "miracles" of Apollonius and tried to show the superiority of pagan wisdom in that they refrained from elevating Apollonius to the rank of God because of these miracles.[14] Porphyry also made use of Apollonius, citing his miracles and opposing his bold defiance of Domitian to the humiliations of Christ in His Passion.[15] St. Augustine bears testimony to this sort of apologetic exploitation of Apollonius on the part of the pagans.[16]

Towards the end of the fourth century Virius Nicomachus Flavianus, a pagan, translated Philostratus' book into Latin, and it was repolished by the grammarian Tascius Victorinus. It seems to have excited some interest in Christian circles, since Sidonius Apollinaris revised it also and speaks of Apollonius with great deference.[17]

Chapter Forty-Three

MIDDLE PLATONISM

We have already seen how the Middle and New Academies inclined to scepticism, and how, when the Academy returned to dogmatism under Antiochus of Ascalon, the latter maintained the theory of the fundamental unity of the Platonic and Peripatetic philosophies. It is, therefore, not surprising to find Eclecticism as one of the leading characteristics of Middle Platonism. Platonists did not possess the lectures of Plato, but the more popular dialogues, and this fact made it more difficult for any rigid orthodoxy to assert itself: it was not as though the founder had left a systematised and carefully-articulated philosophic deposit, which could be passed on as the norm and canon of Platonism. There is no reason, then, to be astonished that Middle Platonism took over the Peripatetic logic, for example, since the Peripatetics had a more carefully-elaborated logical foundation than the Platonists possessed.

Platonism, no less than Neo-Pythagoreanism, felt the influence of contemporary religious interests and demands and the result was that Platonism borrowed from Neo-Pythagoreanism or developed germs latent in itself under the influence of the latter School. Hence we find in Middle Platonism the same insistence on the divine transcendence that we have already observed in Neo-Pythagoreanism, together with the theory of intermediary beings and a belief in mysticism.

On the other hand—and here again Middle Platonism was in line with the contemporary tendencies—much attention was devoted to the work of studying and commenting on the Platonic dialogues.[1] The result of this was a more intense reverence for the person and actual *dicta* of the founder and, consequently, a tendency to stress the differences between Platonism and the other philosophical systems. Thus we find writings directed against the Peripatetics and the Stoics. These two movements, the one towards philosophic "orthodoxy" and the other towards eclecticism, were obviously in conflict, and the consequence is that Middle Platonism does not present the character of a unitary whole: different thinkers amalgamated the various elements in different ways. Middle Platonism is accordingly *Middle* Platonism; that is to say, it bears the mark of a transition-stage: it is only in Neo-Platonism that anything like a real synthesis and fusion of the various currents and tendencies can be found. Neo-Platonism is thus like the sea, to which the various contributing rivers are flowing and in which their waters are at length mingled.

1. The eclectic tendency of Middle Platonism and the orthodox tendency of the same School may be observed together in the thought of *Eudorus of Alexandria* (about 25 B.C.). In accordance with the *Theaetetus* (176 b) Eudorus affirmed that the end of philosophy is ὁμοίωσις θεῷ κατὰ τὸ δυνατόν. In this conception of the end of philosophy Socrates, Plato and Pythagoras are in agreement, said Eudorus. This shows the eclectic side of Eudorus' thought and, in particular, the influence of Neo-Pythagoreanism, in accordance with which he distinguished a threefold One or ἕν. The first is the supreme Godhead and is the ultimate source of being, and from Him proceeds the second ἕν (also called μονάς, together with the ἀόριστος δυάς, the second ἕν being τεταγμένον), περιττόν, φῶς, etc., the ἀόριστος δυάς being ἄτακτον, ἄρτιον, σκότος etc. But though Eudorus obviously felt the influence of Neo-Pythagoreanism and to this extent was eclectic, we learn that he composed a work against the Aristotelian κατηγορίαι, thus showing the "orthodox" as over against the eclectic tendency.

2. A prominent figure of Middle Platonism is the author of the celebrated lives of Greek and Roman worthies, *Plutarch of Chaeronea*. This distinguished man was born about A.D. 45 and was educated at Athens, where he was stimulated to mathematical studies by the Platonist Ammonius. He often visited Rome and was on terms of friendship with important personages in the imperial city. According to Suidas[2] the Emperor Trajan gave him the consular dignity

and told the officials of Achaesa to ask for Plutarch's approval for all their measures. Plutarch also became Archon Eponymos of his native city and was for some years priest to the Delphic Apollo. Besides the *Lives* and the *Moralia* Plutarch wrote commentaries on Plato (e.g. Πλατωνικὰ ζητήματα), books against the Stoics and the Epicureans (e.g. Περὶ Στωϊκῶν ἐναντιωμάτων and Ὅτι οὐδὲ ζῆν ἔστιν ἡδέως κατ' Ἐπίκουρον), works on psychology and astronomy, on ethics and on politics. To these must be added compositions on family life, on pedagogy and on religion (e.g. Περὶ τῶν ὑπὸ τοῦ θείου βραδέως τιμωρουμένων and Περὶ δεισιδαιμονίας). A number of works that pass under his name are not by Plutarch (e.g. the *Placita* and the Περὶ εἱμαρμένης).

Plutarch's thought was decidedly eclectic in character, for he was influenced not only by Plato but also by the Peripatetics, the Stoics and especially the Neo-Pythagoreans. Moreover, while on the one hand the scepticism of the Middle and New Academies led him to adopt a somewhat distrustful attitude towards theoretical speculation and a strong opposition to superstition (the latter due more, perhaps, to his desire for a purer conception of the Deity), he combined therewith a belief in prophecy and "revelation" and "enthusiasm." He speaks of an immediate intuition or contact with the Transcendental, which doubtless helped to prepare the way for the Plotinian doctrine of ecstasy.[3]

Plutarch aimed at a purer conception of God. "While we are here below, encumbered by bodily affections, we can have no intercourse with God save as in philosophic thought we may faintly touch Him, as in a dream. But when our souls are released, and have passed into the region of the pure, invisible, and changeless, this God will be the guide and king of those who depend on Him and gaze with insatiable longing on the beauty which may not be spoken of by the lips of man."[4] This desire for a purer conception of God led him to deny God's authorship of evil. Some other cause had to be found for the evil in the world, and this Plutarch found in the World-Soul. This is postulated as the cause of evil and imperfection in the world and is set over against God as the pure Good, so that a dualism is asserted of two principles, the good and the bad. The evil principle, however, seems to have become the divine World-Soul at creation by participating in, or being filled with, reason, which is an emanation from the

Godhead. The World-Soul is therefore not destitute of reason and harmony, but on the other hand it continues to act as the evil principle and thus the dualism is maintained.

Since God, freed from all responsibility for evil, is elevated far above the world, it is but natural that Plutarch should introduce intermediary beings below God. Thus he accepted the star-gods and followed Xenocrates and Poseidonius in postulating a number of "Demons" who form the connecting link between God and man. Some of these are more akin to God, others are tainted by the evil of the lower world.[5] Extravagant rites, barbarous and obscene sacrifices are really offered to the evil demons. The good demons are the instruments of Providence (on which Plutarch lays great stress). Plutarch, as I have already mentioned, professed himself a foe to superstition and condemned myths that were unworthy of God (like Poseidonius, he distinguished a threefold theology); but that did not prevent him from showing considerable sympathy for the popular religion. Thus according to him the various religions of mankind all worship the same God under different names, and he makes use of allegorical interpretation, in order to justify popular beliefs. For instance, in his *De Iside et Osiride* he tries to show that Osiris represents the good principle and Tryphon the bad principle, while Isis represents matter, which is not evil in Plutarch's view but, though neutral in itself, has a natural tendency and love for the Good.

Plutarch's psychology gives evidence of mythological and fantastic notions of the origin of the soul and its relation with the Demons, into which it is unnecessary to enter. One may, however, point out the dualism asserted between ψυχή and νοῦς, that is superimposed upon the soul-body dualism. Just as ψυχή is better and more divine than the body, so is νοῦς better and more divine than ψυχή, the latter being subject to passions, the former being the "Demon" in man and the element which should rule. Immortality is affirmed by Plutarch and he depicts the happiness of the after-life, when the soul not only attains to a knowledge of the truth but also enjoys once more the company of relatives and friends.[6] In his ethic the philosopher was clearly influenced by the Peripatetic tradition, since he emphasises the need of attaining the happy mean between ὑπερβολὴ and ἔλλειψις, excess and defect. To get rid of the affections is neither possible nor desirable; we should aim rather at moderation and the golden mean. Plutarch, however, follows the Stoics in permitting suicide, and he was influenced too by their Cosmopolitanism, especially when seen under the light of his experience of the Roman Empire. The ruler represents God.

The world was created in time, for this is necessitated by the principle of the soul's priority over the body and of God's priority in regard to the world.[7] There are five elements (adding aether) and five worlds.[8]

3. *Albinus* (A D. second century), a disciple of Gaius the Middle Platonist, distinguished the πρῶτος θεός, νοῦς and ψυχή. The πρῶτος θεός is unmoved (Aristotle) but is not mover, and he would appear to be identical with the ὑπερουράνιος θεός. The first god does not operate immediately—since he is unmoved but not mover—but operates through the Νοῦς or World-Intellect.[9] Between God and the world are the star-gods and others, οἱ γεννητοὶ θεοί. The Platonic Ideas are made eternal ideas of God and are patterns or exemplary causes of things: the Aristotelian εἴδη are subordinated to them as copies.[10] The conception of God as unmoved and as not acting through efficient causality is, of course, Aristotelian in origin, though elements in the conception of God are developments of Platonic doctrine, e.g. the transposition of the Ideas into Ideas of God, a doctrine which we have already met in Neo-Pythagoreanism. Albinus also makes use of the gradual elevation to God through the various degrees of beauty, an ascent suggested by Plato's *Symposium,* while the conception of the World-Soul is obviously to be connected with the *Timaeus.*[11] In this fusion of Platonic and Aristotelian elements Albinus, like Numenius the Neo-Pythagorean, helped to prepare the way for Neo-Platonism. His distinction of πρῶτος θεός, νοῦς and ψυχή was also a direct step on the way to the Neo-Platonic distinction of τὸ ἕν, νοῦς and ψυχή. (In his psychology and ethics Albinus combined Platonic, Aristotelian and Stoic elements, e.g. identifying the Stoic ἡγεμονικόν with the Platonic λογιστικόν, introducing the Aristotelian παθητικόν over against the λογιστικόν, distinguishing with Plato τὸ θυμικόν (Plat. θυμοειδές] and τὸ ἐπιθυμητικόν, making use of the Stoic οἰκείωσις, declaring the end of ethics to be the Platonic end of ὁμοίωσις θεῷ κατὰ τὸ δυνατόν, following the Stoics in making φρόνησις the first of the cardinal virtues and Plato in making δικαιοσύνη the general virtue, opposing the Stoic "Apathy" in favour of the Platonic-Aristotelian "Metriopathy." An eclectic indeed!)

4. Among other Middle Platonists we may mention *Apuleius* (b. *c.* A.D. 125), *Atticus* (*c.* A.D. 176), *Celsus* and *Maximus of Tyre* (*c.* A.D. 180). Atticus represented the more orthodox Platonic tradition in contrast to the eclectic tendency, as we have observed it in Albinus. Thus he attacked Aristotle for neglecting Divine Providence, teaching the eternity of the world, and for denying immortality or not expressing it clearly. But he seems to have been influenced by Stoic doctrine, as he emphasises the Divine Immanence and stresses the all-sufficiency of virtue, in contrast to the Peripatetic doctrine that corporeal and external goods are necessary for happiness. He naturally maintained the Platonic Ideas, but, characteristically of his time, made them thoughts or ideas of God. In addition he identified the Demiurge of the *Timaeus* with the Form of the Good, and he attributed to matter an evil soul as its principle.

Celsus is best known to us as a determined opponent of Christianity: we are acquainted with the content of his Ἀληθὴς λόγος (written about A.D. 179) through Origen's reply to it. He emphasised God's utter transcendence and would not allow that the corporeal is the work of God. To bridge the gulf between God and the world he admitted "Demons," angels and heroes. God's Providence has the universe as its object and is not, as the Christians believe, anthropocentric.

A similar emphasis on the Divine Transcendence, together with the admission of inferior gods and demons, as also the referring of evil to matter, is found in the case of Maximus of Tyre (*c.* A.D. 180). Maximus speaks of the vision of the transcendent God. "Thou shalt see Him fully only when He calls thee, in age or death, but meantime glimpses of the Beauty which eye hath not seen nor can tongue speak of, may be won, if the veils and wrappings which hide His splendour be torn away. But do not thou profane Him by offering vain prayers for earthly things which belong to the world of chance or which may be obtained by human effort, things for which the worthy need not pray, and which the unworthy will not obtain. The only prayer which is answered is the prayer for goodness, peace, and hope in death." [12] The angels are servants of God and helpers of men; "thrice ten thousand are they upon the fruitful earth, immortal, ministers of Zeus." [13]

Chapter Forty-Four

JEWISH-HELLENISTIC
PHILOSOPHY

It was at Alexandria particularly that the influence of Greek
speculation on the Jewish mind became most apparent, although traces of such influence may be seen in Palestine
itself, as in the doctrine of the sect of the Essenes (mentioned by Josephus for the first time in his picture of the
period of Jonathan the Hasmonaean, about 160 B.C.),[1] which
shows Orphic-Pythagorean traits. For example, the Essenes
maintained a clear dualism of soul and body, with which
they coupled a belief, not only in the soul's survival after
death but also in its pre-existence before birth. Blood-
offerings and the consumption of flesh and wine were banned,
and great importance was attached to the belief in angels
or intermediary beings. Moreover it is a significant feature—
even if not to be overstressed—that when Antiochus Epiphanes attempted a forcible Hellenisation of the Palestinian
Jews, he was able to rely on a certain amount of support
among the Jews themselves, though he encountered a determined opposition on the part of the more orthodox, who
resolutely adhered to the tradition of their fathers and
were naturally irreconcilable enemies of the moral abuses
that they considered accompaniments of Hellenism. However, Alexandria, that great cosmopolitan city set on the confines of East and West, became the real centre of the Jewish-
Hellenistic philosophy, which culminated in the thought of
Philo. Away from their native home the Jews were naturally
more prone to accept Greek influence, and this showed
itself largely in an attempt to reconcile Greek philosophy with

Jewish theology, an attempt that led on the one hand to the selection of those elements in Greek speculation that harmonised best with Jewish religion and on the other hand to the practice of allegorising the Jewish Scriptures and interpreting them in such a way that they would harmonise with Greek thought. Thus we even find Jews asserting that the great Greek philosophers were indebted to the Scriptures for their leading ideas. This notion is of course void of historical foundation as it concerns Plato, for instance, but it is symptomatic of the syncretistic tendencies of the Hellenised Jews of the Empire.[2]

The chief figure of the Jewish-Hellenistic philosophy is *Philo of Alexandria,* who was born about 25 B.C. and died some time after A.D. 40, the year in which he was at Rome as ambassador of the Alexandrian Jews to the Emperor Gaius. We possess a large number of his works, though some have perished.[3]

Filled with admiration for the Greek philosophers Philo maintained that the same truth is to be found in both the Greek philosophy and Jewish Scriptures and tradition. While believing that the philosophers had made use of the Sacred Scriptures, he at the same time did not hesitate to interpret the Scriptures allegorically when he deemed it necessary. Thus in his work "Ότι ἄτρεπτον τὸ θεῖον he shows that God cannot properly be said to move, since He is in no way corporeal. We must accordingly recognise two senses in the anthropomorphic passages of the Scriptures, a higher and non-anthropomorphic sense and a lower or anthropomorphic sense, which is suited to ordinary people. It might be supposed that this work of allegorisation and of discerning "higher" meanings would, if pushed far enough, lead to a denial of the necessity of observing literally the ceremonial precepts of the Law, at least for those who are capable of discerning the higher sense. But this Philo would not allow. Soul is above body, yet body is part of man; and though the allegorical sense is higher than the literal, we are not entitled to disregard the literal sense—rather should we pay heed to both letter and spirit. His intention was therefore not that of destroying or superseding Jewish orthodoxy but rather that of reconciling it with philosophy, while at the same time preserving the observance of the Law intact.[4]

God is personal, as the Jewish theology teaches, but He is at the same time Pure Being (τὸ ὄντως ὄν), absolutely simple (φύσις ἁπλῆ), free and self-sufficient.[5] He does not occupy space or place but rather contains all things within Himself.[6] Yet He is absolutely transcendent, transcending even the Idea of the Good and the Idea of Beauty (αὐτὸ τὸ ἀγαθὸν καὶ αὐτὸ τὸ καλόν):[7] Man attains to God, not through scientific understanding (λόγων ἀποδείξει)—"In order to comprehend God we must first become God, which is impossible"[8]—but in immediate intuition (ἐναργείᾳ).[9] God is thus ineffable Being, Who is above thought and can be attained only through ecstasy or intuition. We see how Philo was influenced by the contemporary tendency to exalt the Divine Transcendence—though we must not forget that the transcendence of the Divine Being was clearly maintained in Jewish scriptural theology, even if not expressed in philosophic terminology.

This insistence on the Divine Transcendence and on God's elevation above everything material not unnaturally led, as later on, for example, in Albinus the Middle Platonist and Numenius the Neo-Pythagorean, to the conception of intermediary beings, in order to bridge the gulf between God Himself and the material cosmos. The highest of these intermediary beings is the Logos or Nous. The Logos is spoken of as the first-born of God, being πρεσβύτατος καὶ γενικώτατος τῶν ὅσα γέγονε.[10] The Logos is for Philo definitely inferior to God and is to be placed in the rank of ὅσα γέγονε, which includes many other beings besides the Logos, even if the latter has the primacy. The Philonic conception of the Logos is therefore not identical with the dogma of the Logos as maintained in Christian theology, even if it influenced early Christian thinkers. Sometimes indeed the Logos seems to be conceived as an aspect of God, but even in this case there would still be a clear distinction between the Philonic and the Christian idea of the Logos. It has been well said, that Philo wavered between "Monarchianism" and "Arianism" but never asserted "Athanasianism"—provided, of course, that it is understood that in the Philonic doctrine of the Logos there is no reference to an historic Man. The Platonic Ideas are placed in the Logos, so that the Logos is the Τόπος or place in which the ideal world (ὁ ἐκ τῶν ἰδεῶν κόσμος) is situated.[11] In this conception Philo is at one with Neo-Pythagoreanism, which placed the Ideas in Nous. (Numenius was influenced by the Philonic philosophy.) Generally speaking Philo speaks simply of the Logos, though he distinguishes two aspects or functions of Logos, ὁ λόγος

ἐνδιάθετος and ὁ λόγος προφορικός, the first consisting
in the immaterial world of the Ideas, the second in the
visible things of this world, in so far as they are copies
of the immaterial Ideas.[12] This division of the Logos corresponds to the vision in man between the λόγος ἐνδιάθετος
or faculty of reason itself and the λόγος προφορικός or
spoken word, which proceeds from the λόγος ἐνδιάθετος
as the stream from its source. An example of Philo's allegorising is to be found in the fact that he discovers a symbol
of this twofold Logos in the double breastplate of the
High Priest. The Logos is God's instrument in the formation
of the world, and Philo found a reference to this in
the words of the Pentateuch, καὶ ἐποίησεν ὁ θεὸς τὸν
ἄνθρωπον κατ᾽ εἰκόνα θεοῦ.[13]

It is to be noted that, when the Old Testament mentions
the angel of God in describing the theophanies, Philo
identifies the angel with the Logos, just as, when several
angels are mentioned, he identifies them with the Powers
(see below). This Logos is an incorporeal substance, the
immaterial Word or Voice of God; but, in so far as it is
conceived as really distinct from God, it is conceived as
subordinate to God, as God's instrument. Philo utilised,
not only the conception of the Divine Wisdom, as found in
the Sapiential Books, but also Platonic exemplarism (the
Logos is the image, the shadow, of God and is itself the
exemplar of creation) and Stoic themes (the Logos is the
immanent, yet at the same time, transcendent, principle
of law in the world and organising bond of creatures); but
the general conception seems to be that of a descending
scale of being. In other words, the Philonic Logos, so far as it
is really distinct from the ultimate Godhead, Yahweh, is
a subordinate and intermediary being, through which God
expresses Himself and acts: it is not the consubstantial
Word of the Father, the Second Person of the Blessed Trin-
ity. The Philonic philosophy, in respect to the Logos, is more
akin to Neo-Platonism than to Christian Trinitarianism.[14]

Besides the Logos there are other Powers (δυνάμεις)
or intermediary beings subordinate to God, such as ἡ ποιητική
and ἡ βασιλική or κύριος (sometimes named ἀγαθότης
and ἐξουσία), ἡ προνοητική, ἡ νομοθετική, etc. But just
as Philo seems to have wavered between conceiving the
Logos as an aspect of God and conceiving it as an independent being, so he wavered between conceiving the other
Powers as attributes or powers of God, corresponding to the

Ideas (i.e. as operative functions of the Ideas) and conceiving them as relatively independent beings. They all appear to be comprehended in the Logos, but this does not help much in settling the question as to their personality or lack of it. If the Logos is conceived as an aspect of God, then the Powers will be qualities or ideas of God, while if the Logos is conceived as a relatively independent being, subordinate to God, then the Powers may be minor subordinate beings or forces; but it does not appear that Philo ever came to a settled or clear decision on the matter. Dr. Praechter can thus say, that "Philo wavers between two conceptions, the 'Analoga' of which recur in the Christian Church as Monarchianism and Arianism; but a doctrine analogous to that of Athanasius is wholly foreign to him and would contradict both his religious and his philosophic consciousness." [15] Moreover, it does not require much thought to recognise that the Philonic philosophy could never admit the Christian doctrine of the Incarnation—at least if Philonism were to remain self-consistent—since it lays such stress on the Divine Transcendence that direct "contact" with matter is excluded. It is indeed perfectly true that Christianity itself insists on the Divine Transcendence and that the Incarnation is a mystery; but on the other hand the spirit of the Christian attitude towards matter is not that of the Philonic or Neo-Platonic philosophies.

Influenced by Platonism, Philo maintains a sharp dualism of soul and body or of the rational and sensual elements in man, and insists on the necessity of man's liberating himself from the power of the sensual.[16] Virtue is the only true good, and in regard to the passions apathy is to be aimed at. But though Philo was influenced by Stoic and Cynic ethical teaching, he emphasised trust in God rather than trust in oneself. Virtue then is to be pursued and man's task is to attain the greatest possible likeness to God.[17] This is an interior task and so public life is discouraged because of its distracting influence, while science is to be pursued only so far as it is an aid to the soul's inner life. In this development there are stages, for above conceptual knowledge of God is to be ranked heavenly wisdom or the immediate intuition of the ineffable Godhead. The passive state of ecstasy thus becomes the highest stage of the soul's life on earth, as it was later to be in the Neo-Platonic philosophy.[18]

While Philo's influence on early Christian thought has Philonism helped to prepare the way for Neo-Platonism doubtless been exaggerated,[19] it will be recognised that through its insistence on the utter Transcendence of God, the existence of intermediary beings, and the soul's ascent to God culminating in ecstasy.

Chapter Forty-Five

PLOTINIAN NEO-PLATONISM

1. Life of Plotinus

The birthplace of Plotinus is uncertain, since it is given as Lycon by Eunapius and as Lycopolis by Suidas.[1] In any case he was born in Egypt about A.D. 203 or 204 (Porphyry gives 205/6). Plotinus, we are told by Porphyry, attended the lectures of various professors at Alexandria in turn, but did not find what he was looking for until he came upon Ammonius Saccas, when he was about twenty-eight. He remained a pupil of Ammonius until the year 242 when he joined the Persian expedition of the Emperor Gordian, in order to make the acquaintance of Persian philosophy. However, the expedition came to grief when Gordian was assassinated in Mesopotamia, and Plotinus made his way to Rome where he arrived in his fortieth year. At Rome he opened a school and soon came to enjoy the favour of the highest officials, even of the Emperor Gallienus and his wife. Plotinus conceived the notion of founding a city, Platonopolis, in the Campagna, which was to be the concrete realisation of Plato's Republic, and he seems to have obtained the Emperor's consent to the project; but for some reason or other the Emperor withdrew his consent after a while and so the plan fell through.

When Plotinus was about sixty years old he received as a pupil the celebrated Porphyry, who afterwards wrote the life of the Master whom he so greatly admired. It was Porphyry who attempted to arrange the writings of Plotinus in systematic form, dividing them into six books, each of which contained nine chapters. Hence the name *Enneads*, which is applied to the works of Plotinus. Although the philosopher is said to have had a pleasant and eloquent oral style, his written composition was somewhat difficult and the difficulty was not lessened by the fact that his weak eyesight prevented him from correcting the manuscript. Porphyry had therefore no easy task to start with, and as he made a point of preserving the style of the writer, Plotinus' treatises have always been a source of difficulty to later editors.

At Rome, Plotinus was frequently approached for help and advice, and so exercised the office of a sort of "spiritual director." Moreover he took into his house orphaned children and acted as their guardian—an example of his kindness and amiability. He made many friends and no enemies, and though his personal life was ascetic, he was gentle and affectionate in character. We are told that he was somewhat diffident and nervous, a fact that tended to show itself in his lectures. He led a deep spiritual life and Porphyry relates that his Master experienced ecstatic union with God four times in the six years in which he was his disciple.[2] Plotinus did not enjoy strong health, and his infirmities had a fatal termination in A.D. 269/70, when he died at a country-house in the Campagna. Porphyry was at that time in Sicily, whither he had gone on Plotinus' advice, in order to recover from a state of melancholy and depression into which he had fallen; but a friend of Plotinus, the physician Eustochius, arrived from Puteoli in time to hear the philosopher's last words: "I was waiting for you, before that which is divine in me departs to unite itself with the Divine in the universe."

Although Plotinus attacked the Gnostics, he is silent about Christianity, which he must have known to some extent. But though he never became a Christian, he was a resolute witness to spiritual and moral ideals, not only in his writings but also in his own life, and it was the spiritual idealism of his philosophy that enabled it to exercise such an influence on the great Latin doctor, St. Augustine of Hippo.

2. Doctrine of Plotinus

God is absolutely transcendent: He is the One, beyond all thought and all being, ineffable and incomprehensible, οὗ μὴ λόγος, μηδὲ ἐπιστήμη, ὃ δὴ καὶ ἐπέκεινα λέγεται εἶναι οὐσίας.[3] Neither essence nor being nor life can be predicated of the One, not of course that it is less than any of these things but because it is *more*, τὸ ὑπὲρ πάντα ταῦτα εἶναι.[4] The One cannot be identical with the sum of individual things, for it is these individual things which require a Source or Principle, and this Principle must be distinct from them and logically prior to them. (We might say that, however much you increase the number of contingent things, you cannot thus arrive at a Necessary Being.) Moreover, if the One were identical with each individual thing taken separately, then each thing would be identical with every other and the distinction of things, which is an obvious fact, would be illusion. "Thus the One cannot be any existing thing, but is prior to all existents."[5] The One of Plotinus is not, therefore, the One of Parmenides, a monistic principle, but is the One, whose transcendence we have seen emphasised in Neo-Pythagoreanism and Middle Platonism. Indeed, just as Albinus had set the πρῶτος θεός above νοῦς and distinguished the ὑπερουράνιος θεός from the ἐπουράνιος θεός, and as Numenius had set the πρῶτος θεός above the Demiurge, and as Philo had set God above the world-forming Powers, so Plotinus sets the ultimate Deity, the One or πρῶτος θεός, beyond being, ἐπέκεινα τῆς οὐσίας.[6] This does not mean, however, that the One is nothing or non-existent; rather does it mean that the One transcends all being of which we have experience. The concept of being is drawn from the objects of our experience, but the One transcends all those objects and consequently transcends also the concept that is founded on those objects.

Since God is one, without any multiplicity or division, there can be in the One no duality of substance and accident, and Plotinus is accordingly unwilling to ascribe to God any positive attributes. We should not say that the One is "thus" or "not thus," for if we say this we thereby delimit it and make it a particular thing, whereas in reality, it is beyond all things which can be delimited by such predication, ἄλλο τοίνυν παρ᾽ ἅπαντα τὸ οὕτως.[7] Nevertheless, Goodness may be attributed to the One, provided that it is not attributed as an inhering quality. God is accordingly *The Good* rather than "good."[8] Moreover, we can legitimately ascribe to the One neither thought nor will nor activity. Not thought, since thought implies a distinction between the thinker and the object of his thought;[9] not will, since this also implies distinction; not activity, for then there would be a distinction between the agent and the object on which he acts. God is the One, beyond all distinctions whatsoever: He cannot even distinguish Himself from Himself, and so is beyond self-consciousness. Plotinus allows, as we have seen, the predicates of unity and goodness to be ascribed to God (in the sense that God is the One and the Good); yet he stresses the fact that even these predicates are inadequate and can be applied to God only analogously. For unity expresses the denial of plurality and goodness expresses an effect on something else. All we can say is that the One is—though, indeed, God is beyond being, One, indivisible, unchanging, eternal, without past or future, a constant self-identity.

On this view of God, the ultimate Principle, how can Plotinus account for the multiplicity of finite things? God cannot limit Himself to finite things, as though they were part of Him; nor can He create the world by a free act of His Will, since creation is an activity and we are not justified in ascribing activity to God and so impairing His unchangeability. Plotinus, therefore, had recourse to the metaphor of emanation. But although he makes use of metaphorical terms like ῥεῖν and ἀπορρεῖν, Plotinus expressly rejects the notion that God becomes in any way less through the process of emanation: He remains untouched, undiminished, unmoved. A free creative act would imply that God issues forth from His state of tranquil self-containedness, and this Plotinus would not admit: he maintained, then, that the world issues from God or proceeds from God by necessity, there being a principle of necessity that the less perfect should issue from the more perfect. It is a principle that every nature should make that which is immediately subordinate to it (τὸ μετ᾽ αὐτὴν ποιεῖν), unfolding itself, as a seed unfolds itself, the procession being from an undivided source or principle to a goal in the universe of sense. The prior Principle, however, remains always in its own place (μένοντος μὲν ἀεὶ τοῦ προτέρου ἐν τῇ οἰκείᾳ ἕδρᾳ), the consequent being engendered out of an ineffable power (ἐκ δυνάμεως ἀφάτου) which is in the prior Principles, it being unfitting that this power should be stayed in its operation by any jealousy or selfishness.[10] (Plotinus also uses the metaphors περίλαμψις, ἔλλαμψις, likening the One to the sun, which illuminates, itself undiminshed. He also employs the comparison of the mirror, since the object which is mirrored is reduplicated, yet without itself undergoing any change or any loss.)

We have, therefore, to be careful, if we wish to make the statement that the process of emanation in Plotinus is pantheistic in character. It is quite true that for Plotinus the world proceeds from God *secundum necessitatem naturae* and that he rejects free creation *ex nihilo;* but it should also be remembered that for him the prior Principle remains "in its own place," undiminshed and unimpaired, always transcending the subordinate being. The truth of the matter would seem to be that, while rejecting free creation out of nothing on the ground that this would involve change in God, Plotinus equally rejects a fully pantheistic self-canalisation of the Deity in individual creatures, a self-diremption of God. In other words he tries to steer a middle course between theistic creation on the one hand and a fully pantheistic or monistic theory on the other hand. We may well think that (since an ultimate dualism does not enter into the question) no such compromise is possible; but that is no reason for calling Plotinus a pantheist without due qualification.

The first emanation from the One is Thought or Mind, Νοῦς, which is intuition or immediate apprehension, having a twofold object, (*a*) the One, (*b*) itself. In Nous exist the Ideas, not only of classes but also of individuals,[11] though the whole multitude of Ideas is contained indivisibly in Nous. (τὴν δὲ ἐν τῷ νοητῷ ἀπειρίαν, οὐ δεῖ δεδιέναι πᾶσα γὰρ ἐν ἀμερεῖ, κατ᾽ οἷον προείσιν, ὅταν ἐνεργῇ.) Nous is identified with the Demiurge of the Platonic *Timaeus,* and Plotinus uses the phrase πατὴρ τοῦ αἰτίου of the One, identifying the αἴτιον with the Nous and the Demiurge. That Nous is itself ὁ κόσμος νοητός[12] is a point insisted on by Plotinus against Longinus, who had made the Ideas to be apart from Nous, appealing to the *Timaeus* of Plato, where the Ideas are depicted as being distinct from the Demiurge. (Porphyry held the same opinion as Longinus, until Plotinus persuaded him to change it.) It is in Nous, therefore, that multiplicity first appears, since the One is above all multiplicity, above even the distinction of νοεῖν and νοητόν; yet the distinction in Nous is not to be understood absolutely, for it is one and the same Nous that is both τὸ νοοῦν and τὸ νοούμενον. The Demiurge of Plato and the νόησις νοήσεως of Aristotle thus come together in the Plotinian Nous. Nous is eternal and beyond time, its state of blessedness being not an acquired state but an eternal possession. Nous enjoys, therefore, that eternity which

time does but mimic.[13] In the case of Soul its objects are
successive, now Socrates, now a horse, now some other
thing; but Nous knows all things together, having neither
past nor future but seeing all in an eternal present.

From Nous, which is Beauty, proceeds Soul, corresponding to the World-Soul of the *Timaeus*. This World-Soul is
incorporeal and indivisible, but it forms the connecting-link
between the super-sensual world and the sensual world, and
so looks not only upwards to the Nous but also downwards
towards the world of nature. Whereas Plato, however, had
posited only one World-Soul, Plotinus posited two, a higher
and a lower, the former standing nearer to Nous and being in
no immediate contact with the material world, the latter
(γέννημα ψυχῆς προτέρας) being the real soul of the phenomenal world. This second soul Plotinus termed nature or
φύσις.[14] Moreover, although the phenomenal world owes
all the reality it possesses to its participation in the Ideas,
which are in Nous, these Ideas do not operate in the
sensible world and have no direct connection with it, so
that Plotinus posited reflections of the Ideas in the World-
Soul, calling them λόγοι σπερματικοί and saying that they
are comprised within the λόγος—an obvious adoption of
Stoic doctrine. In order to fit in this conception with his
distinction of two World-Souls, he further distinguished
πρῶτοι λόγοι, comprised within the higher Soul, from the
derivate λόγοι, comprised within the lower Soul.[15]

Individual human souls proceed from the World-Soul, and,
like the World-Soul, they are subdivided into two elements
(in accordance with the Pythagorean-Platonic tripartition
Plotinus admits also a third and mediating element), a
higher element which belongs to the sphere of Nous (cf.
the Aristotelian Nous) and a lower element, which is directly connected with the body. The soul pre-existed before
its union with the body, which is represented as a fall, and
survives the death of the body, though apparently without
memory of the period of earthly existence. (Transmigration
is also admitted.) But although Plotinus speaks of individual
souls as bound together in the unity of the World-Soul,[16]
he is not prepared to deny personal immortality: the soul
is real and nothing that is real will perish. Can we suppose
that Socrates, who existed as Socrates on this earth, will
cease to be Socrates, just because he has reached the best
of all abodes? In the after-life, therefore, each individual

soul will persist, each remaining one, yet all being one together.[17]

Below the sphere of Soul is that of the material world. In accord with his conception of the emanative process as radiation of light, Plotinus pictures light as proceeding from the centre and passing outwards, growing gradually dimmer, until it shades off into that total darkness which is matter-in-itself, conceived as the privation of light, as στέρησις.[18] Matter, then, proceeds from the One (ultimately), in the sense that it becomes a factor in creation only through the process of emanation from the One; but in itself, at its lowest limit, it forms the lowest stage of the universe and is the antithesis to the One. In so far as it is illumined by form and enters into the composition of material objects (Aristotle's ὕλη) it cannot be said to be complete darkness; but in so far as it stands over against the intelligible and represents the ἀνάγκη of the *Timaeus*, it is unilluminated, darkness. Plotinus thus combined Platonic with Aristotelian themes, for though he adopted the Platonic conception of matter as ἀνάγκη, as the antithesis to the intelligible, as the privation of light, he also adopted the Aristotelian conception of matter as the substrate of form, as an integral component of material objects. The transmutation of one element into another shows that there must be some substrate of bodies, which is distinct from the bodies themselves.[19] If we consider bodies and make complete abstraction of form, then the residuum is what we mean by matter.[20] Matter is thus partially illuminated by its information and does not exist separately in the concrete as complete darkness, the principle of not-being. Moreover, just as the phenomenal world in general has its pattern in the intelligible, so does matter in nature correspond to a νοητὴ ὕλη.[21]

In addition to this fusion of Platonic and Aristotelian cosmological themes Plotinus asserts the Orphic and Neo-Pythagorean view of matter as the principle of evil. At its lowest grade, as devoid of quality, as unilluminated privation, it is evil itself (not, however, having evil as an inhering quality any more than the Good has goodness as an inhering quality), and so stands over against the Good as its radical antithesis. (The evil of matter does not, of course, pertain to the νοητὴ ὕλη.) Plotinus thus comes perilously near to asserting a dualism which would be opposed to the real character of his system, though it must be remembered that matter itself is privation and not a positive principle. In any case we might suppose that Plotinus would be led logically to depreciate the visible universe, though in point of fact he does not do so. It is true that a certain tendency to depreciate the visible universe does show itself in his psychological and ethical teaching; but this is offset, so far as his cosmology is concerned, by his insistence on the unity and harmony of the cosmos. Plotinus opposed the Gnostic contempt for the world and praised the latter as the work of the Demiurge and the World-Soul: it is an eternal and unified creature, bound together in a harmony of parts, governed by Divine Providence. He expressly says that we must not allow that the universe is an evil creation, in spite of all the vexatious things that are in it. It is the image of the intelligible, but it is too much to demand that it should be the precise counterpart of the intelligible. What cosmos, he asks, could be better than the one we know, with the exception of the intelligible cosmos?[22] The material world is the exteriorisation of the intelligible, and the sensible and the intelligible are bound together for ever, the former reproducing the latter according to the measure of its capacity.[23] This universal harmony and cosmic unity form the rational basis for prophecy and for the magical influencing of superhuman powers. (Besides the star-gods Plotinus admitted other "gods" and "demons," which are invisible to man.)

In his psychology Plotinus assigns three parts to the individual soul. The highest of these (corresponding to the Nous of Aristotle) is uncontaminated by matter and remains rooted in the intelligible world,[24] but in so far as the soul enters into real union with the body, to form the compositum (τὸ κοινόν), it is contaminated by matter, and so there follows the necessity of an ethical ascent, with the θεῷ ὁμοιωθῆναι as the proximate goal and union with the One as the ultimate goal. In this ascent the ethical element (πρᾶξις) is subservient to the theoretical or intellectual element (θεωρία), as in Aristotle. The first stage of the ascent, undertaken under the impulse of Eros (cf. Plato's Symposium) consists in κάθαρσις, the process of purification by which man frees himself from the dominion of the body and the senses and rises to the practice of the πολιτικαὶ ἀρεταί, by which Plotinus means the four cardinal virtues. (The highest of these is Φρόνησις.[25]) Secondly the soul must rise above sense-perception, turning towards Nous and

occupying herself with philosophy and science.[26] A higher
stage, however, carries the soul beyond discursive thought
to union with Nous which Plotinus characterises as πρώτως
καλός. In this union the soul retains her self-consciousness.
But all these stages are but a preparation for the final stage,
that of mystical union with God or the One (Who transcends beauty) in an ecstasy characterised by the absence
of all duality. In thought *of* God or *about* God the Subject
is separated from the Object; but in ecstatic union there
is no such separation. "There shall a man see, as seeing may
be in Heaven, both God and himself: himself made radiant,
filled with the intelligible light, or rather grown one with
that light in its purity, without burden or any heaviness,
transfigured to godhead, nay, being in essence God. For
that hour he is enkindled; but when once more he is become
heavy, it is as though the fire were quenched." "That
sight is hard to put into words. For how should a man
bring back report of the Divine, as of a thing distinct, when
in the seeing he knew it not distinct but one with his own
consciousness?" [27] (Needless to say, the ascent to God is
not meant to imply that God is spatially present "out there."
In meditation on God it is not necessary to cast one's thought
outwards, as though God were present in any one place in
such a way that He leaves other places destitute of Himself.[28]
On the contrary, God is everywhere present. He is "outside"
no one but is present to all, even if they know it not.[29])
This ecstatic union is, however, of brief duration so far as
this life is concerned: we look for its complete and permanent possession in the future state, when we are freed from
the hindrance of the body. "He will lapse again from the
vision: but let him again awaken the virtue which is in
him, again know himself made perfect in splendour; and he
shall again be lightened of his burden, ascending through
virtue to the Intelligence, and thence through wisdom to the
Supreme. This is the life of gods and of the godlike and
happy among men; a quittance from things alient and earthly,
a life beyond earthly pleasure, a flight of the alone to the
Alone." [30]

In the system of Plotinus, then, the Orphic-Platonic-Pythag-
orean strain of "otherworldliness," intellectual ascent, salvation through assimiliation to and knowledge of God, reach
their most complete and systematic expression. Philosophy
now includes, not only logic, cosmology, psychology, metaphysics and ethics, but also the theory of religion and mysti-

cism: in fact, since the highest type of knowledge is the mystical knowledge of God and since Plotinus, who most probably based his theory of mysticism on his own experience as well as on past speculation, evidently regards mystical experience as the supreme attainment of the true philosopher, we may say that in Plotinian Neo-Platonism philosophy tends to pass into religion—at least it points beyond itself: speculation does not set itself up as the ultimate goal to be achieved. This made it possible for Neo-Platonism to act as a rival to Christianity, though on the other hand its complicated philosophic system and its "anhistorical" spirit prevented it from proving the rival that it might have been: it lacked the popular appeal exercised by the mystery religions, for instance. Neo-Platonism was really the intellectualist reply to the contemporary yearning for personal salvation, those spiritual aspirations of the individual, which are so marked a feature of the period. "Truly the words of counsel 'Let us flee to our own fatherland,'[31] might be uttered with a deep meaning. The Fatherland to us is that place from whence we came; and in that place is the Father."[32] Christianity, rooted in history, combining popular appeal with a growing speculative background, insistence on the Beyond with a sense of a mission to be accomplished in the Here, mystical communion with ethical probity, asceticism with a consecration of the natural, would have a far wider and deeper appeal than the transcendental philosophy of the Neo-Platonists or the fashionable devotions of the mystery cults. Yet, from the point of view of Christianity itself, Neo-Platonism had an important function to fulfil, that of contributing to the intellectual statement of the Revealed Religion, and so the convinced Christian cannot but look with sympathy, and a certain reverence, on the figure of Plotinus, to whom the greatest of the Latin Fathers (and so the Universal Church) owed no inconsiderable debt.

3. School of Plotinus

The tendency to increase the intermediary beings between God and corporeal objects is already observable in Plotinus' disciple *Amelius,* who distinguished three hypostases in Nous, namely τὸν ὄντα, τὸν ἔχοντα, and τὸν ὁρῶντα.[33] A more important philosopher, however, was *Porphyry of Tyre* (A.D. 232/3–after 301), who joined Plotinus in Rome in 262/3. Porphyry's life of his master I have already mentioned: in addition to this he wrote a great number of other works and on a great variety of subjects, his most celebrated book being his *Isagoge* or introduction to the *Categories* of Aristotle. This was translated into Latin (e.g. by Boethius), Syrian, Arabic and Armenian and exercised great influence, not only in Antiquity but on into the Middle Ages, being itself made the subject of many commentaries. The work treats of Αἱ πέντε φωναί—genus (γένος), species (εἶδος), difference (διαφορά), property (ἴδιον) and accident (συμβεβηκός). Porphyry composed many other commentaries both on Plato (e.g. on the *Timaeus*) and on Aristotle (mainly on his logical works), and tried to show—in his Περὶ τοῦ μίαν εἶναι τὴν Πλάτωνος ᾿Αριστοτέλους αἵρεσιν —that the Platonic and Aristotelian philosophies are in essential agreement.

Porphyry set himself to propound the doctrine of Plotinus in a clear and comprehensible manner, but he laid more stress on the practical and religious sides than even Plotinus had done. The end of philosophy is salvation (ἡ τῆς ψυχῆς σωτηρία), and the soul must purify itself by turning its attention from what is lower to what is higher, a purification to be accomplished by asceticism and knowledge of God. The lowest stage of virtue consists in the practice of the πολιτικαὶ ἀρεταί, which are essentially "metriopathic" virtues, i.e. consisting in the reduction of the affections of the soul to the golden mean under the dominion of reason, and concerning man's intercourse with his fellow men. Above these virtues stand the cathartic or purifying virtues, which aim rather at "Apathy." This is realised in the πρὸς θεὸν ὁμοίωσις. In the third stage of virtue the soul turns towards Nous (for Porphyry evil does not lie in the body as such but rather in the soul's conversion to inferior objects of desire),[34] while the highest stage of virtue, that of the παραδειγματικαὶ ἀρεταί, belongs to the νοῦς as such. The four cardinal virtues recur at each stage, but of course at different degrees of elevation. In order to facilitate the soul's ascent Porphyry stresses the need for ascetic practices, such as abstinence from flesh-meat, celibacy, abstinence from theatrical performances, etc. Positive religion occupies an important place in his philosophy. While issuing a warning against the misuse of divination and other such superstitions (which he, however, accepted and permitted in themselves, since he believed in demonology), Porphyry at the same time lent his support to the popular and traditional religion, making the pagan myths allegorical representations of philosophic truth. He insisted on the importance of works, affirming that God does not prize the wise man's words, but his deeds.[35] The truly pious man is not for ever at prayer and sacrifice, but practises his piety in works: God does not accept a man for his reputation or for the empty formulae he employs, but for a life in accordance with his professions.[36]

During his residence in Sicily Porphyry composed fifteen books against the Christians. These polemical works were burnt in the year A.D. 448 under the Emperors Valentinian III and Theodosius II, and only fragments have come down to us: we have to rely largely on the writings of Christians for testimony as to the line of attack adopted by Porphyry. (Answers were composed by, among others, Methodius and Eusebius of Caesarea.) St. Augustine says that if Porphyry had ever had a true love of wisdom and had known Jesus Christ "... nec ab eius saluberrima humilitate resiluisses." [37] This phrase would not seem to be conclusive evidence that Porphyry was ever actually a Christian or even a catechumen, for the Saint gives no further evidence that he looked on Porphyry as an apostate, though it is true that the historian Socrates affirms that Porphyry abandoned Christianity (τὸν χριστιανισμὸν ἀπέλειπε) and attributed the apostasy to the philosopher's indignation at being assaulted by some Christians at Caesarea in Palestine.[38] It seems that we cannot attain absolute certainty on the question whether or not Porphyry ever was a Christian: he is not quoted as saying himself that he ever adhered to the Christian religion. Porphyry wanted to prevent the conversion of cultured people to Christianity, and he endeavoured to show that the Christian religion was illogical, ignoble, involved in contradictions, etc. He made a special point of attacking the Bible and the Christian exegesis, and it is interesting to observe his anticipation of Higher Criticism, e.g. by denying the authenticity of the book of Daniel and declaring the prophecies therein contained to be vaticinia ex eventu, denying that the Pentateuch was by Moses, pointing out apparent inconsistencies and contradictions in the Gospels, etc. The Divinity of Christ was a particular point of attack, and he brought many arguments against the Divinity of Christ and the doctrines of Christ.[39]

Chapter Forty-Six

OTHER NEO-PLATONIC SCHOOLS

1. The Syrian School

The chief figure of the Syrian School of Neo-Platonism is Iamblichus (d. c. A.D. 330), a pupil of Porphyry. Iamblichus carried much further the Neo-Platonic tendency to multiply the members of the hierarchy of beings, which he combined with an insistence on the importance of theurgy and occultism in general.

1. The tendency to multiply the members of the hierarchy of being was present in Neo-Platonism from the very beginning, as a consequence of the desire to emphasise the transcendence of the Supreme Godhead and remove God from all contact with the world of sense. But while Plotinus had restrained this tendency within reasonable bounds, Iamblichus gave it wings. Thus above the One of Plotinus he asserted yet another One, which exceeds all qualifications whatsoever and stands beyond the good.[1] This One, which transcends all predicates or indeed any statements on our part—except that of unity—is therefore superior to the One of Plotinus, which is identical with the Good. From the One proceeds the world of ideas or intelligible objects —ὁ κόσμος νοητός— and from this again the world of intellectual beings—ὁ κόσμος νοερός[2]—consisting of Νοῦς, an intermediary hypostasis and the Demiurge, though Iamblichus seems not to have been content with this complication, but to have distinguished further the members of the κόσμος νοερός.[3] Below the κόσμος νοερός is the Superterrestrial Soul, and from this Soul proceeds two others. As for the gods of the popular religion and the "heroes,"

these—together with a host of angels and demons—belong to the world, and Iamblichus tried to arrange them according to numbers. But while endeavouring to establish this fantastic scheme by means of the speculative reason, Iamblichus insisted on the immediate and innate character of our knowledge of the gods, which is given us together with our innate psychical impulse towards the Good.

2. The religious interest of Iamblichus is apparent in his ethical doctrine. Accepting Porphyry's distinction of the political, cathartic and paradigmatic virtues he then proceeds to introduce, between the two last, the *theoretical* virtues, by which the soul contemplates Nous as its object and views the procession of the orders from the final Principle. By the paradigmatic virtues the soul identifies herself with Nous, the place of ideas and παράδειγμα of all things. Finally, above these four types of virtue stand the *priestly* virtues, in the exercise of which the soul is ecstatically united to the One. (These virtues are therefore also called ἑνιαῖαι). As we must look to divine revelation in order to ascertain the means of entering upon union with God, the priest is superior to the philosopher. Purification from the sensual, theurgy, miracles, divination, play an important part in the system of Iamblichus.

2. *The School of Pergamon*

The Pergamene School was founded by *Aedesius,* a pupil of Iamblichus, and is characterised mainly by its interest in theurgy and in the restoration of polytheism. Thus while *Maximus,* one of the Emperor Julian's tutors, gave particular attention to theurgy, Sallustius wrote a work *On the gods and the world* as propaganda for polytheism, while the rhetorician Libonius, another of Julian's tutors, wrote against Christianity, as did also *Eunapius* of Sardes. *Julian* (322-363) was brought up as a Christian but became a pagan. In his short reign (361-363), Julian showed himself to be a fanatical opponent of Christianity and adherent of polytheism, combining this with Neo-Platonic doctrines, for which he relied largely on Iamblichus. He interpreted, for example, the worship of the sun according to the Neo-Platonic philosophy, by making the sun the intermediary between the intelligible and the sensible realms.[4]

3. *The Athenian School*

In the Athenian School of Neo-Platonism there flourished a lively interest in the writings of Aristotle, as well of course as in those of Plato, an interest that showed itself in the commentary on the *De Anima* composed by Plutarch of Athens, the son of Nestorius and Athenian Scholarch (d. A.D. 431/2) and in the commentaries on the *Metaphysics* by Syrianus (d. *c.* 430), the successor of Plutarch in the headship of the School at Athens. But Syrianus was no believer in the agreement of Plato and Aristotle: on the contrary not only did he account the study of the philosophy of Aristotle merely a preparation for the study of Plato, but—in his commentary on the *Metaphysics*—he defended the Platonic ideal theory against Aristotle's attacks, clearly recognising the difference between the two philosophers on this point. Yet that did not prevent him from trying to show the agreement between Plato, the Pythagoreans, the Orphics and the "Chaldaic" literature. He was succeeded by *Domninus,* a Syrian of Jewish origin, who wrote on mathematics.

Much more important, however, than any of these men is the celebrated *Proclus* (410-485), who was born at Constantinople and was Athenian Scholarch for many years. He was a man of untiring diligence, and though much of his work has perished, we still possess his commentaries on the *Timaeus, Republic, Parmenides, Alcibiades I* and *Cratylus,* in addition to his works Στοιχείωσις Θεολογική, Εἰς τὴν Πλάτωνος Θεολογίαν and the *De decem dubitationibus circa providentiam,* the *De providentia et fato et eo quod in nobis* and the *De malorum subsistentia*—the last three works being preserved in the Latin translation of William of Moerbeke. Possessed of a wide knowledge concerning the philosophies of Plato and Aristotle and of his Neo-Platonic predecessors, Proclus combined with this knowledge a great interest in and enthusiasm for all sorts of religious beliefs, superstitions and practices, even believing that he received revelations and was the reincarnation of the Neo-Pythagorean Nicomachus. He had, therefore, an immense wealth of information and learning at his disposal, and he attempted to combine all these elements in one carefully articulated system, a task rendered all the easier by his dialectical ability. This has won for him the reputation of being the greatest Scholastic of Antiquity, in that he brought his dialectical ability and genius for subtle systematisation to bear on the doctrines that he had received from others.[5]

The main *motif* of Proclus' dialectical systematisation is that of triadic development. This principle was certainly used by Iamblichus, but Proclus employed it with considerable dialectical subtlety and made it the dominant principle in the procession of beings from the One, i.e. in the emanation of the orders of being from the highest Ἀρχή down to the most inferior stage. The effect, or being that proceeds, is partly similar to the cause or source of emanation and partly dissimilar. In so far as the being that proceeds is similar to its origin, it is regarded as being in some degree identical with its principle, for it is only in virtue of the self-communication of the latter that the procession takes place. On the other hand, since there *is* a procession, there must be something in the proceeding being that is not identical with, but different from, the principle. We have, therefore, at once two moments of development, the first being that of remaining in the principle (μονή), in virtue of partial identity, the second being that of difference, in virtue of external procession (πρόοδος). In every being that proceeds, however, there is a natural tendency towards the Good, and, in virtue of the strictly hierarchical character of the development of beings, this natural tendency towards the Good means a turning-back towards the immediate source of emanation on the part of the being that emanates or proceeds. Proclus thus distinguishes three moments of development, (i) μονή or remaining in the principle; (ii) πρόοδος or proceeding out of the principle, and (iii) ἐπιστροφή or turning-back towards the principle. This triadic development, or development in three moments dominates the whole series of emanations.[6]

The original principle of the whole process of development is the primary one, τὸ αὐτὸ ἕν.[7] Beings must have a cause, and cause is not the same as effect. Yet we cannot admit a *regressus ad infinitum*. There must be, therefore, a First Cause, whence the multiplicity of beings proceed "as branches from a root," some being nearer to the First Cause, others more remote. Moreover, there can be only one such First Cause, for the existence of a multiplicity is always secondary to unity.[8] This must exist since we are logically compelled to refer all multiplicity back to unity, all effects to an ultimate Cause and all participated good to an Absolute Good; yet as a matter of fact the primary Principle transcends the predicates of Unity, Cause and Good, just as it transcends Being. It follows that we are really not entitled to predicate anything positively of the ultimate Principle: we can only say what it is *not*, realising that it stands above all discursive thought and positive predication, ineffable and incomprehensible.

From the primary One proceed the Units or ἑνάδες, which are nevertheless looked on as super-essential and incomprehensible gods, the source of providence, and of which goodness is to be predicated. From the Henads proceeds the sphere of Nous, which subdivides into the spheres of the νοητοί, the νοητοὶ καὶ νοεροί and the νοεροί (cf. Iamblichus), the spheres corresponding respectively to the concepts of Being, Life and Thought.[9] Not content with these divisions Proclus introduces further subdivisions in each of the three spheres of Nous, the first two being subdivided into three triads, the third into seven hebdomads, and so on.

Below the general sphere of Nous is the sphere of the Soul, which is the intermediary between the supersensible and the sensible worlds, mirroring the former as a copy (εἰκονικῶς) and serving as a pattern for the latter (παραδειγματικῶς). This sphere of soul is subdivided into three sub-spheres, that of divine souls, that of "demonic" souls, and that of ψυχαί or human souls. Each subsphere is again subdivided. The Greek gods appear in the sphere of divine souls, but the same name is found in different groups according to the different aspect or function of the god in question. For instance, Proclus seems to have posited a threefold Zeus. The sphere of demonic souls, which serves as a bridge between gods and men, is subdivided into angels, demons and heroes.

The world, a living creature, is formed and guided by the divine souls. It cannot be evil—nor can matter itself be evil—since we cannot refer evil to the divine. Rather is evil to be thought of as imperfection, which is inseparable from the lower strata of the hierarchy of being.[10]

In this process of emanation the productive cause, Proclus insists, remains itself unaltered. It brings into actuality the subordinate sphere of being, but it does so without movement or loss, preserving its own essence, "neither transmuted into its consequents nor suffering any diminution." The product, therefore, does not arise through the self-diremption of the producer, nor by its transformation. In this way Proclus tries, like Plotinus, to steer a middle course between *creatio ex nihilo* on the one hand and true monism or pantheism on the other hand, for, while the productive being is neither related nor diminished through the production of the subordinate being, it nevertheless furnishes the subordinate being out of its own being.[11]

On the principle that like can only be attained by like, Proclus attributed to the human soul a faculty above thought, by which it can attain the One.[12] This is the unitary faculty, which attains the ultimate Principle in ecstasy. Like Porphyry, Iamblichus, Syrianus and others, Proclus also attributed to the soul an ethereal body composed of light, which is midway between the material and the immaterial and is imperishable. It is with the eyes of this ethereal body that the soul can perceive theophanies. The soul ascends through the different grades of virtue (as in Iamblichus) to ecstatic union with the primary One. Proclus distinguishes three general stages in the soul's ascent, Eros, Truth and Faith. Truth leads the soul beyond love of the beautiful and fills it with knowledge of true reality, while Faith consists in the mystical silence before the Incomprehensible and Ineffable.

Proclus was succeeded in the headship of the School by *Marinus,* a native of Samaria. Marinus distinguished himself in mathematics and through his sober and restrained interpretation of Plato. For instance, in his commentary on the *Parmenides* he insisted that the One and so on denote *ideas* and not gods. However, that did not prevent him from following the contemporary fashion of attributing great importance to religious superstitions, and at the summit of the scale of virtues he placed the θεουργικαὶ ἀρεταί. Marinus was succeeded as Scholarch by Isidorus.

The last of the Athenian Scholarchs was Damascius (Sch. from *c.* A.D. 520), whom Marinus had instructed in mathematics. Having been forced to the conclusion that the human reason cannot understand the relation of the One to the proceeding beings, Damascius seems to have considered that human speculation cannot really attain the truth. All the words we employ in this connection, "cause" and "effect," "processions," etc., are but analogies and do not properly represent the actuality.[13] Since on the other hand he was not prepared to abandon speculation, he gave full rein to theosophy, "Mysticism" and superstition.

A well-known disciple of Damascius is *Simplicius,* who wrote valuable commentaries on the *Categories, Physics,*

De Caelo and *De Anima* of Aristotle. That on the *Physics* is particularly valuable because of the fragments of the pre-Socratics therein contained.

In the year 529 the Emperor Justinian forbade the teaching of philosophy at Athens, and Damascius, together with Simplicius and five other members of the Neo-Platonic School, went to Persia, where they were received by king Chosroes. In 533, however, they returned to Athens, apparently disappointed with the cultural state of Persia. It does not appear that there were any more pagan Neo-Platonists surviving shortly after the middle of the century.

4. The Alexandrian School

1. The Alexandrian School of Neo-Platonism was a centre for investigation in the department of the special sciences and for the labour of commenting on the works of Plato and Aristotle. Thus *Hypatia* (best known for her murder in A.D. 415 by a fanatical mob of Christians) wrote on mathematics and astronomy and is said to have lectured on Plato and Aristotle, while *Asclepiodotus* of Alexandria (second half of A.D. fifth century), who later resided at Aphrodisias in Caria, studied science and medicine, mathematics and music. *Ammonius, Ioannes Philoponus, Olympiodorus* and others commented on works of Plato and Aristotle. In the commentaries of the School special attention was paid to the logical works of Aristotle, and in general it may be said of these commentaries that they show moderation and a desire on the part of their authors to give the natural interpretation of the works on which they are commenting. Metaphysical and religious interests tend to retreat from the foreground, the multiplication of intermediary beings, so characteristic of Iamblichus and Proclus, being abandoned and little attention being paid to the doctrine of ecstasy. Even the pious and somewhat mystically inclined Asclepiodotus, who was a pupil of Proclus, avoided the latter's complicated and highly speculative metaphysic.

2. Characteristic of Alexandrian Neo-Platonism is its relation to Christianity and the thinkers of the celebrated Catechetical School. The result of the abandonment of the speculative extravagancies of Iamblichus and Proclus was that the Neo-Platonic School at Alexandria gradually lost its specifically pagan character and became rather a "neutral" philosophical institute: logic and science were obviously subjects

on which Christians and pagans could meet on more or less
common ground. It was this growing association of the
School with Christianity which made possible the continuation of Hellenic thought at Constantinople. (Stephanus of
Alexandria migrated to Constantinople and there expounded
Plato and Aristotle in the university in the first half of the
seventh century, during the reign of the Emperor Heraclius,
i.e. a century after Justinian had closed the School at
Athens.) An instance of the close relation between Neo-
Platonists and Christians at Alexandria is the life of Hypatia's disciple, Synesius of Cyrene, who became bishop
of Ptolemais in A.D. 411. Another striking instance is the conversion of Ioannes Philoponus to Christianity. As a con-
vert he wrote a book against Proclus' conception of the eternity of the world and supported his own view by an appeal
to Plato's *Timaeus* which he interpreted as teaching creation
in time. Philoponus also held the view that Plato drew
his wisdom from the Pentateuch. One may mention also
Nemesius, bishop of Emesa in Phoenicia, who was influenced
by the Alexandrian School.

3. But if Neo-Platonism exercised a profound influence
on Christian thinkers at Alexandria, it is also true that Christian thinkers were not without influence on non-Christian
philosophers. This can be seen in the case of *Hierocles of
Alexandria,* who lectured at Alexandria from about A.D. 420.
Hierocles shows affinity with Middle Platonism rather than
with his Neo-Platonist predecessors, for, neglecting the
Plotinian hierarchy of beings which had been so exaggerated
by Iamblichus and Proclus, he admits only one super-ter-
restrial being, the Demiurge. But what is particularly striking
is that Hierocles asserts *voluntary creation out of nothing* by
the Demiurge.[14] He rejects indeed creation in time, but that
does not militate against the very great probability of Christian influence, especially as Fate or ʿΑιμαρμένη denotes for
Hierocles, not mechanical determinism, but the apportioning
of certain effects to man's free actions. Thus petitionary
prayer and providential ʿΑιμαρμένη are not mutually exclusive,[15] and the doctrine of Necessity or Fate is brought
more into harmony with the Christian insistence on human
freedom on the one hand and Divine Providence on the
other.

5. Neo-Platonists of the Latin West

One would scarcely be justified in speaking of a "School" of
Neo-Platonism in the Latin West. However, there is a characteristic common to those thinkers who are usually classed
as "Neo-Platonists of the Latin West" and that is, that the
speculative side of Neo-Platonism is no longer in evidence
while the learned side is very much to the fore. By their
translation of Greek works into Latin and by their commentaries on Platonic and Aristotelian writings, as well as on
writings of Latin philosophers, they helped to spread the
study of philosophy in the Roman world and at the same
time constructed a bridge whereby Ancient Philosophy passed
to the Middle Ages. Thus in the first half of the fourth
century A.D. *Chalcidius* (who probably was or became a
Christian) made a Latin translation of Plato's *Timaeus* and
wrote a Latin commentary on it—apparently in dependence
on Poseidonius' commentary (with the possible use of intermediate writings). This translation and its commentary were
much used in the Middle Ages.[16] In the same century
Marius Victorinus (who became a Christian when of advanced years) translated into Latin Aristotle's *Categories* and
De Interpretatione, Porphyry's *Isagoge* and some Neo-Platonist works. He also wrote commentaries on Cicero's *Topics*
and *De Inventione* and composed original works *De Defi-
nitionibus* and *De Syllogismis Hypotheticis.* As a Christian
he also composed some theological works, of which a great
part are still extant. (St. Augustine was influenced by Marius
Victorinus.) One may also mention *Vettius Agonius Prae-
textatus* (d. 384), who translated Themistius' paraphrase of
Aristotle's *Analytics,* and *Macrobius* (he seems to have become a Christian in later years), who wrote the *Saturnalia*
and also a commentary on Cicero's *Somnium Scipionis* about
A.D. 400. In this commentary the Neo-Platonist theories of
emanation appear and it seems that Macrobius made use of
Porphyry's commentary on the *Timaeus,* which itself made
use of that of Poseidonius.[17] Fairly early in the fifth century
Martianus Capella composed his (still extant) *De Nuptiis
Mercurii et Philologiae,* which was much read in the Middle
Ages. (For instance, it was commented on by Remigius
of Auxerre.) This work, which is a kind of Encyclopaedia,
treats of each of the seven liberal arts, books three to nine
being each devoted to one of the arts. This was of importance for the Middle Ages, which made the seven liberal

arts the basis of education as the *Trivium* and *Quadrivium*.

More important, however, than any of the afore-mentioned writers is the Christian *Boethius* (c. A.D. 480-524/5), who studied at Athens, held high office under Theodoric, king of the Ostrogoths, and was finally executed on a charge of treason after a term of imprisonment, during which he composed the famous *De Consolatione Philosophiae*. As it is more convenient to treat of the philosophy of Boethius by way of introduction to Mediaeval Philosophy, I shall content myself here with mentioning some of his works.

Although it was the aim of Boethius to translate into Latin, and to furnish with commentaries, all the works of Aristotle (*De Interpret.* 1, 2), he did not succeed in carrying his project to completion. He did, however, translate into Latin the *Categories*, the *De Interpretatione*, the *Topics*, both *Analytics* and the *Sophistical Arguments*. It may be that Boethius translated other works of Aristotle besides the *Organon*, in accordance with his original plan; but this is uncertain. He translated Porphyry's *Isagoge*, and the dispute concerning universals which so agitated the early Middle Ages took its *point de départ* in remarks of Porphyry and Boethius.

Besides furnishing the *Isagoge* (in the translation of Marius Victorinus) with a double commentary, Boethius also commented on the *Categories*, the *De Interpretatione*, the *Topics*, the *Analytics* and *Sophistical Arguments* (probably) and on Cicero's *Topics*. In addition to these commentaries he composed original treatises, the *Introductio ad categoricos syllogismos*, *De categoricis syllogismis*, *De hypotheticis syllogismis*, *De divisione*, *De topicis differentiis*, *De Consolatione Philosophiae*, *De Institutione arithmetica*, etc. In the last period of his life several theological opuscula came from his pen.

On account of this extensive labour expended on translation and commenting, Boethius may be called the principal mediator between Antiquity and the Middle Ages, "the last Roman and the first Scholastic," as he has been called. "Down to the end of the twelfth century he was the principal channel by which Aristotelianism was transmitted to the West." [18]

Chapter Forty-Seven

CONCLUDING REVIEW

When we look back at the philosophy of Greece and of the Greco-Roman world, as we watch its naïve beginnings on the shore of Asia Minor, as we see the intellectual power and comprehensive mind of a Heraclitus or a Parmenides struggling with a crippling poverty of philosophic language, as we trace the development of two of the greatest philosophies the world has ever seen, the philosophies of Plato and of Aristotle, as we see the broadening influence of the Stoic School and witness the evolution of the final creative effort of ancient thought, the system of Plotinian Neo-Platonism, we cannot but acknowledge that we have before us one of the supreme achievements of the human race. If we gaze with admiration at the Greek temples of Sicily, at the Gothic cathedrals of the Middle Ages, at the work of a Fra Angelico or a Michelangelo, a Rubens or a Velasquez, if we treasure the writings of a Homer or a Dante, a Shakespeare or a Goethe, we should pay the tribute of a like admiration to what is great in the realm of pure thought and count it as one of the greatest treasures of our European heritage. Mental effort and perseverance are no doubt required in order to penetrate the riches of Greek thought, but any effort that is expended in the attempt to understand and appreciate the philosophy of those two men of genius, Plato and Aristotle, is amply rewarded: it can no more be wasted than the effort we expend to appreciate at its full value the music of Beethoven or Mozart or the beauty of the cathedral at Chartres, Greek drama, Greek architecture, Greek sculpture, are imperishable memorials of the Greek genius and culture, of the glory of

Hellas; but that glory would be incomplete without Greek philosophy and we cannot appreciate fully the culture of the Greeks unless we know something of Greek philosophy. It may be of help towards the appreciation of that philosophy if, in these concluding remarks, I make a few suggestions (some of them already touched upon) concerning different ways in which we may regard Greek philosophy as a whole.

1. I have already mentioned, particularly in connection with the pre-Socratic philosophers, the problem of the One and the Many; but the theme of the relation between the One and the Many and of the character of both may be discerned running through the whole of Greek philosophy, just as it runs indeed through the whole of philosophy, owing to the fact that while the Many are given in experience, the philosopher strives to see the Many with a synoptic vision, to arrive, so far as is possible, at a comprehensive view of Reality, i.e. to see the Many in the light of the One or in some sense to reduce the Many to the One. This attempt at a synoptic vision is very clear in the case of the pre-Socratic cosmologists and there is no need to dwell on this point again, beyond recalling to mind that their attempt to reconcile the Many of experience with the One demanded by thought was pursued predominantly on the material plane; the Many are material and the One also, the Unity-in-difference is material, water or the indeterminate or air or fire. Sometimes the aspect of Unity is predominant, as in the Eleatic system, sometimes the Many are triumphant, as in the atomistic philosophy of Leucippus and Democritus; but mind, partly no doubt owing to poverty of language, hardly rises above the material plane, though in Pythagoreanism we see, for example, a much clearer distinction between soul and body, while with Anaxagoras the concept of Nous tends to liberation from materialism.

So far as we can speak of the Sophists as occupying themselves at all with this problem, it is rather the aspect of multiplicity that is stressed (the multiplicity of ways of life, of ethical judgments, of opinions), while with Socrates the aspect of unity is stressed, inasmuch as the basic unity of true judgments of value is set in clear light; but it is Plato who really develops the complexity and richness of the problem. The fleeting multiplicity of phenomena, the data of experience, is seen against the background of the unitary realities of the exemplary Ideas, apprehended by the human mind in the concept, and this assertion of the Ideal realm of reality forces the philosopher to consider the problem of the One and the Many not only in the logical sphere, but also in the ontological sphere of immaterial being. The result is that the immaterial unities (themselves a multiplicity) are viewed in function of the One, the synthesising reality of the transcendental sphere and the ultimate Exemplar. Moreover, although the particulars of sense-experience, the Many of the older Cosmologists, are "dismissed," precisely in regard to their particularity considered as impenetrable by conceptual thought, into the infinite or indeterminate, the whole material world is regarded as ordered and informed by Mind or Soul. On the other hand a "chorismos" is left between exemplary Reality and the fleeting particulars, while —apparently at least—no satisfactory answer is given as to the precise relation between the Exemplary and Efficient Causes, so that, although Plato brings the complexity of the problem into greater relief and definitely transcends the pre-Socratic materialism, he fails to give any adequate solution to the problem and leaves us with a dualism, the sphere of Reality on the one hand and the sphere of semi-reality or Becoming on the other hand. Not even his assertion of the immaterial, which sets him above both Parmenides and Heraclitus, can suffice to explain the relation of Being and Becoming or of the One and the Many.

With Aristotle we find a greater realisation of the wealth and richness of the material world and he attempts, through his doctrine of immanent substantial form, to effect some synthesis of the realities of the One and the Many, the multiplicity of members within a species being united in the possession of a similar specific form, though there is no numerical identity. Again, the doctrine of hylomorphism enabled Aristotle to assert a real unifying principle in the terrestrial world, while at the same time he avoided any over-emphasis of unity, such as would conflict with the evident multiplicity given in experience: he thus provided a principle of stability and a principle of change and so did justice to both Being and Becoming. Moreover, Aristotle's Unmoved Mover, the ultimate Final Cause of the universe, served in some degree as a unifying and harmonising Principle, drawing the multiplicity of phenomena into an intelligible unity. On the other hand, however, Aristotle's dissatisfaction with the Ideal Theory of Plato and his perception of its weaknesses led him into an unfortunate rejection of the Platonic Exemplarism as a whole, while his insistence on final causality to the apparent exclusion of cosmic efficient causality meant the assertion of an ultimate dualism between God and an *independent* world.

In post-Aristotelian philosophy it is perhaps not fanciful to see in Stoicism an over-stressing of the One, resulting in cosmic pantheism (which has its noble reflection in ethical cosmopolitanism), and in Epicureanism an over-assertion of the Many, appearing in a cosmology built on an atomistic basis and in a (theoretically at least) egoistic ethic. In Neo-Pythagoreanism and Middle Platonism we see that growing syncretism of Pythagorean, Platonic, Aristotelian and Stoic elements which culminated in the Neo-Platonic system. In that system the only possible way of settling the problem of the One and the Many is apprehended, namely that the Many must issue in some way from the One, the dualism between God and an independent world being avoided on the one hand and monism being avoided on the other hand, so that justice could be done to the reality of the One and the Many, to the supreme reality of the One and the dependent reality of the Many. But, while the Neo-Platonists rejected cosmic monism through their doctrine of the hierarchy of being and rejected any self-diremption of the transcendent One and while they admitted a "manifold Many" and did not attempt to dismiss the cosmos and the subordinate degrees of Being as illusory, they failed to see the unsatisfactory character of their attempt to steer a middle way between a true creation and monism and that their theory of "emanation," given their denial of creation out of nothing on the one hand and their denial of the self-diremption of God on the other hand, could possess no intelligible significance, but remained a mere metaphor. It was left for Christian philosophy to assert the true solution of *creatio ex nihilo sui et subiecti*.

2. Under a slightly different aspect we might regard Greek philosophy in its totality as an attempt to discover the ultimate cause or causes of the world. The pre-Socratics in general, as Aristotle observes, were concerned with the material cause, the *Urstoff* of the world, that which remains permanent beneath the constant changes. Plato, however, gave special emphasis to the Exemplary Cause, ideal and supra-material Reality, while he also asserted the Efficient operative Cause, Mind and Soul, developing the first steps of the pre-Socratic Anaxagoras. Nor did he, in spite of what Aristotle says, neglect final causality, since the exemplary causes are also

final causes: they are not only Ideas, but also Ideals. God acts in the world with a view to an end, as is clearly stated in the *Timaeus*. But Plato seems to have left a dichotomy between the Exemplary Cause and the Efficient Cause (at least this is suggested by what he actually says and we have not sufficient warrant to state categorically that he brought the two ultimate Causes together), while in the terrestrial world he does not give that clear place to the immanent formal cause that Aristotle supplied. Yet while Aristotle developed a clear theory concerning the immanent formal and material causes in the terrestrial world, his system is sadly deficient in relation to the ultimate Efficient and Exemplary Causes. The Aristotelian God works as ultimate Final Cause, but, since the philosopher did not see how God's changelessness and self-sufficiency could be reconciled with the exercise of efficient causality, he neglected to provide an ultimate Efficient Cause. He thought, no doubt, that the exercise of final causality by the Unmoved Mover was also all the ultimate efficient causality that was requisite; but this meant that for Aristotle the world was not only eternal, but also onologically independent of God: the Unmoved Mover could scarcely be regarded as drawing the world into existence through the unconscious exercise of final causality.

A synthesis of Plato and Aristotle was, therefore, necessary, and in Neo-Platonism (as also, to a greater or less extent, in the intermediate philosophies leading up to it) the God of Aristotle and the Exemplary and Efficient Causes of Plato were brought more or less together, even if not in a thoroughly satisfactory manner. In Christian philosophy on the other hand the ultimate Efficient, Exemplary and Final Causes are explicitly identified in the one spiritual God, supreme Being and Reality and the Source of all created and dependent Being.

3. Again, we might look on Greek philosophy as a whole from the humanistic viewpoint, according to the position attributed to man in the individual systems. The pre-Socratic cosmology, as I pointed out earlier, was particularly concerned with the Object, the material cosmos and man was regarded as an item in that cosmos, his soul being, for example, a contraction of the primal Fire (Heraclitus) or composed of a particular type of atoms (Leucippus). On the other hand, the doctrine of transmigration of souls, as found for instance in the Pythagorean philosophy and in the teaching of Empedocles, implied that there was in man a prin-

ciple superior to matter, an idea which bore splendid fruit
in the philosophy of Plato.

With the Sophists and with Socrates we find a swing-over,
due to various causes, from the Object to the Subject, from
the material cosmos as such to man. But it is in the Platonic
philosophy that the first real attempt is made to combine
both realities in a comprehensive synthesis. Man appears
as the knowing and willing subject, the being who realises, or
should realise, true values in his individual life and in the
life of society, the being endowed with an immortal soul;
and human knowledge, human nature, human conduct and
human society, are made the subject of profound and pene-
trating analyses and considerations. On the other hand man
appears as a being set between two worlds, the full immaterial world of Reality above him and the merely material
limit below him: he thus appears, in his dual character
of embodied spirit, as what Poseidonius, the outstanding
thinker of the Middle Stoa, was later to term the δεσμός
or bond between the two worlds of the immaterial and the
material.

In Aristotle's philosophy man is again a midway being,
as it were, for neither Plato nor Aristotle considered man
to be the highest being: the founder of the Lyceum, no
less than the founder of the Academy, was convinced that
above men there is unchanging Being and that contemplation of unchanging Being is the exercise of man's highest
faculty. Again, Aristotle, no less than Plato, gave profound
consideration to human psychology, human conduct and
human society. Yet of Aristotle's philosophy we may perhaps
say that it was at once more and also less human than that
of Plato: more human in that, for example, he knits together
soul and body more closely than does Plato and so produces
a more "realistic" epistemology, attributes a greater value to
human aesthetic experience and artistic production, and is
more "commonsense" in his treatment of political society,
less human in that his identification of the active intellect
in all man (according to what seems the more probable
interpretation of the *De Anima*) would result in denial of
personal immortality. Moreover, there is nothing in Aristotle
to suggest that man can ever become united to God in any
real sense.

Yet, although it is true that Plato and Aristotle attribute
an important position to the study of man and his conduct,
as individual and as a member of society, it is also true that

both of them (notwithstanding Aristotle's trend towards empirical science) are great metaphysicians and speculative philosophers and of neither of them could we say that he fixes his attention exclusively in man. In the Hellenistic and Roman periods, however, man comes to occupy more and more the centre of the picture: cosmological speculation tends to flag and is unoriginal in character, while in Epicureanism and the developed Stoa the philosopher is concerned above all with human conduct. This preoccupation with man produces the noble doctrine of the later Stoa, of Seneca, Marcus Aurelius and—most strikingly perhaps—of Epictetus, in which all men, as rational beings, appear as brethren, children of "Zeus." But if it is man's moral conduct that is most insisted on in the Stoic School, it is man's religious capacity, need and yearning that come to occupy a prominent position in the Schools and thinkers that are influenced by the Platonic tradition: a doctrine of "salvation," of knowledge of God and assimilation to God, culminates in the Plotinian doctrine of ecstatic union with the One. If Epicureanism and Stoicism (the latter with some qualification perhaps) concern themselves with man on what we might call the horizontal level, Neo-Platonism concerns itself rather with the vertical, with man's ascent to God.

4. Epistemology or the theory of knowledge is generally regarded as a branch of philosophy, the study of which is peculiar to our modern era, and for some modern thinkers it has constituted practically the whole of philosophy. There is, of course, a good deal of truth in the assertion that it was modern philosophy that first made epistemology a really serious and critical study, but it is not a completely true statement, if asserted without qualification. Leaving out of account the philosophy of the Middle Ages, which also dealt with epistemological themes, it can scarcely be denied that the great thinkers of Antiquity concerned themselves to some extent with epistemological questions, even if it was not recognised as a separate branch of philosophy or accorded that critical importance which has generally been attributed to it in modern times, since the time of Immanuel Kant at least. Without attempting to give anything like a complete survey of the development of epistemology in ancient philosophy, I will suggest one or two points which may help to throw into relief the fact that important epistemological problems at least raised their heads above the ground in the ancient world, even if they did not emerge into full

light of day and receive that close attention which they deserve.

The pre-Socratic philosophers were, in the main, "dogmatists," in the sense that they assumed that man can know reality objectively. It is true that the Eleatic philosophy made a distinction between the way of truth and the way of belief or opinion or appearance; but the Eleatics themselves did not realise the importance of the problems involved in their philosophy. They adopted a monistic position on rationalistic grounds and, since this position conflicted with the data of sense-experience, cavalierly denied the objective reality of phenomena: they did not question their general philosophical position or the power of the human mind to transcend phenomena, but rather assumed this power. Nor did they realise apparently that, by rejecting the objective reality of appearance, they were undermining their metaphysic. In general, therefore, the thinkers of the Eleatic School cannot be termed exceptions to the generally uncritical attitude of the pre-Socratics, in spite of the dialectical ability of a man like Zeno.

The Sophists did indeed assert relativism to a greater or less extent, and the assertion of relativism involved an implicit epistemology. If Protagoras' dictum that man is the measure of all things is to be taken in a broad sense, it is tantamount to an assertion, not only of the independence of man in the ethical sphere, as a creator of moral values, but also of the inability of man to attain metaphysical truth. Did not Protagoras adopt a sceptical attitude in regard to theology and did not the Sophists in general regard cosmological speculation as little more than waste of time? Now, if the Sophists had gone on to institute a critique of human knowledge and had attempted to show why human knowledge is necessarily confined to phenomena, they would have been epistemologists; but in point of fact their interests were, for the most part, other than philosophical and their relativistic theories do not seem to have been based on any profound consideration either of the nature of the subject or of that of the object. The epistemology involved in their general position remained, therefore, implicit and was not elaborated into an explicit theory of knowledge. *We*, of course, can discern the germs of epistemological theories or problems, not only in Sophism but also in pre-Socratic philosophy; but that is not to say that either the Sophists or the pre-Socratic cosmologists had a reflective realisation of these problems.

When we turn to Plato and Aristotle, however, we find explicit theories of knowledge. Plato had a clear notion what he meant by knowledge and sharply distinguished the nature of true knowledge from the nature of opinion and of imagination, he possessed a clear reflective knowledge of the relativistic and variable elements in sense-perception and he discussed the question, how error of judgment takes place and in what it consists. His whole theory of the ascending degrees of knowledge and the corresponding objects of knowledge entitles him without a doubt to rank as an epistemologist. The same is true of Aristotle, who asserted a theory of abstraction, of the function of the image, of the active and passive principle in cognition, of the distinction between sense-perception and conceptual thought, of the different functions of reason. Of course, if we wished to restrict the scope of epistemology to consideration of the question, "*Can* we attain knowledge?", then the Aristotelian epistemology would belong rather to psychology, since it purports to answer the question, "*How* do we come to know?", rather than the question, "*Can* we know?"; but if we are willing to extend the scope of epistemology to cover the nature of the process of coming to know, then we must certainly reckon Aristotle an epistemologist. He may have treated the questions he raises in his psychology and we might to-day include most of them under the heading of psychology, but, labels apart, it remains an undoubted fact that Aristotle had a theory of knowledge.

On the other hand, though both Plato and Aristotle elaborated theories of knowledge, there is no use in pretending that they were not "dogmatists." Plato, as I have said, had a clear idea of what he meant by knowledge; but that such knowledge was possible for man, he assumed. If he accepted from Heraclitus his insistence on the changing character of the material world and from the Sophists the relativity of sense-perception, he accepted also from the Eleatics and the Pythagoreans the rationalistic assumption that the human mind can transcend phenomena and from Socrates the starting-point of his metaphysics of essence. Moreover, it was essential for Plato's ethical and political aims that the possibility of knowing the unchanging values and exemplary essences should be admitted: he never really questioned this possibility nor did he ever seriously raise the question of a purely subjective *a priori* element in human cognition: he attributed the *a priori* element (which he admitted) to "reminiscence," i.e. to previous objective knowledge. Nor did Aristotle ever raise the "critical problem": he assumed that the human mind can transcend phenomena and attain to a certain knowledge of unchanging and necessary objects, the objects of theoretic contemplation. Plato was an untiring dialectician, Aristotle was always ready to consider fresh problems and was careful in the statement of his own theories, even if not in that of other people's theories; but of neither the one nor the other can we say that he was the Kant of the anti-Kantian of the ancient world, for Kant's problem was not considered by them. Nor is this really surprising, since both men were dominated by the problem of Being (whereas in modern philosophy so many thinkers have started from *Consciousness*), so that their theories of knowledge were elaborated in function of their metaphysics and general philosophic positions rather than as a necessary *prolegomenon* to any metaphysic.

In the post-Aristotelian philosophy, if we except the Sceptics, we find in general the same "dogmatic" attitude, though it is also true that considerable attention was devoted to the question of the criteria of truth, e.g. by the Stoics and Epicureans. In other words, thinkers were alive to the difficulty that arises through the variability of sense-perception and attempted to meet this difficulty; in fact they had to meet it, in order to be able to erect their several philosophical structures. They were much more critical than the pre-Socratics; but that does not mean that they were critical philosophers in the Kantian sense, for they confined themselves more or less to a particular problem and tried to differentiate between, e.g. objective sense-perception, imagination and hallucination. In the New Academy, however, a radical scepticism showed itself, as when Carneades taught that there is no criterion of truth and that knowledge is impossible, on the ground that no sense-presentation is certainly true and that conceptual reasoning, since it is founded on sense-experience, is no more reliable than the latter, and the later Sceptics elaborated a systematic criticism of dogmatism and argued the relative character of both sensation and judgment, so that they were determined anti-metaphysicians. Dogmatism indeed won the final victory in ancient philosophy; but in view of the attacks of the Sceptics it cannot be said that ancient philosophy was altogether uncritical or that epistemology had no place in the consideration of Greek philosophers. This is the point I want to make: I am not concerned to admit that the attacks on metaphysics were justified, for I believe that they can be answered. I only wish to point out that not all Greek philosophers were naïve "dogmatists" and that, even if this can be legitimately asserted of the pre-Socratics, it would be a far too sweeping assertion in regard to Greek philosophers in general.

5. Closely allied with epistemology is psychology, and it may be as well to make a few remarks on the development of psychology in ancient philosophy. It is the Pythagorean School which stands out among the pre-Socratics as possessing a definite concept of the soul as a permanent principle, persisting in its individuality, even after death. The philosophy of Heraclitus recognised, of course, a part of man which is more akin to the ultimate Principle of the universe than the body, and Anaxagoras asserted that Nous is present in man; but the latter did not succeed in transcending, *verbally* at least, the materialism of the pre-Socratic system, while for Heraclitus the rational element in man was but a purer manifestation of the fiery Principle. The Pythagorean psychology, however, by its distinction between soul and body at least implied a distinction between the spiritual and corporeal. Indeed, the doctrine of metempsychosis over-emphasised the distinction between soul and body, since it involved the conclusion that the soul stands in no intrinsic relation to any particular body. Moreover, acceptance of metempsychosis involves the acceptance of the theory that memory and reflective consciousness of continued self-identity are not essential to individual persistence. (If Aristotle held that there is a separate active intellect in each man and that the active intellect persists in its individuality, his notion that memory perishes with death may have been due not only to his own psychology and physiology, but to relics of the Pythagorean doctrine and its implication.) As to the Pythagorean theory of the tripartite nature of the soul, this was doubtless ultimately due to empirical observation of man's rational and emotional functions and of the conflict between reason and passion.

The Pythagorean conception of the soul exercised a very considerable influence on the thought of Plato. Rejecting epiphenomenalism, he made the soul the principle of life and movement in man, a principle that does not depend essentially on the body for the exercise of its highest intellectual functions, a principle that comes from "without" and survives the death of the body. Tripartite in nature, the soul has various functions or "parts," the hierarchy of which was fitted by Plato into his general metaphysical position. The lower parts or functions depend essentially on the body, but the rational soul belongs to the sphere of abiding Reality: in its proper dialectical and intuitive processes its activity is on a higher plane than that of phenomena and demonstrates the "divine" or immortal character of the soul. But Plato was not primarily interested in the soul from the strictly psychological aspect, still less from the point of view of the biologist: he was interested first and foremost in the soul as apprehending values and as realising values, in its ethical aspect. Hence the tremendous importance that he attached to education and culture of the soul. If he sharpened, as he did, the anthesis between soul and body and spoke of the soul as inhabiting the body, as being lodged in the body like a captain in a ship, destined to rule the body, it was mainly his ethical interest that led him to do so. It is true that he attempted to prove the soul's pre-existence, intrinsic independence of the body and immortality, with epistemological arguments, arguing, e.g. from the *a priori* element in human knowledge; but all the time he was under the sway of ethical, and to a certain extent religious interests, and at the close of his life we find him still insisting that the soul is man's dearest possession and tendance of the soul man's highest task and duty. This is what we might call the characteristic side of Plato's psychology, for, though he certainly attributed a biological function to the soul, i.e. as source of movement and vital principle, he placed the emphasis on ethical and metaphysical aspects to such a degree that it may well be doubted if his treatment of these aspects really squares with his treatment of the soul in its biological function.

Aristotle began with the Platonic conception of the soul and the Platonic metaphysico-ethical picture of the soul and features of this conception are salient features of his psychology as represented in the pedagogical works. Thus, according to Aristotle, the highest part of man's soul, the active intellect, comes from without and survives death, while insistence on education and on moral culture is prominent in the philosophy of Aristotle as in that of Plato. Nevertheless, one can hardly avoid the impression that this

aspect of his doctrine of the soul is not the really characteristic aspect of the Aristotelian psychology. However much
he may have insisted on education and however prominent
his intellectualist attitude may be in the picture of the
ideal life for man as given in the *Ethics,* it would seem true
to say that Aristotle's characteristic contribution to psychology
is to be found rather in his treatment of the soul in its
biological aspects. The sharp antithesis drawn by Plato between soul and body tends to retreat into the background,
to give place to the conception of the soul as the immanent
form of the body, as wedded to this particular body. The
active intellect (whether monistically conceived or not) survives death, but the soul in its generality, including the
passive intellect and including the functions of memory, etc.,
depends on the bodily organism and perishes at death.
Where does it come from, this soul of man (excluding the
active intellect)? It does not come from "without," it is not
"made" by any Demiurge: is it perhaps a function of the
body, little more than an epiphenomenon? Aristotle gave an
extensive empirical treatment of such psychical functions
as memory, imagination, dreams, sensations, and it would
appear that his realisation of the dependence of so many of
these functions on physiological factors and conditions was
leading him towards an epiphenomenalist view of the soul,
even if he never explicitly repudiated the totality of his
Platonic inheritance or realised the tension between what
he had retained of the Platonic psychology and that view
of the soul to which his own researches and bent of mind
were leading him.

The most important contribution of post-Aristotelian philosophy to psychology in a broad sense was perhaps the
emphasis it laid on the religious aspect of the human soul:
this is true at least of Neo-Platonism and of the Schools
that led up to Neo-Platonism, though not, of course, of all
post-Aristotelian Schools. The thinkers of the movement which
culminated in Neo-Platonism working from the viewpoint
of the Platonic tradition, set in clear relief man's kinship
to the Divine, the soul's transcendental orientation and
destiny. In other words, it was the characteristically Platonic
attitude that triumphed in ancient philosophy rather than the
characteristically Aristotelian attitude. As for the Stoics and
Epicureans, the former could not achieve a really unified
psychology owing to the simple fact that their dogmatic materialism demanded one psychology and their ethic another.

Moreover, they did not investigate the nature and function of the psyche for their own sake and endeavour to establish a rational psychology on sure empirical foundations; but, adopting and adapting a pre-Socratic cosmology and centering their attention on ethical conduct, fitted a rationalist psychology, as best they could, to a hybrid system. Nevertheless, the tendency of Stoic doctrine and the effect of its influence was certainly to increase the direction of interest to the ethical and religious aspects of the soul rather than to its biological aspects. The Epicureans denied the immortality of the soul and asserted its atomic character; but they did so in the interest of their own ethic and not, of course, because they had discovered that the soul is in reality composed of atoms, though it must be admitted that the Epicurean psychology fits in better with their banal ethic than the Stoic psychology with the Stoic idealist ethic. Both Stoic psychology and Stoic ethic were constantly striving, as it were, to break the bonds of the traditional materialistic monism in which they were bound, and the Stoics could no more explain rational though in terms of their system than the Epicureans could explain thought in terms of the motion of atoms. The Epicureans may have anticipated to some extent the psychology of Hobbes or of thinkers of the French Enlightenment, but neither in the ancient world nor in eighteenth-century France, nor even in the twentieth century, can the psychical be satisfactorily explained in terms of the corporeal, the rational in terms of irrational, the conscious in terms of the unconscious. On the other hand, if the psychical cannot be reduced to the corporeal, no more can the corporeal be reduced to the psychical: the two remain distinct, though in man, the bond between the purely spiritual and the purely material spheres, the two elements are intimately related. Plato laid the emphasis on the fact of distinction, Aristotle on that of the intimate relationship: both factors need to be borne in mind if one would avoid occasionalism or modern idealism on the one hand and epiphenomenalism on the other hand.

6. A few remarks on the development of ethics in ancient philosophy, particularly in regard to the relationship between ethical norms and a transcendental foundation of morality. I am quite aware that the question of the relation between ethics and metaphysics is hotly debated, and I do not propose to discuss the problem on its own merits: I wish to

do no more than indicate what I consider one of the main trends in Greek ethical thought.

We have to distinguish between moral philosophy as such and the unsystematised moral judgments of mankind. Moral judgments had been made by Greeks long before the Sophists, Socrates, Plato, Aristotle, the Stoics, etc., reflected on them, and the fact that the ordinary moral judgments of man formed the material for their reflection meant that the theories of the philosophers mirrored to a greater or less extent the ordinary moral consciousness of the time. These moral judgments, however, are in turn dependent, in part at least, on education, social tradition and environment, are moulded by the community, so that it is only natural that they should differ somewhat from community to community, nation to nation. Now, in face of this difference two ways of reaction at any rate lie open to the philosopher.

(i) Perceiving that a given community holds fast to its own traditional code and considers it the only one, the "natural" one, while on the other hand not all communities have exactly the same code, he may react by drawing the conclusion that morals are relative, that though one code may be more useful, more expedient, than another, there exists no absolute code of morals. This was the line taken by the Sophists.

(ii) The philosopher may attribute a good deal of the observed differences to *error* and assert a sure standard and norm of morality. This was the way taken by Plato and Aristotle. In fact the ethical intellectualism, particularly characteristic of Socrates, though also of Plato to a less extent, bears witness to the fact that they ascribed differences in moral judgment to mistake, to error. Thus to the man who thinks, or professes to think, that the natural and proper procedure is to injure one's enemies or to pursue a career of unabashed egoism, Plato attempts to show that he is quite mistaken in his notion. He may at times appeal to self-interest, even if only in *argumentum ad hominem;* but, whatever he appeals to in order to prove his view, Plato was certainly no relativist in ethics: he believed in abiding standards, objectively true and universally valid.

Now, if we look at the moral philosophies of Plato and Aristotle, this fact is apparent, that in either case the standard of conduct is measured by their conception of human nature. The ideal was regarded by Plato as something fixed, eternal and transcendent, not subject to relativity and variation. The different faculties of man are faculties of activity according to certain habits or virtues, and of each virtue there is an ideal pattern, comprised in the all-embracing ideal, the Ideal of the Good. There is an ideal of man and ideals of man's virtues, and it is man's moral function to conform himself to those ideals. When he does so, when his nature is harmoniously developed and perfected according to the ideal, he is a "just" or good man, he is a true example of a man and has attained true well-being. Moreover, for Plato God is constantly operative in the world, striving to realise the ideal in the concrete and actual world. God Himself never departs from the ideal, but always has the ideal, the best, in view: He is the Reason, Divine Providence, operative in the cosmos. God is also the source of the human reason and is depicted symbolically in the *Timaeus* as forming the human reason Himself, so that man's rational soul is akin to the Divine and has as its task the same task as the Deity, the realisation of the ideal, of value, in the world. Man is thus by nature a co-operator with God: in that consists his vocation, to work towards the realisation of the ideal, of value, in his personal life and in that of society or the State. It is God Who sets the standard, not man, says Plato against Protagoras, and man's end is the greatest possible likeness to God. Plato says little of moral obligation, it is true, but he evidently considered, even if without a fully reflective consciousness of the fact, that man is under an obligation to act as truly befits a man. The ethical intellectualism which he inherited from Socrates, was doubtless a hindrance in the way of a clear realisation of moral obligation and responsibility; but do not the myths of the future life, of reward and punishment, clearly imply some realisation of moral obligation? Plato certainly gave a transcendental foundation to the *content* of the moral law and, though the same cannot be said in regard to the *form* of the moral law, the categorical imperative, he does seem to have had a dim awareness of the fact that a moral law, if its morally binding and universally valid character is to be substantiated, must be given a transcendental foundation, not only in regard to its content, but also in regard to its form.

When we turn to Aristotle, we find a very fine analysis of the good life, of the moral and intellectual virtues, which were analysed by Aristotle much more completely and systematically than by Plato; but the transcendental values of

Plato have been swept away or been replaced by the immanent form. It is true that Aristotle calls on man to think
divine things, to imitate, as far as he can, God's contemplation of the highest object, so that in a sense there is,
even for Aristotle, an eternal pattern of human life; but
the theoretic life is inaccessible to most men, while on the
other hand Aristotle affords no ground for a man thinking
that he is called upon to co-operate with the Divine, since
the God of the *Metaphysics* at least does not operate consciously and efficiently in the world. Aristotle never really
synthesised satisfactorily the life of the moral virtues and
the theoretic life, and the moral law for Aristotle is, it would
seem, devoid of any real transcendental foundation, in regard to both content and form. What could he say to anyone
who questioned the obligation of living in the manner proposed in the *Ethics?* He could appeal to aesthetic standards,
to good form, to "fairness," and he could reply that to act
otherwise is to miss the goal of happiness, which all necessarily seek, with the consequence that one would be acting
irrationally; but he left no place for an appeal to a specifically moral obligation with a firm foundation in absolute
Reality.

Later Greek philosophers, if we except, e.g. the Epicureans, seem to have seen the necessity of founding a standard morality on an absolute basis. The Stoics insist on duty,
on the Divine Will, on the life of reason which is life in
accordance with nature, since man's rational nature proceeds
from God, the all-pervasive Reason, and returns to Him.
Their pantheism certainly involved them in ethical difficulties;
but, none the less, they viewed morality as ultimately the
expression of the Divine in man and in human life. As God
is one, as human nature is constant, there can be but one
morality. It would be an anachronism to read into their
expression for "duty" all the meaning that the term has
acquired in modern times; but at least they had some conception of duty and of moral obligation, even if the clear
statement of this conception was hampered by the determinism consequent on their pantheism. In the Neo-Platonic
system or systems ethics proper was subordinated to insistence on the religious aspect of human life and man's
ascent to God; but the practice of the moral life was regarded as an integral part of that ascent and, in practising
it, man conforms himself to transcendentally-grounded standards. Moreover, the fact that those Romans who aspired to a

moral life and attached importance to moral values, saw the necessity of purifying the idea of God and of empha- sising Divine Providence serves to illustrate the practical benefit of founding ethics ultimately on metaphysics and so serves as an empirical confirmation of the theoretical asser- tion of that foundation.

7. The mention of ethics and of an ascription to morality of a transcendental foundation naturally leads one on to a brief consideration of Greek philosophy viewed as a prepara- tory intellectual instrument for Christianity, as a *preparatio evangelica*. Only a few suggestions can be made, however: any adequate treatment of the subject would require more space than I can devote to it in this concluding chapter. (Consideration of the doctrines actually borrowed directly or indirectly by Christian philosophy from Greek thinkers is best reserved for the next volume, that dealing with mediaeval philosophy.)

In the philosophy of Heraclitus we find the beginnings of the doctrine of an immanent Reason operative in the world, though the Logos is conceived on the material plane, as identical with the primal Fire (a conception that was elaborated in later times by the Stoics), while Anaxagoras contributes the theory of Nous as the primary moving Prin- ciple. But in both cases there is but a hint of the develop- ments that were to come later, and it is not until Plato that we find anything like a natural theology. But, if among the pre-Socratics we find little more than hints of the doc- trine of (what we would call) God, as First Efficient Cause (Anaxagoras) and as Providence or immanent Reason (Hera- clitus), we find in Pythagoreanism a somewhat clearer enun- ciation of the distinction between soul and body, the superior- ity of soul to body and the necessity of tending the former and preserving it from contamination. However, in regard to pre-Socratic philosophy as a whole, it is the search for the ultimate nature of the world and its conception of the world as a law-ordered world, rather than any specific doctrines (with the exception perhaps of the Orphic-Pythagorean psy- chology), which entitles it to be regarded in any sense as a remote *preparatio evangelica,* a preparation of the pagan mind for the reception of the revealed religion. For it is the conception of a law-ordered world that naturally leads on to the conception of a Lawgiver and Orderer. Before this further step could be taken, however, it was necessary to arrive at a clear distinction between soul and body, the immaterial and the material, and for the apprehension of this distinction the Orphics and Pythagoreans paved the way, though it was really Plato who extended the Pythagorean anthropological distinction between the transcendental and the phenomenal, the immaterial and the material.

It would be difficult to exaggerate the importance of Plato in the intellectual *preparatio evangelica* of the pagan world. By his doctrine of exemplarism, his theory of the transcendental Exemplary Cause, by his doctrine of Reason or Mind operative in the world and forming the world for the best, he obviously remotely paved the way for the ultimate acceptance of the one Transcendent-Immanent God. Again, by his doctrine of the immortal and rational soul of man, of retribution, of moral purification, he made easier the intellectual acceptance of Christian psychology and asceticism, while his insistence on absolute moral standards in accordance with the teaching of his great Master, Socrates, and the hints he drops as to the assimilation with God were a remote preparation for the acceptance of the Christian ethic. Nor must we forget that in the *Laws* Plato gave reasons why we should admit the existence of Mind operative in the universe, thus foreshadowing the later natural theologies. But it is rather the total attitude fostered by the Platonic philosophy—I refer to the belief in transcendental Reality, eternal values, immortality, righteousness, Providence, etc., and the characteristic mental and emotional attitude that is logically fostered by such belief—rather than any specific arguments which helped to lead up to the acceptance of Christianity. It is true that the doctrine of the Transcendental, as developed in Middle and Neo-Platonism, was used *against* Christianity, under the plea that the dogma of the Incarnation is incompatible with the transcendent character of God: but the transcendent character of God is an integral doctrine of Christianity and it can scarcely be denied that the Platonic ascent above pre-Socratic materialism was a predisposing factor towards the acceptance of a religion which insists on the supreme reality of the transcendental and on the abiding character of spiritual values. Early Christian thinkers certainly recognised in Platonism a certain kinship, even if more or less remote, with their own *Weltanschauung* and, though Aristotle was later to become the philosopher *par excellence* of Scholasticism, Augustinianism stands rather in the line of the Platonic tradition. Moreover, Platonic-Augustinian elements are very far from being entirely absent in the philosophy of that very Scholastic who adopted—and adapted—Aristotelianism, St. Thomas Aquinas. Thus, if Platonism helped in some degree to prepare the way for Christianity, even if largely through succeeding Schools that developed the Platonic tradition, Christianity may also be said to have borrowed some of its philosophic "outfit" from Platonism.

By mediaeval philosophers of the Augustinian tradition, such as St. Bonaventure (one of whose main objections against Aristotle was that he rejected exemplarism), Aristotelianism tended to be regarded as inimical to the Christian religion, largely because he became known to the West principally through the Arabian commentators. (Thus Averroes interpreted Aristotle—probably rightly—as denying, for example, the *personal* immortality of the human soul.) But though it is true, for instance, that the conception of God in the *Metaphysics* as entirely self-engrossed and caring nought for the world and man, is not that of Christianity, it must surely be admitted that the natural theology of Aristotle was a preparation for the acceptance of Christianity. God appears as transcendent, immaterial Thought, the absolute Final Cause, and when the Platonic Ideas came later to be placed in the Mind of God and a certain syncretism of Platonism and Aristotelianism took place, the ultimate Efficient, Exemplary and Final Causes tending to coalesce, a conception of reality was provided that made it easier than it might otherwise have been to accept Christianity from the intellectual standpoint.

Of the post-Aristotelian philosophy much might be said in the present connection; I can but select a few points for mention. Stoicism, with its doctrine of the immanent Logos and its "providential" operation in the world, with its noble ethic, was an important factor in the world in which Christianity was implanted and grew. It is quite true that the Stoic philosophy remained theoretically materialist and more or less determinist; but, from the practical viewpoint, the insistence on man's kinship with God, on purification of the soul by self-control and moral education, on submission to the "Divine Will," together with the broadening influence of its cosmopolitanism, served as a preparation in some minds for the acceptance of the universal religion which, while transcending the materialism of the Stoics, insisted on the brotherhood of men as children of God and introduced a dynamic influence which was wanting in the Stoic system. Moreover, in so far as ethical Stoicism was an answer to the contemporary need for moral guidance and direction as to the right course to be pursued by the individual, swamped in the great cosmopolitan Empire, this need was far better met by the Christian doctrine, which could appeal to the uneducated and simple in a way that Stoicism could hardly do and which held out the prospect of complete happiness in the future life as the term of moral endeavour in a way that Stoicism, by its very system, was debarred from doing.

Besides the strictly ethical needs of man there were also his religious capacity and need to be satisfied. While the State cult was unable to meet this need, the mystery-religions and even philosophy (in a far less popular form, e.g. in Neo-Platonism) catered for its satisfaction. By attempting to cater for man's deeper spiritual aspirations they at the same time tended to develop and intensify those aspirations, with the result that Christianity fell on an already prepared ground. Christianity, with its doctrine of salvation, its sacramental system, its dogmas, its doctrine of incorporation with Christ through membership of the Church and of the final vision of God, its offer of supernatural life, was *the* "mystery-religion"; but it had the inestimable advantage over all pagan mystery-religions that it was an *historical* religion, based on the Life, Death and Resurrection of the God-Man, Jesus Christ, Who lived and suffered in Palestine in a certain historical period: it was based on historical fact, not on myth. As to the doctrine of "salvation" as found in philosophical Schools and the doctrine of ecstatic union with God as developed in Neo-Platonism, this was far too intellectualist in character to admit of its having a popular appeal. Through the Sacraments and the reception of the supernatural life Christianity offered to *all* men, educated and uneducated alike, union with God, imperfect in this life, perfect in the next, and so, even from the purely natural viewpoint, was obviously destined to exercise a far wider influence than philosophy as such could ever exercise, even a philosophy that was strongly tinctured with religious elements. Moreover, the Neo-Platonic philosophy was unhistorical, in the sense that a doctrine like that of the Incarnation was alien to its spirit, and an historical religion is bound to have a wider popular appeal than a metaphysical philosophy. Nevertheless, in spite of the shocked and scandalised attitude that some early Christian writers adopted (very naturally) in regard to the mystery-religions, particularly that of Mithras, with its quasi-sacramental rites, both the more or less popular mystery-religions and intellectualist Neo-Platonism served the purpose of preparing men's minds for the acceptance of Christianity. They may have tended to set themselves up as rivals to Christianity and they may have kept some individuals from embracing Christianity who would otherwise have done so; but that does not mean that they could not and did not serve as a way to Christianity. Porphyry attacked Christianity, but was not St. Augustine brought to Christianity by way of Plotinus? Neo-Platonism was the last breath, the last flower, of ancient pagan philosophy; but in the thought of St. Augustine it became the first stage of Christian philosophy. Christianity was not, of course, in any sense the outcome of ancient philosophy, nor can it be called a philosophic system, for it is the revealed religion and its historical antecedents are to be found in Judaism; but when Christians began to philosophise, they found ready at hand a rich material, a store of dialectical instruments and metaphysical concepts and terms, and those who believe that divine Providence is operative in history will hardly suppose that the provision of that material and its elaboration through the centuries was simply and solely an accident.

SOME ABBREVIATIONS
USED IN THIS VOLUME

AËTIUS. Collectio placitorum (philosophorum).
ALBINUS. Didask. (Didaskalikos).
AMMIANUS MARCELLINUS. Rerum gest. (Rerum gestarum libri 18).
AUGUSTINE. Contra Acad. (Contra Academicos).
  C.D. (De Civitate Dei).
BURNET. E.G.P. (Early Greek Philosophy).
  G.P., I. (Greek Philosophy. Part I, Thales to Plato).
CAPITOLINUS, JULIUS. Vit. M. Ant. (Vita Marci Antonini Pii).
CHALCIDIUS. In Tim. (Commentary on Plato's *Timaeus*).
CICERO. Acad. Prior. (Academica Priora).
  Ad Att. (Letters to Atticus).
  De Div. (De Divinatione).
  De Fin. (De Finibus).
  De Nat. D. (De Natura Deorum).
  De Off. (De Officiis).
  De Orat. (De Oratore).
  De Senect. (De Senectute).
  Somn. Scip. (Somnium Scipionis).
  Tusc. (Tusculanae Disputationes).
CLEMENS ALEXANDRINUS. Protrep. (Protrepticus).
  Strom. (Stromata).
DAMASCIUS. Dubit. (Dubitationes et solutiones de primis principiis).
DIOGENES LAËRTIUS. Lives of the Philosophers.
EPICTETUS. Disc. (Discourses).
  Ench. (Enchiridion).
EUDEMUS. Phys. (*Physics*, of which only fragments remain).

EUNAPIUS. Vit. Soph. (Lives of the Sophists).

EUSEBIUS. Hist. Eccl. (Historia Ecclesiastica).
Prep. Evan. (Preparatio Evangelica).

GELLIUS, AULUS. Noct. Att. (Noctes Atticae).

GREGORY OF NAZIANZEN. adv. Max. (adversus Maximum).

HIPPOLYTUS. Ref. (Refutationis omnium haeresium libri X).

JOSEPHUS. Ant. Jud. (Jewish Antiquities).

LACTANTIUS. Div. Inst. (Institutiones divinae).

LAMPRIDIUS. Alex. (Life of Alexander Severus).
Aurel. (Life of Aurelian).

LUCIAN. De morte Peregr. (De morte Peregrini).

MARCUS AURELIUS. Med. (Meditations or To Himself).

MAXIMUS OF TYRE. Diss. (Dissertationes).

ORIGEN. c. Cels. (Contra Celsum).

P.G. Patrologia Graeca (ed. Migne).

P.L. Patrologia Latina (ed. Migne).

PHILO. De conf. ling. (De confusione linguarum).
De gigant. (De gigantibus).
De human. (De humanitate).
De migrat. Abrah. (De migratione Abrahami).
De mutat. nom. (De mutatione nomium).
De opif. mundi (De opificio mundi).
De post. Caini (De posteritate Caini).
De somn. (De somniis).
De vita Mos. (De vita Moysis).
Leg. alleg. (Legum allegoriarum libri).
Quis rer. div. her. (Quis rerum divinarum heres sit).
Quod Deus sit immut. (Quod Deus sit immutabilis).

PHOTIUS. Bibliotheca (about A.D. 857).

PLUTARCH. Cat. Mai. (Cato Maior).
De anim. proc. (De animae procreatione in Timaeo).
De comm. notit. (De communibus notitiis adversus
Stoicos).
De def. orac. (De defectu oraculorum).
De gloria Athen. (Bellone an pace clariores fuerint
Athenienses).
De Is. et Osir. (De Iside et Osiride).
De prim. frig. (De primo frigido).
De ser. num. vind. (De sera numinis vindicta).
De sol. animal. (De sollertia animalium).
De Stoic repug. (De repugnantiis Stoicis).
Non p. suav. (Ne suaviter quidem vivi posse secundum
Epicurum).

PSEUDO-PLUTARCH. Strom. (Fragments of the stromateis conserved in Eusebius' *Preparatio Exangelica*).

PORPHYRY. Isag. (Isagoge, i.e. introd. to Aristotle's *Categories*).

PROCLUS. De Prov. (De providentia et fato et eo quod in nobis).

In Alcib. (Commentary on *Alcibiades* I of "Plato").

In Remp. (Commentary on *Republic* of Plato).

In Parmen. (Commentary on *Parmenides* of Plato).

In Tim. (Commentary on *Timaeus* of Plato).

Instit. Theol. (Institutio Theologica).

Theol. Plat. (In Platonis Theologiam).

SENECA. Nat. Quaest. (Naturalium Quaestionum libri VII).

SEXTUS EMPIRICUS. adv. math. (Adversus mathematicos).

Pyrr. Hyp. (Pyrrhonenses Hypotyposes).

SIMPLICIUS. In Arist. Categ. (Commentary on Aristotle's *Categories*).

Phys. (Commentary on Aristotle's *Physics*).

STACE, W. T. Crit. Hist. (A Critical History of Greek Philosophy).

STOBAEUS. Flor. Florilegium.

TACITUS. Ann. (Annales).

Hist. (Historiae).

THEOPHRASTUS. Phys. Opin. (Physicorum Opiniones).

XENOPHON. Cyneg. (Cynegeticus).

Mem. (Memorabilia).

Appendix Two

A NOTE ON SOURCES

Since on the one hand some philosophers did not write at all, while on the other hand the works of many philosophers who did write have been lost, we have to rely in very many cases on the testimony of later writers for information as to the course of Greek philosophy.

The chief source of knowledge in the ancient world concerning the pre-Socratic philosophy was the work of Theophrastus entitled *Physicorum Opiniones*, a work which, unfortunately, we possess only in fragmentary form. Theophrastus' work became the source of various other compilations, epitomes or "doxographies," in some of which the opinions of the philosophers were arranged according to theme, while in others the opinions were set forth under the names of the respective philosophers. Of the former type were the *Vetusta Placita*, written by an unknown disciple of Poseidonius in the first half of the first century A.D. We do not possess this work, but that it existed and that it was based on Theophrastus' work, has been shown by Diels. The *Vetusta Placita* in turn formed the main source of the so-called *Aëtii Placita* or Συναγωγὴ τῶν Ἀρεσκόντων (about A.D. 100). Aetiüs' work in turn served as a basis for the *Placita philosophorum* of the Pseudo-Plutarch (compiled about A.D. 150) and the doxographical extracts given by John Stobaeus (A.D. fifth century) in the first book of his *Eclogae*. These two last works are the most important doxographical compilations which we possess, and it has become evident that the main ultimate source for both was the work of Theophrastus, which was also ultimately the

chief, though not the only, source for the first book of
Hippolytus' *Refutation of all heresies* (in which the subject-
matter is arranged under the names of the respective philosophers concerned), and for the fragments, falsely attributed
to Plutarch, which are quoted in the *Preparatio Evangelica*
of Eusebius.

Further information on the opinions of Greek philosophers
is provided by such works as the *Noctes Atticae* of Aulus
Gellius (about A.D. 150), the writings of philosophers like
Plutarch, Cicero and Sextus Empiricus, and the works of
the Christian Fathers and early Christian writers. (Care
must be exercised, however, in the use of such historical
sources, since, for example, Cicero drew his knowledge of
early Greek philosophers from intermediate sources, while
Sextus Empiricus was mainly concerned to support his own
sceptical position by drawing attention to the contradictory
opinions of the dogmatic philosophers. In regard to Aristotle's testimony as to the opinions of his predecessors we
must not forget that Aristotle tended to look on earlier
philosophies simply from the viewpoint of his own system
and to see in them preparatory work for his own achievement. His attitude on this matter was doubtless largely
justified, but it does mean that he was not always concerned to give what we should consider a purely objective
and scientific account of the course of philosophic thought.)
The commentaries composed by authors of Antiquity on the
works of eminent philosophers are also of considerable importance, for instance, the commentary by Simplicius on the
Physics of Aristotle.

In regard to the lives of the philosophers the most important work which we possess is that of Diogenes Laërtius
(A.D. third century). This work is a compilation of material
taken from various sources and is of very unequal merit,
much of the biographical material being anecdotal, legendary
and valueless in character, "tall stories" and different, sometimes contradictory, accounts of an event being included by
the author, accounts which he had collected from previous
writers and compilers. On the other hand it would be a
great mistake to allow the unscientific character of the work
to obscure its importance and very real value. The indices
of the works of the philosophers are important, and we are
indebted to Diogenes for a considerable amount of valuable
information on the opinions and lives of the Greek philosophers. In assessing the historical value of Diogenes' state-

ments it is obviously necessary to know (as far as this is possible) the particular source to which he was indebted on any given occasion, and no little painstaking and fruitful labour has been expended by scholars, in order to attain this knowledge.

For the chronology of the Greek philosophers the chief source is the *Chronica* of Apollodorus, who based the first part of his chronicle on the *Chronographia* of Eratosthenes of Cyrene (third century before Christ), but added a supplement, carrying it down to about the year 110 B.C. Apollodorus had not, of course, exact material at his disposal, and he had recourse to the arbitrary method of linking up some event of importance which was supposed to have occurred during the period of a philosopher's life, with the philosopher's prime or ἀκμή (taken as the fortieth year) and then reckoning backward to the date of the philosopher's birth. Similarly, it was taken as a general rule that a disciple was forty years younger than his master. Accuracy, therefore, was not to be expected.

(On the general subject of sources see e.g. Ueberweg-Praechter, *Die Philosophie des Altertums,* pp. 10-26 (Apollodorus' Chronicle is given on pp. 667-71), A. Fairbanks, *The First Philosophers of Greece,* pp. 263-88, L. Robin, *Greek Thought and the Origins of the Scientific Spirit,* pp. 7-16, and the *Stellenregister* to Diels' *Fragmente der Vorsokratiker.*

Appendix Three

A FEW BOOKS

1. *General Histories of Greek Philosophy*

ADAMSON, R. (ed. Sorley and Hardie). The Development of Greek Philosophy. London, 1908.

BENN, A. W. The Greek Philosophers. London, 1914.

BRÉHIER, E. Histoire de la philosophie. Tome I. Paris, 1943.

BURNET, J. Greek Philosophy, Part I. Thales to Plato. Macmillan.

(This scholarly work is indispensable to the student).

ERDMANN, J. E. A History of Philosophy, vol. I. Swan Sonnenschein, 1910.

(Erdmann was an eminent historian of the Hegelian School.)

GOMPERZ, TH. Greek Thinkers, 4 vols. (Trs. L. Magnus.) John Murray.

ROBIN, D. La pensée grecque et les origines de l'esprit scientifique. Paris, 1923.

Greek Thought and the Origins of the Scientific Spirit. London, 1928.

RUGGIERO, G. DE. La filosofia greca. 2 vols. Bari, 1917.

(Professor de Ruggiero writes from the viewpoint of an Italian Neo-Hegelian.)

STACE, W. T. A Critical History of Greek Philosophy. Macmillan, 1920.

STENZEL, J. Metaphysik des Altertums. Berlin, Oldenbourg, 1929.

(Particularly valuable for the treatment of Plato.)

STÖCKL, A. A Handbook of the History of Philosophy. Part I. Pre-Scholastic Philosophy. Trs. by T. A. Finlay, S.J. Dublin, 1887.

UEBERWEG-PRAECHTER. Die Philosophie des Altertums. Berlin, Mittler, 1926.

WERNER, C. La philosophie grecque. Paris, Payot, 1938.

ZELLER, E. Outlines of the History of Greek Philosophy. Kegan Paul, 1931.
> (Revised by W. Nestle, translated by L. R. Palmer.)

2. Pre-Socratic Philosophy

The best collection of the fragments of the pre-Socratics is to be found in Hermann Diels' *Vorsokratiker*, fifth edition. Berlin, 1934-5.

BURNET, J. Early Greek Philosophy. Black, 3rd edition, 1920; 4th edition, 1930.
> (This extremely useful work includes very many fragments.)

COVOTTI, A. I Presocratici. Naples, 1934.

FAIRBANKS, A. The First Philosophers of Greece. London, 1898.

ZELLER, E. A History of Greek Philosophy from the earliest period to the time of Socrates. Trs. S. F. Alleyne. 2 vols. Longmans, 1881.

3. Plato

The Works of Plato are published, under the editorship of J. Burnet, in the *Oxford Classical Texts*. A well-known translation, in five volumes, is that by B. Jowett, O.U.P., 3rd edition, 1892. There are also more literal translations.

ARCHER-HIND, R. D. The Timaeus of Plato. Macmillan, 1888.

CORNFORD, F. M. Plato's Theory of Knowledge. Kegan Paul, 1935.
> (A translation of the *Theaetetus* and *Sophist*, with commentary.)

Plato's Cosmology. Kegan Paul, 1937.
> (A translation of the *Timaeus*, with running commentary.)

Plato and Parmenides. Kegan Paul, 1939.
> (Translation of the *Parmenides*, with commentary and discussion.)

The Republic of Plato. Translated with Introduction and Notes. O.U.P.

DEMOS, R. The Philosophy of Plato. Scribners, 1939.

DIÈS, AUGUSTE. Autour de Platon. Beauchesne, 1927.
Platon. Flammarion, 1930.

FIELD, G. C. Plato and his Contemporaries. Methuen, 1930.

GROTE, C. Plato and the other Companions of Socrates. John Murray, 2nd edition, 1867.

HARDIE, W. F. R. A Study in Plato. O.U.P., 1936.

HARTMANN, N. Platons Logik des Seins. Giessen, 1909.

LODGE, R. C. Plato's Theory of Ethics. Kegan Paul, 1928.

LUTOSLAWSKI, W. The Origin and Growth of Plato's Logic. London, 1905.

MILHAUD, G. Les philosophes-géomètres de la Grèce. 2nd edition, Paris, 1934.

NATORP, P. Platons Ideenlehre. Leipzig, 1903.

NETTLESHIP, R. L. Lectures on the Republic of Plato. Macmillan, 1898.

RITTER, C. The Essence of Plato's Philosophy. George Allen & Unwin, 1933.
(Translated by Adam Alles.)
Platon, sein Leben, seine Schriften, seine Lehre. 2 vols. Munich, 1910 and 1923.

ROBIN, L. La théorie Platonicienne des idées et des nombres. Paris, 1933.
Platon. Paris, 1936.
La physique de Platon. Paris, 1919.

SHOREY, P. The Unity of Plato's Thought. Chicago, 1903.

STENZEL, J. Plato's Method of Dialectic. O.U.P., 1940.
(Translated by D. G. Allan.)
Zahl und Gestalt bei Platon und Aristoteles. 2nd edition. Leipzig, 1933.
Platon der Erzieher. 1928.
Studien zur Entwicklung der Platonischen Dialektik. Breslau, 1917.

STEWART, J. A. The Myths of Plato. O.U.P., 1905.
Plato's Doctrine of Ideas. O.U.P., 1909.

TAYLOR, A. E. Plato, the Man and his Work. Methuen, 1926.
(No student of Plato should be unacquainted with this masterly work.)
A Commentary on Plato's Timaeus. O.U.P., 1928.
Article on Plato in Encyc. Brit., 14th edition.
Platonism and its Influence. U.S.A. 1924 (Eng. Harrap).

WILAMOWITZ-MOELLENDORF, U. VON. Platon. 2 vols. Berlin, 1919.

4. *Aristotle*

The Oxford translation of the works of Aristotle is published in eleven volumes, under the editorship of J. A. Smith and W. D. Ross.

BARKER, E. The Political Thought of Plato and Aristotle. Methuen, 1906.

Article on Aristotle in the Encyc. Brit., 14th edition.

CASE, T. Article on Aristotle in the Encyc. Brit., 11th edition.

GROTE, G. Aristotle. London, 1883.

JAEGER, WERNER. Aristotle. Fundamentals of the History of his Development. O.U.P., 1934. (Translated by R. (Translated by R. Robinson.)

LE BLOND, J. M. Logique et Méthode chez Aristote. Paris, Vrin, 1939.

MAIER, H. Die Syllogistik des Aristoteles. Tübingen, 1896. New edition, 1936.

MURE, G. R. G. Aristotle. Benn, 1932.

PIAT, C. Aristote. Paris, 1912.

ROBIN, L. Aristote. Paris, 1944.

ROSS, SIR W. D. Aristotle. Methuen, 2nd edition, 1930.
    (A survey of Aristotle's thought by a great Aristotelian scholar.)
    Aristotle's Metaphysics. 2 vols. O.U.P., 1924.
    Aristotle's Physics. O.U.P., 1936.
    (These two commentaries are invaluable.)

TAYLOR, A. E. Aristotle. Nelson, 1943.

ZELLER, E. Aristotle and the earlier Peripatetics. 2 vols. Longmans, 1897.

5. *Post-Aristotelian Philosophy*

ARMSTRONG, A. P. The Architecture of the Intelligible Universe in the Philosophy of Plotinus. Cambridge, 1940.
    (A very careful study of the origins and nature of Plotinian Neo-Platonism.)

ARNOLD, E. V. Roman Stoicism. 1911.

BAILEY, C. The Greek Atomists and Epicurus. O.U.P.

BEVAN, E. E. Stoics and Sceptics. O.U.P., 1913.
    Hellenistic Popular Philosophy. Cambridge, 1923.

BIGG, C. Neoplatonism. S.P.C.K., 1895.

BRÉHIER, 5. Philon d'Alexandrie. Paris, 1908.
    La philosophie de Plotin. Paris, 1928.

CAPES, W. W. Stoicism. S.P.C.K., 1880.

DILL, SIR S. Roman Society from Nero to Marcus Aurelius. Macmillan, 1905.

DODDS, E. R. Select Passages illustrating Neoplatonism. S.P.C.K., 1923.

FULLER, B. A. G. The Problem of Evil in Plotinus. Cambridge, 1912.

HENRY, PAUL (S.J.). Plotin et l'Occident. Louvain, 1934.
  Vers la reconstitution de l'enseignement oral de Plotin. Bulletin de l'Academie royale de Belgique, 1937.

HICKS, R. D. Stoic and Epicurean. Longmans, 1910.

INGE, W. R. The Philosophy of Plotinus. 2 vols. 3rd edition. Longmans, 1928.

KRAKOWSKI, E. Plotin et le Paganisme Religieux. Paris, Denoël et Steele, 1933.

LEBRETON, J. (S.J.). Histoire du Dogme de la Trinité. Beauchesne, 1910.

MARCUS AURELIUS. The Meditations of the Emperor Marcus Aurelius.
  Edited with Translation and Commentary by A. S. L. Farquharson. 2 vols., O.U.P., 1944.

PLOTINUS. The *Enneads* have been translated into English, in five vols. by S. MacKenna and B. S. Page. 1917-30.

PROCLUS. The Elements of Theology. O.U.P.
  (A Revised Text with Translation, Introduction and Commentary by E. R. Dodds.)

REINHARDT, K. Poseidonios. Munich, 1921.

ROBIN, L. Pyrrhon et le Scepticisme Grec. Paris, 1944.

TAYLOR, T. Select Works of Plotinus (ed. G. R. S. Mead). G. Bell & Sons, 1929.

WHITTAKER, T. The Neo-Platonists. 2nd edition, Cambridge, 1901.

WITT, R. E. Albinus and the History of Middle Platonism. Cambridge.

ZELLER, E. Plato and the Older Academy. Longmans, 1876.
  (Translated by O. J. Reichel.)
  A History of Eclecticism in Greek Philosophy. Longmans, 1883.
  (Translated by S. F. Alleyne.)

NOTES

CHAPTER TWENTY-SEVEN

[1] Frag. 623. (Rose, *Aristotelis Fragmenta*. Berlin, 1870 edit.)
[2] Werner Jaeger, *Aristotle, Fundamentals of the History of His Development*, p. 34. (Trans. R. Robinson. Clarendon Press, 1934.)
[3] Diog. Laërt. 5, 7 and 8.
[4] Cf. *De Orat.*, I, xi, 49.   [5] *De virt. mor.*, c. 7.
[6] Euseb. *Prep. Evang.*, XIV, 6, following Numenius.
[7] Frag. 41. (Rose.)   [8] Frag. 35. (Rose.)
[9] Iambl., *Protr.*, assuming that chapters 6-12 of Iamblichus' work consist of passages from Aristotle's *Protrepticus*. (Cf. Jaeger, *Aristotle*, pp. 60 ff.)
[10] *Metaph.*, A, 983 a 33-4.   [11] Frag. 11. (Rose.)
[12] Frag. 21. (Rose.) It must be admitted that this fragment implies that Aristotle had not yet definitely stated the existence of the First Mover or broken with his former views.
[13] Frag. 15. (Rose.) Professor Jaeger thinks that the dialogue contained also the proofs from motion and causality.
[14] Frags. 12 and 14. (Rose.) Cf. *Laws*, 966 d 9-967 a 5.
[15] Cf. Frag. 17. (Rose.)   [18] *Physics*, VIII, 251 a 9, 253 b 8,
[16] Jaeger, *Aristotle*, p. 192.   267 b 21.
[17] Cf. *Eud. Eth.*, 1249 b.   [19] *Metaph.*, 989 a 24.
[20] Cf. H. von Arnim, *Die drei arist. Ethiken*. (Sitz. Wien. Ak, 2 Abl., 1924.)   [21] Jaeger, *Aristotle*, p. 273.

CHAPTER TWENTY-EIGHT

[1] Cf. *Top.*, A 14, 105 b 19 ff.
[2] Cf. *Top.*, Z 6, 145 a 15 ff. *Metaph.*, E 1, 1025 b 25.
[3] Cf. *Metaph.*, K 7, 1064 b 1 ff.
[4] Cf. *Metaph.*, E 1, 1026 a 10 ff.   [5] Cf. *Eth. Nic.*, A 1, 1094 a 18 ff.
[6] Determining the rank of the branches of philosophy according to the rank of their object, Aristotle gives the palm to "Theology." Cf. *Metaph.*, K 7, 1064 b 1 ff. It has been argued that the threefold division has no adequate warrant in Aristotle's own words and that he conceived the *Poetics*, not as a philosophical aesthetic theory, but simply as a practical manual.
[7] Cf. e.g. *Anal. Post.*, A 22, 83 a 21 ff., b 15 ff.
[8] *Metaph.*, 1017 a 23-4. ὁσαχῶς γὰρ λέγεται, τοσαταυχῶς τὸ εἶναι σημαίνει.
[9] *Anal. Post.*, B 13.   [16] *Anal. Post.*, I 31.
[10] *Anal. Post.*, B 8 and 10.   [17] *Anal. Priora*, I 1, 24 b.
[11] *Anal. Post.*, I 2, 71 b.   [18] I, 100 a b.
[12] *Anal. Post.*, 71 b-72 a.   [19] Cf. *Anal. Post.*, I 3, 72 b.
[13] *Anal. Post.*, II 19, 100 b.   [20] Cf. *Metaph.*, 1005 b 35 ff.
[14] *Anal. Priora*, II 23, 68 b.   [21] *Anal. Post.*, A 1, 71 a.
[15] *Anal. Priora*, II 23, 68 b.   [22] Ia, 78, 4. Cf. IIa, IIae, 2, 1.
[23] Susan Stebbing, *A Modern Introd. to Logic*, p. 102. (London, 1933.)   [24] *Geschichte der Logik*, p. 27. (Berlin, 1931.)

CHAPTER TWENTY-NINE

[1] *Metaph.*, A, 980 a 1.

[2] The name *Metaphysics* simply refers to the position of the *Metaphysics* in the Aristotelian Corpus, i.e. as coming after the *Physics*. But the book is metaphysical also in the sense that it concerns the first and highest principles and causes, and so involves a higher degree of abstraction than does the *Physics*, which deals predominantly with a particular type of being—that which is subject to motion. Still, it is true to say that if we wish to know Aristotle's doctrine on the themes treated of to-day under the heading *Metaphysics*, we must consult not only the *Metaphysics* itself but also the *Physics*.

[3] *Metaph.*, 982 a 11-12.   [7] *Metaph.*, 985 a 21-3.

[4] *Metaph.*, 982 a 26-8.   [8] *Metaph.*, 988 a 8-10.

[5] *Metaph.*, 984 b 15-18.   [9] *Metaph.*, 988 b 6-16.

[6] *Metaph.*, 985 a 18-21.

[10] *Metaph.*, 1026 a 6-32. Cf. 1064 a 28-b 6.

[11] *Metaph.*, VI (E) 2. E.g. a confectioner aims at giving pleasure; if his productions produce health, that is "accidental."

[12] *Metaph.*, VI (E), 4.   [16] *Metaph.*, 991 a 12-13.

[13] *Metaph.*, IV (Γ), 3 ff.   [17] *Metaph.*, 991 a 8-10.

[14] *Metaph.*, 990 b 8-11.   [18] *Metaph.*, 997 b 5-12.

[15] *Metaph.*, 990 a 34-b 8.   [19] *Metaph.*, 991 b 1-3.

[20] *Metaph.*, M, 1079 b 24-6; A, 991 a 20-2.

[21] *Metaph.*, A, 991 a 19-20.

[22] *Metaph.*, A, 990 b 15-17; K, 1059 b 8-9.

[23] *Metaph.*, 992 a 32-b 1.   [26] *Metaph.*, b 1077-1214.

[24] *Metaph.*, 991 b 9 ff.   [27] *Metaph.*, 1076 b 28-34.

[25] *Metaph.*, e.g. 991 b 27-31.   [28] *Metaph.*, A, 992 b 7-9.

[29] St. Thomas Aquinas, who quotes St. Augustine as to the Divine Ideas, teaches that there is a plurality of ideas in the Divine Mind (*S.T.*, I, 15, 2), rejecting the opinion of Plato that they are "outside" the Divine Mind (cf. *S.T.*, I, 15, 1, ad 1). He explains that he does not mean that there is a plurality of accidental *species* in God, but that God, knowing perfectly His Essence, knows it as imitable (or *participabilis*) by a plurality of creatures.

[30] *Metaph.*, M, 1086 b 2-7. We may compare K, 1059 b 25-6 ("every formula and every science is of universals") and Z 1036 a 28-9 ("definition is of the universal and of the form").

[31] *Categ.* 5. It is to be noted that the terms *first* and *second* in this respect are not valuations but mean first or second *in regard to us*, πρὸς ἡμᾶς. We come to know the individuals first and the universals only secondarily by abstraction, but Aristotle does not depart from his view that the universal is an object of science and has a higher reality than the individual as such.

[32] Professor Zeller remarks: "It is, of course, a contradiction to attribute a higher reality to form, which is always a universal, in comparison to that which is a compound of form and matter, and at the same time to assert that only the universal is the object of knowledge which is in itself the prior and better known. The results of this contradiction are to be observed throughout the whole Aris-

totelian system." (*Outlines*, p. 274.) This is scarcely a fortunate statement of the alleged contradiction.

[33] *Metaph.*, VII (Z), 15.   [34] *Ibid.*, 17.

[35] Cf. *Physics*, 193 a 29 and 191 a 31-2. λέγω γὰρ ὕλην τὸ πρῶτον ὑποκείμενον ἑκάστῳ, ἐξ οὗ γίγνεταί τι ἐνυπάρχοντος μὴ κατὰ συμβεβηκός.

One might also approach prime matter from this point of view. Take any material substance and think away all its definite characteristics, all that it possesses in common with other substances—colour, shape, etc. You are ultimately left with a substratum that is absolutely formless, characterless, that cannot exist by itself, but is logically to be presupposed. This is prime matter. Cf. Stace, *Critical History*, p. 276.

[36] Cf. e.g. *Physics*, I, 6; III, 5.

[37] *Physics*, I, 7 ff.

[38] *Metaph.*, 1034 a 5-8.

[39] *Metaph.*, 1074 a 33-8.

[40] *Metaph.*, 1036 a 2-6.

[41] *Metaph.*, 1049 b 5.

[42] *Metaph.*, 1051 a 20-1.

[43] *Metaph.*, 1051 a 17-18.

[44] *Metaph.*, 985 a 9-10.

[45] For a discussion of potentiality and act, cf. *Metaph.*, Δ, 12 and Θ.

[46] *De Caelo*, 311 a 1-6.

[47] *Metaph.*, H, 1044 a 36-b 11. Cf. *Physics*, B, 7, 198 a 24 ff.

[48] *De Caelo*, A 4, 271 a 33.

[49] *Anal. Post.*, 94 b 27-31. Cf. *De Gen. An.*, 743 b 16 f.

[50] *De Gen. An.*, 778 a 16-b 19; 789 b 19 f. *De Part. An.*, 642 a 2; 677 a 17-19.   [51] *Metaph.*, 1049 b 24 ff.

[52] For First Mover, see *Metaph.*, Δ and *Physics*, Θ, 6, 258 b 10 f.

[53] *Physics*, 258 b 11; 259 a 6-13; 259 b 28-31. (Jaeger thinks that these three passages are later additions, but as it is only in the third passage that A. assumes the actual existence of a plurality of unmoved movers, Ross [*Physics*, pp. 101-2] reasonably concludes that this passage alone was added after the completion of *Metaph.*, Λ).

[54] *Metaph.*, Λ 8.

[55] *Metaph.*, 1074 a 31-8.   [56] *Metaph.*, Λ 9, 1074 b 33-5.

[57] *In Met.*, xii, lect. xi: *Nec tamen sequitur quod omnia alia a se ei sunt ignota; nam intelligendo se intelligit omnia alia.*

[58] Ross, *Aristotle*, p. 184.

[59] *In De Caelo*, A 4, 271 a 33. Aristotle says that God and nature do nothing in vain, but he had not yet elaborated his theory of the Unmoved Mover.   [60] *Metaph.*, Λ 7.

[61] *Eth. Nic.*, e.g. 1170 b 8 ff. and 1179 a 24-5. Cf. *Eth. Nic.*, 1179 a 24-5.

[62] *M.M.*, 1208 b 26-32.   [63] Frag. 14. (Rose.)   [64] Frag. 15. (Rose.)

[65] *Metaph.*, 993 b 23-31. Cf. 1008 b 31-1009 a 5.

[66] St. Thomas, *Summa Theologica*, 1a, q., 2, art. 3, in corp.

CHAPTER THIRTY

[1] *Physics*, B 1, 192 b 13 ff.

[2] Aristotle's words in *Physics*, H 1, 241 b 39 ff. and Θ 4, 254 b 7 ff., may seem to be somewhat ambiguous. He says that whatever is moved is moved by something, either by itself or by something else,

not that every moving thing is moved by something else; but the discussion that follows these words, when understood in the light of his principle of the priority of act to potency and in the light of his arguments for the existence of the Unmoved Mover shows clearly enough that in his eyes no moving thing can be the *absolute* initiator of motion. Whatever initiates motion *absolutely* must be itself *unmoved*. Whether there is a plurality of unmoved movers or not is, of course, another question. The principle, however, is clear.

³ *Physics*, 254 b 33-256 a 3. Cf. *De Caelo*, 311 a 9-12.

⁴ *Physics*, E 2, 226 a 24 ff.; Θ 7, 260 a 26 ff.

⁵ *Physics*, Δ 1, 208 a 27 ff.   ⁸ *Physics*, 215 a 14 ff.; 266 b 27 ff.

⁶ *Physics*, Δ 4, 212 a 20 ff.   ⁹ *Physics*, Δ 10 11, 218 a 30 ff.

⁷ *Physics*, Δ 4, 212 a 19-20.

¹⁰ *Physics*, Δ 11, 219 b 1-2 ff.; 220 a 24-5 ff.

¹¹ Cf. Ross, *Physics*, p. 65.   ¹⁵ Ross, *Physics*, p. 69.

¹² *Physics*, 223 a 29-224 a 2.   ¹⁶ *Physics*, 5, 204 a 34-206 a 7.

¹³ *Physics*, 223 a 21-9.   ¹⁷ *Physics*, 204 b 7-10.

¹⁴ Ross, *Physics*, p. 68.   ¹⁸ *Physics*, 206 a 9 ff.

¹⁹ *De Caelo*, A 4, 217 a 33.ὁ θεὸς καὶ ἡ φύσις οὐδὲν μάτην ποιοῦσιν.

²⁰ *De Gen. An.*, 767 b 13-23.

²¹ *Physics*, B, 4-6. Cf. *Metaph.*, E, 2-3.

²² Cf. *Metaph.*, Δ, 8.   ²⁴ *De An.*, 402 a 10 ff.

²³ *De An.*, 402 a 1-9.   ²⁵ *De An.*, 412 a.

²⁶ Aristotle insists that the soul is badly defined if it is assigned motion as its characteristic. The soul moves actively but does not itself move. This is against the Platonic doctrine of the soul as a self-moving entity. Cf. *De An.*, A, 3.   ²⁷ *De An.*, B 3.

²⁸ *De An.*, 3, 427 b 29 ff.; *Rhet.*, A 11, 1370 a 28-31; *De Mem.*, 1; *Anal. Post.*, B 19, 99 b 36 ff.   ²⁹ *De An.*, 3, 12. Cf. *De Sensu*, 1.

³⁰ *De Gen. et Corrupt.*, B 3, 738 b 27 ff.

³¹ *De An.*, 3, 5, 430 a 17 ff.   ³⁴ *De An.*, 3, 5, 430 a 17 ff.

³² *De An.*, 414 a 19 ff.   ³⁵ *Aristotle*, p. 153.

³³ Ross, *Aristotle*, p. 132.   ³⁶ *De An.*, 408 b 24-30.

³⁷ St. Thomas Aquinas, in his Commentary on Aristotle's *De Anima* (3, lect. 10), does not interpret Aristotle in the Averroistic sense, i.e. as denying individual immortality. The active intellect is essentially and only an *active* principle: hence it is unaffected by passions and emotions and is not retentive of *species*. The separated human reason cannot, therefore, function as it does in the state of union with the body, and the mode of its functioning after death is not treated by Aristotle in the *De Anima*; but this omission does not mean that Aristotle denied individual immortality or condemned the separated intellect to a state of enforced and absolute inactivity.

CHAPTER THIRTY-ONE

¹ *E.N.*, 1094 a 1-3.

² *E.N.*, 1094 a 27-b 11. Cf. *M.M.*, 1181 a and b.

³ *E.N.*, 1094 b 11-27. Cf. *E.E.*, I, 6.

⁴ In the *Eudemian Ethics* Aristotle says that we start with "true but obscure judgments" (1216 b 32 ff.) or "the first confused judg-

ments" (1217 a 18 ff.), and go on to form clear ethical judgments. In other words Aristotle starts with the ordinary moral judgments of men as the basis of argument.

[5] *E.N.*, 1094 b 27 ff.   [6] *E.N.*, A 4 and ff.

[7] *E.N.*, 1100 a 4 ff.; 1101 a 14-20.

[8] Aristotle remarks that the truly happy man must be sufficiently equipped with external goods. He thus rejects extreme Cynicism, but he warns us (cf. *E.E.*, 1214 b 25 f.) not to mistake indispensable conditions of happiness for essential elements of happiness.

[9] *E.N.*, B 1, 1103 a 14-b 26; B 4, 1105 a 17-b 18.

[10] Aristotle thus insists that a completely right action must be not only "externally" the right thing to do in the circumstances, but also done from a right motive, proceeding from a moral agent acting precisely as a moral agent. (Cf. *E.N.*, 1105 b 5 ff.).

[11] *E.N.*, B, 6 ff.   [12] *E.N.*, 1106 b 36-1107 a 2.

[13] *Ethics*, by Nicolai Hartmann, vol. 2, p. 256. (Trans., Dr. Stanton Coit; George Allen & Unwin, Ltd.)

[14] Hartmann, *Ethics*, 2, p. 424.   [15] *E.N.*, e.g. 1102 b 14 ff.

[15] *E.N.*, Γ 1, 1100 a 8-19.   [19] *E.N.*, H.

[16] *E.N.*, Γ 1, 1110 b 24-7.   [20] *E.N.*, 1139 b 4-5.

[17] *E.N.*, Γ 1110 b 18 ff.   [21] *E.N.*, 1113 a 9-11.

[22] *E.N.*, e.g. 1111 b 26 ff. But cf. e.g. 1144 a 20 ff.

[23] *E.N.*, 1106 a 36-b 4.

[24] The conception of a man claiming honour from others as a due to his "virtue" and nobility is somewhat repugnant to us, but it was a lineal descendant of the Homeric hero's expectation of honour as due to his ἀρετή.

[25] *E.N.*, 1124 b 9-1125 a 16.

Sir David Ross gives the following tabulation of the moral virtues as treated by Aristotle. (*Aristotle*, p. 203.)

Feeling	Action	Excess	Mean	Defect
Fear Confidence }		{ Cowardice { Rashness	Courage Courage	Unnamed Cowardice
Certain pleasures of touch		Profligacy	Temperance	Insensibility
(Pain arising from desire of such pleasures)	Giving of money } Taking of money }	{ Prodigality { Illiberality	Liberality Liberality	Illiberality Prodigality
	Giving of money on large scale	Vulgarity	Magnificence	Meanness
	Claiming of honour on large scale	Vanity	Self-respect	Humility
	Pursuit of honor on small scale	Ambition	Unnamed	Unambition
Anger		Irascibility	Gentleness	Unirascibility
Social Intercourse {	Telling truth about oneself	Boastfulness	Truthfulness	Self-depreciation
	Giving of pleasure: By way of amusement	Buffoonery	Wittiness	Boorishness
	in life generally	Obsequiousness	Friendliness	Sulkiness
Shame		Bashfulness	Modesty	Shamelessness
Pains at good fortune of others or bad for-		Envy	Righteous Indignation	Malevolence

²⁶ *E.N.*, 1133 b 30-2.   ²⁷ *E.N.*, 1133 b 32 ff.

²⁸ *E.N.*, E, 8, 1135 a 15-36 a 9. Cf. *Rhet.*, 1374 a 26-b 22.

²⁹ *E.N.*, 1137 b 26-7.   ⁴⁵ *E.N.*, 1105 b 12-18.

³⁰ *E.N.*, 1139 b 31-2.   ⁴⁶ *E.N.*, 1174 a 7-8.

³¹ *E.N.*, Z, 6, 1140 b 31-1141 a 8.   ⁴⁷ *E.N.*, 1173 b 20-31.

³² *E.N.*, 1141 a 9-2.   ⁴⁸ *E.N.*, 1173 b 16-19.

³³ *E.N.*, 1141 a 33-b 3.   ⁴⁹ *E.N.*, 1172 a 19-25.

³⁴ *E.N.*, 1140 a 9-10, 20-21.   ⁵⁰ *E.N.*, 1176 a 22-9.

³⁵ *E.N.*, 1140 b 4-6.   ⁵¹ *E.N.*, 1155 a 3-5.

³⁶ *E.N.*, 1141 b 14-22.   ⁵² *E.N.*, 1169 a 27-30.

³⁷ *E.N.*, 1144 b 19-21.   ⁵³ *E.N.*, 1166 a 30-2.

³⁸ *E.N.*, 1144 b 26-8.   ⁵⁴ *E.N.*, 1159 a 27-8.

³⁹ *E.N.*, 1145 a 2-6.   ⁵⁵ *E.N.*, 1157 b 31-2.

⁴⁰ *E.N.*, 1144 a 23 ff.   ⁵⁶ *E.N.*, 1156 a 10-12.

⁴¹ *E.N.*, 1144 a 13 ff.   ⁵⁷ *E.N.*, 1156 a 31-3.

⁴² *E.N.*, 1144 b 32-45 a 2.   ⁵⁸ *E.N.*, 1157 b 28-31.

⁴³ *E.E.*, 1216 b 3-26.   ⁵⁹ *E.N.*, 1156 b 31-2.

⁴⁴ *M.M.*, 1183 b 15-16.

God, says Aristotle, does not need a friend, since "the deity is his own well-being," but we need a friend or friends, since "with us welfare involves a something beyond us." (*E.E.*, 1245 b 14-19.)

⁶⁰ *E.N.*, 1177 a 12-13.   ⁶² *E.N.*, 1177 b 26-1178 a 8.

⁶¹ *E.N.*, K, 7.   ⁶³ *Metaph.*, 1005 b 1-2, 1026 a 18-19.

⁶⁴ Cf. e.g. *Metaph.*, 1069 a 30 ff., where Aristotle says that physics has to do not only with eternal objects, but also with perishable sensible objects.

⁶⁵ *E.E.*, 1249 b 20. I have already mentioned (when treating of Aristotle's metaphysics) the philosopher's dictum in the *Magna Moralia* (1208 b 26-32) that there can be no question of friendship towards God, since, even if it were possible for us to love Him, He could not return our love.

⁶⁶ Cf. e.g. *Summa Theologica*, Ia, q. 26, art. 2.

CHAPTER THIRTY-TWO

¹ *Pol.*, 1252 b 13-14.   ⁴ *Pol.*, 1253 a 1-4.   ⁶ *Pol.*, 1254 a 23-4.

² *Pol.*, 1252 b 28 ff.   ⁵ *Pol.*, 1253 a 27-9.   ⁷ *Pol.*, 1255 a 1-3.

³ *Pol.*, 1252 a 8-23.

⁸ *Pol.*, cf. 1255 b 9-15, 1278 b 33-8. (In 1260 b 5-7 Aristotle criticises Plato's notion that masters should not converse with their slaves.)   ⁹ *Pol.*, 1330 a 32-3.

¹⁰ *Pol.*, 1254 b 32-4, 1255 a 3-28.   ¹³ *Pol.*, 1264 b 15-23.

¹¹ *Pol.*, 1256 a ff. (A, 8-11).   ¹⁴ *Pol.*, cf. 1277 b.

¹² *Pol.*, 1262 a 13-14.   ¹⁵ *Pol.*, 1275 b 18-19.

¹⁶ *Pol.*, cf. 1277 a 33-1278 a 15, 1328 b 33-1329 a 21.

¹⁷ *Pol.*, 1279 a 17-21.

¹⁸ *Pol.*, 1288 a 12-15.   ²³ *Pol.*, 1326 b 25-1327 b 18.

¹⁹ Cf. *Athen. Polit.*, 28 and 33.   ²⁴ *Pol.*, 1328 b 2-1331 b 23.

²⁰ *Pol.*, 1295 b 1-1296 a 21.   ²⁵ *Pol.*, 1332 b-1333 a 16.

²¹ *Pol.*, Bk. 5.   ²⁶ *Pol.*, 1340 b 29-31.

²² *Pol.*, 1325 b 33-1326 b 24.   ²⁷ *Pol.*, 1333 b 37.

CHAPTER THIRTY-THREE

[1] 896 b 10-28.   [4] 1078 a 31-2.   [6] 1450 b 40-1.
[2] 1078 a 31-b 6.   [5] 1078 a 36-b 1.   [7] 1449 a 32-4.
[3] 1366 a 33-6.

[8] CF. "Beautiful art shows its superiority in this, that it describes as beautiful things which may be in nature ugly or displeasing." Kant, *Critique of Judgment*, I. 1, 48.   [9] *Physics*, B 8, 199 a 15 ff.

[10] *Poetics*, 1448 a 16-18.   [14] 919 b 26.
[11] *Poetics*, 1448 b 10-19.   [15] 1447 a 26-8.
[12] *Poetics*, 1451 b 5-8.   [16] 1338 a 17-19.
[13] 1448 a 5-6.   [17] 1340 b 10-13.

[18] *A History of Aesthetic*, p. 63.

[19] Aristotle certainly regarded the giving of enjoyment as one of the functions of tragedy. The question is, how far was this enjoyment specifically aesthetic in character?   [20] *Poetics*, 1449 b 25-9.

[21] 1449 b 12-14.   [23] *Poetics*, 1450 a 17-26.
[22] *Poetics*, 1450 a 4-16.   [24] *Poetics*, 1451 b 32-5.

[25] Ross, *Aristotle*, p. 282. On this subject see e.g. *Aristotle's Theory of Poetry and Fine Art*, by S. H. Butcher (Macmillan); *Aristotle on the Art of Poetry*, by Ingram Bywater (Oxford).

[26] *Pol.*, 1341 a 17 ff.
[27] *Pol.*, 1342 a 1-16.   [32] Porph., Περὶ ἀποχῆς ἐμψύχων.
[28] *Crit. Hist.*, p. 331.   [33] Cic., *Tusc.*, 1, 10, 19.
[29] *Poetics*, 1449 a 9-30.   [34] Cic., *Tusc.*, 1, 10, 21; 31, 77.
[30] Simplic. *Phys.*, 411, 14.   [35] Cic., *Ad Att.*, 2, 16, 3.
[31] Diog. Laërt., 5, 36.   [36] Diog. Laërt., 5, 80-1.

CHAPTER THIRTY-FIVE

[1] Cf. Ueberweg-Praechter, pp. 32-3.

CHAPTER THIRTY-SIX

[1] Diog. Laërt., 7, 2 and 31.   [4] Plut., *Cat. Mai.*, 22.
[2] Diog. Laërt., 7, 2.   [5] Diog. Laërt., 7, 41-2.
[3] Diog. Laërt., 7, 183.
[6] Sext. Emp., *Pyrr. Hyp.*, 2, 105; *Adv. Math.*, 8, 449.
[7] Sext. Emp., *Adv. Math.*, 7, 254 ff.
[8] Pope, *Essay on Man*, I, 267.   [10] Plut., *De Comm. Notit.*, 1073 e.
[9] Cic., *Acad. Post.*, 1, 11, 39. [11] Cic., *Acad. Prior.*, 2, 41, 126.
[12] Apud Gellium, *Noctes Atticae*, 6, 1.

[13] An act, i.e. a human act, one proceeding from the free will of the human agent, is *materialiter* (or *objectively*) good or evil, in so far as it is objectively in conformity with, or not in conformity with, right reason, with the objective Natural Law. The agent's conscious intention cannot alter the objective or material character of a human act, even though, in the case of an objectively evil act, it may excuse him from formal moral fault.

[14] Plut., *De Stoic. Repugn.*, 1051 c.
[15] Plut., *De Comm. Notit.*, 1065 d; Marcus Aurel., *To Himself*, VI, 42.

[16] Trans. by Dr. James Adam, quoted in Hicks' *Stoic and Epicurean*, pp. 14-16 (Longmans, 1910).   [17] Seneca, Frag. 17.
[18] Plut., *De Stoic. Repugn.*, c. 9 (1035 a 1-f 22).
[19] Diog. Laërt., 7, 86 ff.
[20] Von Arnim, *Stoic. Vet. Frag.*, Vol. I, pp. 59-60. (Pearson, pp. 210 ff.)   [21] Cf. Origen, *c. Cels*, 4, 45 (*P.G.*, 11, 1101).
[22] Frag. 91. (Pearson, *The Fragments of Zeno and Cleanthes*, 1891.)   [23] Seneca, *Ep.*, 107, 11.   [24] Diog. Laërt., 7, 89.
[25] Von Arnim, I, 529, p. 119 (i.e. Sext. Empir., *Adv. Math.*, 9, 90, of Cleanthes).   [26] Seneca, *Nat. Quaest.*, III, Praef., 10-17.

CHAPTER THIRTY-SEVEN

[1] Diog. Laërt., 10, 14.
[2] Cic., *De Nat. D.*, I, 26, 73; Diog. Laërt., 10, 8.
[3] Diog. Laërt., 10, 2.   [4] Diog. Laërt., 10, 12.
[5] Frag. 24. (Metrodori Epicurei Fragmenta, A. Körte, 1890.) But cf. Sext. Emp., *Adv. Math.*, 1, 49.   [6] Diog. Laërt., 10, 146.
[7] Cf. *De Rerum Nat.*, IV, 478-99.
[8] Diog. Laërt., 10, 86.   [12] Diog. Laërt., 10, 38-9.
[9] Diog. Laërt., 10, 33.   [13] *De Rerum Nat.*, I, 265-6.
[10] Diog. Laërt., 10, 31.   [14] Diog. Laërt., 10, 39-40.
[11] Diog. Laërt., 10, 139.   [15] *De Rerum Nat.*, III, 18-22.
[16] *De Rerum Nat.*, V, 1198-1203.
[17] *Georgics*, II, 490-2.   [18] Diog. Laërt., 10, 129.
[19] Diog. Laërt., 10, 128 and 129.   [22] Diog. Laërt., 10, 118.
[20] Diog. Laërt., 10, 129 and 131-2.   [23] Cic., *Tusc.*, 2, 7, 17.
[21] Diog. Laërt., 10, 141.   [24] Diog. Laërt., 10, 131.
[25] Diog. Laërt., 10; Maxims, 5, 17, 37, 42.
[26] Diog. Laërt., 10, 154.
[27] Diog. Laërt., 10, 132.   [28] Diog. Laërt., 10, 148.

CHAPTER THIRTY-EIGHT

[1] Diog. Laërt., 9, 61.   [4] *Adv. Math.*, 1, 53.
[2] Diog. Laërt., Proem., 16.   [5] Cic., *Acad. Post.*, I, 12, 45.
[3] Diog. Laërt., Proem., 16; 9, 102.   [6] Cic., *de Orat.*, 3, 18, 67.
[7] Cf. Sext. Emp., *Adv. Math.*, 7, 159 and 166 ff.; Cic., *Acad. Prior.*, 2, 30, 98 ff.
[8] Cf. Sext. Emp., *Adv. Math.*, 9, 13 ff.; Cic., *De Nat. D.*, 3, 17, 44; 3, 29 ff.
[9] Cic., *Acad. Prior.*, 2, 22, 69; Numenius cited by Euseb., *Prep. Evang.*, 614, 9, 2 (*P.G.* 21, 1216-17); Aug., *contra Acad.*, 2, 6, 15; 3, 18, 41.   [10] Cic., *Acad. Prior.*, 2, 43, 132.
[11] *De Civit. Dei*, 6, 4.   [12] *Ad. Att.*, 12, 52, 3.
[13] *De Fin.*, 5, 32, 95; *De Off.*, 3, 3, 11; cf. *De Fin.*, 5, 26, 77 ff., and *Tusc.*, 5, 13, 39 ff.
[14] *Tusc.*, 4, 18, 41 ff.   [18] *De Nat. D.*, 2, 37, 93.
[15] *Tusc.*, 4, 6, 11; 4, 21, 47.   [19] *Tusc.*, 1, 26, 65; 4, 33, 71.
[16] *De Off.*, 1, 44, 158.   [20] *Tusc.*, 1, 12, 26 ff.; 1, 49, 117 ff.
[17] *Acad. Prior.*, 2, 41, 127.   [21] *De Fin.*, 2, 14, 45.

CHAPTER THIRTY-NINE

[1] Ad. Att., 16, 11, 4.
[2] Cic., Tusc., 1, 32, 79.
[3] Cic., De Div., 1, 3, 6.
[4] St. Aug., De Civit. Dei, 4, 27.
[8] Cic., De Div., 1, 49, 110; 1, 57, 129-30.
[9] Cic., De Div., 1, 49, 110; 1, 55, 125.
[10] Cf. Seneca, Epist., 90; Lucr., De Rerum Nat., V.
[11] Simplic., Phys., 965, 16 a.
[12] Plut., de sol. animal., 3 (961 a).
[13] C.A.G., 11/1, 4; 30 and 6 : 8.
[14] Eunap., Vit. Soph., II.

[5] Outlines, p. 249.
[6] Cic., De Nat. D., 2, 33 ff.
[7] Cf. Plat. Tim., 31 b c.

CHAPTER FORTY

[1] Ep., 75, 5.
[2] Ep., 88, 36.
[7] Nat. Q., 6, 4.
[9] Ep., 120, 14; 65, 16. Cf. Dies iste, quem tamquam extremum reformidas, aeterni natalis est. Ep., 102, 26.
[10] Ep., 62, 3.
[12] Does he not himself admit, Non de me loquor, qui multum ab homine tolerabili nedum a perfecto absum? Ep., 57, 3.

[3] Ep., 88, 2.
[4] Ep., 71, 6.

[5] Ep., 73, 13.
[6] Nat. Q., 6, 32.
[8] Ep., 66, 12; 117, 2; 57, 8.

[11] Cf. Dion Cassius, 61, 10.

[13] Ep., 116, 7.
[14] Ep., 73, 15; 43, 5.
[15] Ep., 90, 46.
[16] Ep., 75, 8.
[17] De Ira, 3, 36, 3.
[18] Ep., 78, 16, 4.
[19] Ep., 48, 2.
[33] Disc., 3, 2; cf. 1, ch. 18 (end).
[34] Disc., 4, 11, 25.
[35] Ench., 24.
[36] Ench., 31.
[41] Ueberweg-Praechter, p. 498, Note.
[42] Med., 1, 7.
[43] Med., 7, 26.
[44] Med., 7, 22.
[50] Capitol, Vit. M. Ant., 3, 3.
[52] Med., 5, 27.
[55] Med., 4, 14; 4, 43; 5, 23.

[20] De Vita Beata, 24, 3.
[21] Fr. 114.
[22] Disc., 4, 1, 22.
[23] Disc., 3, 1, 8.
[24] Disc., 3, 6, 8.
[25] Disc., 1, 22.
[26] Ibid.
[37] Disc., 1, 12.
[38] Cf. Disc., 3, 22; 3, 26, 67.
[39] Disc., 1, 13.
[40] Stob., Flor., 20, 61.
[45] Med., 9, 42.
[46] Med., 7, 31.
[47] Med., 4, 23.
[53] Med., 2, 11.

[27] Ibid.
[28] Disc., 1, 29.
[29] Ibid.
[30] Disc., 4, 9, 16.
[31] Disc., 4, 9, 13.
[32] Disc., 1, 30.

[48] Med., 5, 27.
[49] Med., 12, 1.

[51] Med., 2, 13 : 11, 20; 9, 1.
[54] Med., 9, 3; 11, 3.
[56] Med., 4, 21.

CHAPTER FORTY-ONE

[1] Philostr., Apoll. Tyan., 4, 8; 4, 31.
[2] Tac., Hist., 3, 81.
[3] Epict., Disc., 1, 25.
[6] Suet., Vesp., 13; Dion Cass., 66, 13; Luc., De Morte Peregr., c. 18.
[7] Cf. Dio. Cass., 66, 15.
[8] De Morte Peregr., 4; 20 ff.

[4] Tac., Ann., 16, 34.
[5] E.g. Or., 32, 9.

[9] Cf. Demonax (Lucian).
[10] Demonax, 11.

[11] Julian, *Or.*, 7, 209.   [14] Philostr., *Vit. Soph.*, 1, 7.

[12] *Or.*, 33.   [15] Cf. *Or.*, 1-4.

[13] *Or.*, 32.

[16] *Or.*, 12, 61. ὥσπερ νήπιοι παῖδες πατρὸς ἢ μητρὸς ἀπεσπασμένοι δεινὸν ἵμερον ἔχοντες καὶ πόθον ὀρέγουσι χεῖρας . . .

[17] Greg., *Adv. Maxim.*, P.G., 37, 1339 ff.

[18] Diog. Laërt., *Proem.*, 21.   [19] Sen., *Ep.*, 108, 17.

[20] Sext. Emp., *Pyrr. Hyp.*, 1, 36 ff.

[21] Sext. Emp., *Pyrr. Hyp.*, 1, 164 ff.

[22] Sext. Emp., *Pyrr. Hyp.*, 1, 178 ff.

[23] Sext. Emp., *Pyrr. Hyp.*, 2, 190 ff.

[24] Sext. Emp., *Adv. Math.*, 9, 207 ff. Cf. 8, 453 ff.

[25] Sext. Emp., *Adv. Math.*, 9, 148 ff.

[26] Sext. Emp., *Pyrr. Hyp.*, 3, 9 ff.

[27] Sext. Emp., *Pyrr. Hyp.*, 1, 3; 1, 226; *Adv. Math.*, 7, 435 ff.

CHAPTER FORTY-TWO

[1] See Note on Apoll. Tyana, pp. 193-194.

[2] *Adv. Math.*, 10, 281 ff.

[3] Clem. Alex., *Strom.*, 1, 22, 148. (*P.G.*, 8, 895.)

[4] Cf. Plato, *Ep.*, 2.   [5] Procl. *in Tim.*, I, 303, 27 ff.

[6] Chalcid., *in Tim.*, c. 295.

[7] Cf. Ed. Meyer, *Hermes*, 197, pp. 371 ff.

[8] Orig., *Contra Celsum*, 6, 41 (*P.G.*, 11, 1357).

[9] Dion Cass., 77, 18.   [11] Lamprid., *Aurel.*, 24.

[10] Lamprid., *Alex.*, 29.   [12] Ed. Boissonade, p. 500, Didot.

[13] *Rerum gest.*, 21, 14, 5.

[14] Lact., *Div. Inst.*, V, 3; *P.L.* 6, 556 ff.

[15] St. Jerome, in Ps. 81 (*P.L.* 26, 1130).

[16] Cf. *Ep.*, 136, I; 102, 32; 138, 18.

[17] *Ep.*, 8, 3; ed. Mohr, p. 173.

CHAPTER FORTY-THREE

[1] The tetralogic arrangement of the Platonic Dialogues was attached to the name of Thrasyllus, the court-astronomer of Tiberius, who joined the Platonic School.

[2] Suid., Πλούταρχος.   [4] *De Is. et Osir.*, 78.

[3] *De Is. et Osir.*, 77.   [5] *De Is. et Osir.*, 26.

[6] *Non p. suav.*, 28 ff.; *De ser. num. vind.*, 18.

[7] *De anim. procr.*, 4 ff.

[8] *De def. orac.*, 32 ff., 37; cf. Plat., *Tim.*, 31 a b, 34 b, 55 cd, where Plato opts for one world.   [9] *Didaskalikos*, 164, 21 ff.

[10] *Didask.*, 163-4.   [12] *Diss.*, 17, 11: 11, 2 and 7.

[11] *Didask.*, 169, 26 ff.   [13] *Diss.*, 14, 8.

CHAPTER FORTY-FOUR

[1] *Ant. Jud.*, 13, 5, 9.

[2] Consideration of the question, What influence was exercised by Greek speculation on Jewish Apocryphal writings and even on certain books of the O.T. itself, is here omitted.

[3] Cf. Euseb., *Hist. Eccles.*, 2, 18. References to the works of Philo are given according to the edition of Leopold Cohen and Paul Wendland, Berlin (Vol. 6, Cohen and Reiter).

[4] Cf. *De migrat. Abrah.*, 16, 92.

[5] Cf. *De post. Caini*, 48, 167; *Leg. alleg.*, 2, 1, 2 f.; *De Mutat nom.*, 4, 27.

[6] *De conf. ling.*, 27, 136; *De somniis*, I, 11; 63.

[7] *De opif. mundi.*, 2, 8.   [10] *Leg. alleg.*, 3, 61, 175.

[8] Frag. a 654.   [11] *De opif. mundi.*, 4, 17 ff.

[9] *De post. Caini*, 48, 167.

[12] *Quod Deus sit immut.*, 7, 34; cf. *De vita Mos.*, 2 (3), 13, 127.

[13] *De opif. mundi.*, 6, 25.

[14] On this subject, cf. Jules Lebreton, S.J., *Histoire du Dogme de la Trinité.* (Beauchesne, 1910.)

[15] Ueb.-P., p. 577.   [16] E.g. *De somn.*, 123, 149.

[17] *De opif. mundi.*, 50, 144; *De human.*, 23, 168.

[18] Cf. *Quis rer. div. her.*, 14, 68 ff.; *De gigant.*, II, 52 f.

[19] It is probable, however, that Origen's habit of allegorising is due in large measure to Philo.

CHAPTER FORTY-FIVE

[1] Eunap., *Vit. Soph.*, 6; Porph., *Isag.*, 12b; Suid., *Plot.*

[2] "Ἔτυχε δὲ τετράκις που, ὅτε συνήμην αὐτῷ, τοῦ σκόπου, ἐνεργείᾳ ἀρρήτῳ, καὶ οὐ δυνάμει. *Plotini Vita*, 23, 138.

[3] *Enn.*, 5, 4, 1 (516 b-c).   [6] Cf. *Rep.*, 509 b 9.

[4] *Enn.*, 3, 8, 9 (352 b).   [7] *Enn.*, 6, 8, 9 (743 e).

[5] *Enn.*, 3, 8, 8 (351 d).   [8] *Enn.*, 6, 7, 38.

[9] *Enn.*, 3, 8, 8.' Ἐι οὖν τοῦτο νοῦν ἐγγένησεν, ἁπλούστερον νοῦ δεῖ αὐτὸ εἶναι (351 c).

[10] *Enn.*, 4, 8, 6 (474 b-c). The assertion that the prior Principle is not stayed by jealousy is an echo of Plato's words in the *Timaeus*. Plotinus' comparison of the One or the Good with the sun is a development of the comparison already given by Plato in the *Republic*. The view of God as the uncreated Light and of creatures as participated lights, hierarchically ordered according to their degree of luminosity, which we find in some Christian philosophers comes from Neo-Platonism.

[11] *Enn.*, 5, 7, 1 ff.

[12] *Enn.*, 5, 9, 9. ἀναγκαῖον καὶ ἐν νῷ τὸ ἀρχέτυπον πᾶν εἶναι, καὶ κόσμον νοητὸν τοῦτον τὸν τοῦν εἶναι, ὃν φησὶν ὁ Πλάτων, ἐν τῷ δ ἐστι ζῷον.

[13] *Enn.*, 5, 1, 4. ὁ ὄντως αἰὼν ὁ μιμεῖται χρόνος περιθέων ψυχὴν (485 b).

[14] *Enn.*, 3, 8, 3. ἡ λεγομένη φύσις ψυχὴ οὖσα γέννημα ψυχῆς προτέρας. (345 e).

[15] *Enn.*, 4, 3, 10; 5, 9, 3; 5, 9, 9; 2, 3, 17.

[16] *Enn.*, 3, 5, 4. οὔκ ἀποτετμημένη, ἐμπεριεχομένη δέ, ὡς εἶναι πάσας μίαν.   [17] *Enn.*, 4, 3, 5 (375 c-f).   [18] *Enn.*, 2, 4; 3, 67; 6, 3, 7.

[19] *Enn.*, 2, 4, 6 (162 c-e).   [20] *Enn.*, 1, 8, 9 (79 a b).

[21] *Enn.*, 2, 4, 4-5; 3, 5, 6 (ὕλην δεῖ νοητὴν ὑποθέσθαι, 296 e).

[22] *Enn.*, 2, 9, 4 (202 d-e).

[23] Procl., *in Plat. Tim.*, I, 306, 1 ff.   [25] *Enn.*, 1, 2, 1.

[24] *Enn.*, 4, 8, 8 (476 a-d).   [26] *Enn.*, 1, 3, 4.

[27] *Enn.*, 6, 9, 9 (768 f-769 a); 6, 9, 10 (769 d). (Professor Dodds' translation.)

[28] *Enn.*, 6, 9, 7 (765 c).   [29] *Enn.*, 6, 9, 7 (766 a).

[30] *Enn.*, 6, 9, 11 (771 b). (Professor Dodds' translation.)

[31] *Iliad*, 2, 140.

[32] *Enn.*, 1, 6, 8 (56 g). (Professor Dodds' translation.)

[60] Procl., in *Plat. Tim.*, I, 306, 1 ff.   [33] *Ad Marc.*, 16.

[34] *Ad Marcellam*, 29.   [36] *Ad Marc.*, 17.

[37] *De Civit. Dei.*, 10, 28. (P. knew Origen while a youth. Euseb., *Hist. Eccl.*, 6, 19, 5.)

[38] *Hist. Eccl.*, 3, 23, (*P.G.*, 67, 445).

[39] "Obscurity, incoherence, illogicality, lying, abuse of confidence and stupidity, Porphyry saw scarcely anything else in Christianity, to judge by the *membra disiecta* of his work." (Pierre de Labriolle, *La Réaction Païenne*, p. 286, 1934.)

CHAPTER FORTY-SIX

[1] ἡ πάντη ἄρρητος ἀρχή Damasc., *Dubit.*, 43.

[2] Procl., *in Tim.*, 1308, 21 d.

[3] Procl., *in Tim.*, 1308, 21 ff. d. Damasc., *Dubit.*, 54.

[4] Julian, *Or.*, 4.

[5] In his commentary on Euclid I Proclus gives much valuable information concerning Platonic, Aristotelian, Neo-Platonic and other positions in mathematical philosophy (ed. Friedlein, Leipzig, 1873).

[6] *Instit. Theol.*, 30 ff.; *Theol. Plat.*, 2, 4; 3, 14; 4, 1.

[7] *Instit. Theol.*, 4, 6; *Theol. Plat.*, 2, 4.

[8] *Instit. Theol.*, 11.   [9] *Theol. Plat.*, 3, 14; 4, 1.

[10] *Theol. Plat.*, 1, 17; in *Remp.*, I, 37, 27 ff.

[11] *Instit. Theol.*, 27.   [12] *In Alcib.*, III; *de Prov.*, 24.

[13] *Dubit.*, 38, I 79, 20 ff.; 41, I 83, 26 ff.; 42, I 85, 8 ff.; 107, I 278, 24 f.

[14] Phot., 460 b 23 ff.; 461 b 6 ff.   [15] Phot., 465 a 16 ff.

[16] As this work contains extracts from other dialogues of Plato, as well as extracts and texts and opinions from other Greek philosophers, it came about that up to the twelfth century A.D. Chalcidius was regarded as one of the chief sources for a knowledge of Greek philosophy.

[17] As Macrobius introduces into his Commentary ideas on number-symbolism, emanation, the Plotinian gradation of virtues, and even polytheism, the work is "really a syncretic product of Neo-Platonist paganism." (Maurice de Wulf, *Hist. Med. Phil.*, I, p. 79. Trans. E. Messenger, Ph.D., Longmans, 3rd Eng. edit., 1935.)

[18] M. De Wulf, *Hist. Med. Phil.*, I, p. 109.

INDEX

(A small *n* after a number indicates that the reference
is to a note on the page in question.)

Aedesius, II: 220

Aenesidemus, II: 187

Aeschines, I: 124, 135

Aeschylus, I: 55, 117; II: 110

Aëtius, I: 90; II: 254

Agrippa, II: 187–88

Albinus, II: 199, 200, 203, 209

Al Bitrogi, II: 64

Alcidamas, I: 307 *n*. 26

Alexander, Aphrod., II: 71, 72, 170–71

Alexander the Great, II: 10–11, 93, 123, 157

Alexander Severus, II: 193

Alfred, I: 15

Amelius, II: 216

Ammianus Marcellinus, II: 194

Ammonius, II: 196, 225

Ammonius Saccas, II: 207

Anatolius, II: 171

Anaxagoras, I: 66, 82, 83–88, 91–92, 94, 118, 134, 227; II: 32, 230, 232, 239, 246

Anaximander, I: 40–42, 49, 56, 95

Anaximenes, I: 36, 42–44, 57, 68, 79, 80, 92, 93–95; II: 32

Andronicus, II: 12, 15, 170

Androtion, I: 105

Angelico, Fra, I: 15; II: 229

Anniceris, I: 144; II: 155

Antiochus of Ascalon, II: 161, 162, 186, 195

Antiochus Epiphanes, II: 201

Antipater of Tarsus, II: 130, 165

Antiphon, I: 115

Antisthenes, I: 139–41; II: 130

Antoninus Pius, II: 183

Antony, II: 128

Apollodorus, II: 256

Apollonius of Tyana, II: 182, 190, 191, 193–94

Apuleius, II: 200

Aquinas, St. Thomas, I: 15, 16, 20, 21–22, 191, 236, 269, 288; II: 19, 27, 51, 59, 60, 64, 71, 91, 248, 264 *n*. 29, 267 *n*. 37

Arcesilaus, II: 158, 159

Archelaus, I: 118

Archytas, I: 47, 153, 303 *n*. 25

Aristippus, I: 142–44; II: 155

Aristocles, II: 171

Ariston, II: 129, 170

Aristophanes, I: 112, 118, 119, 120, 134

Aristophanes Byz., I: 158

Aristotle, I: 15, 16, 25, 33, 38, 39, 47, 49, 50, 51, 52, 55, 62–63, 64, 66, 69, 70, 74, 81, 84, 85, 88, 89, 90, 91, 92, 93, 95, 97, 115, 120–33 (*passim*, on Socrates), 145, 154–55, 159, 175, 180–83 (on Plato), 188 (on Plato), 192–96 (on Plato), 198, 202 (on Plato), 205 (on Plato), 207–8 (on Plato), 211, 218–21 (on Plato), 228 (on Plato), 249, 269, 272, 274, 276, 287 (last three on Plato), 290, 291, 310 *n*. 8, 313–14 *n*. 47; II: 9–120 (and Plato esp., 35–44, 113–14), 123–24, 130, 132, 161, 165, 169–71, 180, 186, 190, 196, 199, 200, 211, 214, 217, 221, 225, 226–28, 229–50 (*passim*), 255

Aristoxenus, I: 46, 196, 202; II: 111

Arnim, H. von, II: 262 *n*. 20, 271 *n*. 20, 272 *n*. 25

Arrianus, F., II: 172, 175

Asclepiodotus, II: 225

Athanasius, St., II: 205

Athenaeus, I: 158

Atticus, II: 274, 200
Augustine, St., I: 15, 16, 26, 236, 288; II: 41, 71, 127, 133, 136, 194, 208, 218, 227, 247–48, 250, 264 n. 29, 273 n. 4
Aulus Gellius, II: 162, 255
Aurelian, II: 194
Averroes, II: 248, 267 n. 37
Avicenna, II: 30

Bacon, F., I: 15
Bacon, R., I: 15
Beethoven, II: 229
Berenice, II: 183
Bergson, I: 22, 304 n. 11
Berkeley, I: 15; II: 136
Bernays, II: 108
Bias, I: 54
Bion, II: 156
Boethius, II: 217, 228
Bonaventure, St., I: 16, 223; II: 19, 51, 248
Bosanquet, II: 93, 103
Bradley, I: 20; II: 93
Brentano, II: 59
Burnet, I: 43, 46, 51, 55, 68, 70, 85, 86, 87, 89, 107, 111, 117, 121–24, 301 n. 12, 301 n. 2, 308 n. 18, 309 n. 45, 48, 49, 310 n. 1; II: 83
Butcher, S. H., II: 270 n. 25
Bywater, I., II: 270 n. 25

Calderón, I: 33
Caligula, II: 173
Calippus, II: 68
Callicles, I: 115
Callisthenes, II: 11
Calvin, I: 46
Campanella, I: 288
Capella, Martianus, II: 162, 227
Caracalla, II: 193
Carneades, II: 159–61, 238
Cato (elder), II: 130
Celsus, II: 200
Cephisodorus, II: 12
Cercides, II: 156
Chalcidius, II: 227

Chestov, L., I: 303 n. 24
Chosroes, II: 225
Christianity, I: 18, 25, 26, 61, 236, 256–57, 269; II: 71, 124–25, 127, 180, 192, 193–94, 203–6, 208, 216, 218, 220, 225–26, 232, 246–50, 277 n. 10
Chrysippus, II: 129, 130, 132, 134–37, 139, 141, 142, 160
Cicero, I: 90, 143, 311 n. 12, 315 n. 9; II: 12, 146, 158, 161, 162–64, 166, 227, 255
Claudius, II: 173
Claudius Severus, II: 180
Cleanthes, II: 129, 130, 132, 137, 140, 141
Clement, Alex., II: 192
Cleopatra, II: 128
Collingwood, R. G., I: 319 n. 24
Cornford, F. M., I: 272, 308 n. 22, 318 n. 43
Covotti, A., I: 301–2 n. 4, 302 n. 1, 306 n. 11
Crantor, I: 291
Crashaw, I: 223
Crates (Acad.), I: 289
Crates (Cynic), I: 141; II: 129, 182
Cratylus, I: 152
Critolaus, II: 170
Croce, B., I: 319 n. 13
Cromwell, I: 15
Cynics, I: 139–41; II: 77, 124, 129, 156, 162, 170, 179, 182–86, 205
Cyrenaics, I: 142–44; II: 124, 151, 155, 156, 157

Damascius, II: 224–25
Damon, I: 83
Dante, I: 15; II: 229
De Burgh, I: 34
Demetrius (Cynic), II: 183
Demetrius (Perip.), II: 111–12
Demiurge (of Plato), I: 203, 214–18, 225, 235, 273 ff.; II: 33,

Demiurge (*cont'd*)
38, 42–44, 67, 192, 200, 211, 214, 219, 226
Democritus, I: 43, 68, 69, 89–92, 97, 145–47, 212, 271, 273; II: 69, 124, 145, 147, 148, 155, 157, 169, 230
Demonax, II: 184
Descartes, I: 15, 17, 234, 236; II: 71
De Wulf, M., II: 278 *n*. 17, 18
Dicaearchus, II: 111
Diels, H., I: 12; II: 254, 256
Diocletian, II: 194
Diodorus Cronus, I: 138
Diodorus of Tyre, II: 170
Diodotus, II: 162
Diogenes (Apoll.), I: 118, 119
Diogenes (Cynic), I: 140, 141; II: 139, 156, 182
Diogenes Laërt., II: 255 (and *passim* as source)
Diogenes (Seleuc), II: 129
Dion, I: 153, 155–56
Dion Chrysostom, II: 183, 184–85
Dionysius I, I: 142, 153, 155
Dionysius II, I: 155–56
Dionysius (artist), II: 103
Dionysius (Herac.), II: 129
Dionysodorus, I: 116
Dittenberger, I: 160
Domitian, II: 175, 184, 185, 194
Domninus, II: 221
Döring, I: 121
Duns Scotus, I: 15, 16; II: 19

Ecphantus, I: 291
Elizabeth, I: 15
Empedocles, I: 60, 68, 78–82, 84, 90, 91, 94, 113, 118, 145, 272; II: 32, 147, 233
Epicharmus, I: 305 *n*. 1
Epicrates, I: 210
Epictetus, I: 26; II: 172, 175–79, 183, 235
Epicureanism, I: 85, 90, 273; II: 124, 125, 126, 145–56, 235,

238, 241–42
Epicurus, I: 90, 142; II: 145 ff., 156
Eratosthenes, II: 256
Erymneus, II: 170
Essenes, II: 201
Eubulides, I: 138
Euclid of Megara, I: 137–38, 153
Eudemus, II: 18, 110
Eudorus, II: 196
Eudoxus, I: 52, 154, 289, 291; II: 68, 87, 88
Eunapius, II: 194, 207, 220
Euripides, I: 35, 105, 117, 153, 240; II: 105, 107
Eurytus, I: 47, 50
Eusebius, I: 142; II: 218, 262 *n*. 6
Eustochius, II: 208

Fairbanks, A., II: 256
Fichte, I: 19, 160
Field, G. C., I: 123
Frederick the Great, I: 15

Gaius (Caligula), II: 173, 202
Gaius (phil.), II: 199
Galen, II: 171
Gallienus, II: 207
Gellius, II: 162
Gilson, E., I: 20
Goethe, I: 15; II: 19, 229
Gomperz, I: 114
Gordian, II: 207
Gorgias, I: 113–15, 139
Gregory Naz., St., II: 186

Hackforth, R., I: 123–24
Hardie, W. R. F., I: 210, 312 *n*. 14, 313 *n*. 35
Hartmann, N., I: 139, 288, 301 *n*. 4; II: 79–80
Hecataeus, I: 54
Hegel, I: 16, 17, 19–20, 22, 23, 24, 56, 63, 215, 221, 269, 301 *n*. 5, 306 *n*. 12, 307 *n*. 6; II: 32, 38, 43, 93
Hegesias, I: 143–44; II: 155

Heraclides, I: 289, 291
Heraclitus, I: 19, 36, 54–63, 68,
    69–70, 76–77, 93–96, 97, 101,
    109, 167, 168, 174, 226; II:
    32, 124, 132, 133, 155, 168,
    229, 231, 233, 237, 239, 246
Heraclius, II: 226
Herillus, II: 129
Hermann, K., I: 311 n. 17
Hermarchus, II: 146
Hermias, II: 10
Hermodorus, I: 54
Herodotus, I: 30, 38, 105; II:
    102, 145
Heros, II: 183
Hesiod, I: 29–30, 33, 54, 61, 252;
    II: 158
Hierocles, II: 194
Hierocles (Alex.), II: 226
Hipparchia, I: 141
Hippias, I: 113, 132
Hippolytus, II: 255
Hobbes, II: 242
Hölderlin, I: 305 n. 3
Homer, I: 29–30, 47, 48, 54, 56,
    225, 234, 252–53, 279–80; II:
    102, 158, 229, 268 n. 24
Hume, I: 15, 20, 22; II: 189
Hypatia, II: 225, 226

Iamblichus, I: 45; II: 171, 219–
    20, 223, 225, 226, 262 n. 9
Ioannes Philoponus, II: 64, 225,
    226
Isidorus, II: 224
Ismenias, I: 161
Isocrates, I: 114, 154, 160

Jaeger, W., I: 11, 32, 159, 301 n.
    2; II: 14, 17, 58, 262 n. 2, 9, 13
Joel, K., I: 121
John of the Cross, St., I: 223
Josephus, II: 201
Julia Domna, II: 193
Julian, II: 184, 194, 220
Justinian, II: 225, 226

Kant, I: 16, 17, 19–20, 21, 22,
    159, 167, 238; II: 21, 65, 100,

    102, 141, 235, 238
Körte, II: 272 n. 5

Labriolle, P. de, II: 278 n. 39
Laelius, II: 165
Lebreton, J., II: 276 n. 14
Leibniz, I: 237, 240; II: 134, 136
Leon of Salamis, I: 134
Lessing, II: 107
Leucippus, I: 89–92, 95–97, 145,
    147; II: 69, 155, 230, 233
Levy, O., I: 12
Libonius, II: 220
Lindsay, A. D., I: 124
Locke, I: 15, 269; II: 93
Logos, the, esp., I: 59; II: 203–5,
    245–48
Longinus, II: 211
Lucian, II: 156, 183–84
Lucilius, II: 173
Lucretius, II: 146, 148–50
Lycon, II: 170
Lycophron, I: 115
Lysias, I: 105

Macrobius, II: 162, 227
Malebranche, II: 40
Mallarmé, I: 229–30
Marcus Aurelius, I: 26; II: 172,
    179–81, 235
Maréchal, J., I: 301 n. 9
Marinus, II: 224
Marius Victorinus, II: 227
Marlborough, I: 15
Martial, II: 183
Marxism, I: 17
Maximus, II: 220
Maximus, Alex., II: 186
Maximus of Tyre, II: 200
Melissus, I: 68, 70, 114
Menedemus, I: 139
Menippus, II: 156
Meno, II: 18
Menoeceus, II: 145
Methodius, II: 218
Metrodorus, I: 145, 146
Michelangelo, I: 16; II: 229
Mill, J. S., I: 15; II: 48, 188, 189

Moeragenes, II: 193
Monimus, I: 141
More, St. Thomas, I: 288
Mozart, II: 229
Musonius, II: 183

Napoleon, I: 15
Nausiphanes, II: 145
Nelson, I: 15
Nemesius, II: 226
Neo-Kantians, I: 197, 229
Neo-Platonism, I: 187, 203–4,
    217–18, 226, 236, 274, 275,
    288, 289; II: 18, 40, 41, 58,
    119, 125–26, 127, 133, 136,
    168, 171, 191, 192, 196, 204–
    6, 207–28, 232, 233, 241, 245,
    247–50
Neo-Pythagoreans, II: 126, 182,
    190–94, 195, 196, 197, 199,
    203, 209, 213, 232
Nero, II: 172, 173, 183
Nestorius, II: 221
Nettleship, R. L., I: 179, 312 n.
    31
Newman, II: 27
Nicomachus, II: 9
Nicomachus (younger), II: 17
Nicomachus of Gerasa, II: 191,
    221
Nietzsche, I: 23, 35, 93–94, 230–
    31, 306 n. 8, 316 n. 12; II: 76,
    82, 133
Numenius, II: 191, 192, 199,
    203, 209

Ockham, I: 20
Oenomaus, II: 184
Olivi, II: 64
Olympiodorus, II: 225
Onesicritus, I: 141
Origen, II: 200, 271 n. 21, 277 n.
    19, 278 n. 37
Orphicism, I: 46, 48–49, 240; II:
    193–94, 201, 213, 215, 221,
    246–47

Pamphilus, II: 145
Panaetius, I: 142, 165–66, 167

Parmenides, I: 19, 56, 64–70, 71–
    72, 73, 76, 78–80, 82, 84, 85,
    86, 89, 90, 92, 94, 96, 101,
    209–10, 226; II: 53–54, 209,
    229, 231
Pascal, I: 222
Paul, St., II: 175
Pauson, II: 103
Pearson, II: 271 n. 20
Peregrinus, II: 183–84
Pericles, I: 83, 107, 151
Person, II: 129
Petronius, II: 183
Phaedo, I: 139
Phaedrus, II: 146, 162
Philip (Mac.), II: 10
Philoponus, II: 64
Philippus of Opus, I: 159, 289,
    290
Philiscus, I: 141
Philo, II: 127, 192, 201–6
Philolaus, I: 47, 303 n. 20
Philon, II: 162
Philostratus, II: 191, 193–94
Pindar, I: 55
Pirandello, I: 55
Piso, II: 145
Plato, I: 15, 16, 19, 24, 25, 31,
    33, 35, 48, 53, 55, 60–61, 66,
    69, 70, 72, 81, 83, 95, 97, 101,
    104–6 (on Sophists), 108–10
    (on Protag.), 112, 113, 115–
    16, 117, 119, 120 ff. (and Soc-
    rates), 127, 136, 138, 140,
    142, 145, 151–291; II: 9–19
    (passim), 33, 35–44 (Aristot-
    le's criticism), 45, 48, 51, 52,
    53, 58, 60–61, 67, 69, 71, 81,
    95, 98, 99, 101, 102, 108, 113–
    20 (and Aristotle), 123–24,
    130, 132, 158, 165–66, 167,
    171, 180, 186, 190, 191, 192,
    195, 196, 197, 199, 200, 202,
    207, 211, 212, 213, 214, 215,
    217, 221, 225, 229–48 (pas-
    sim), 269 n. 8, 277 n. 10
Platonism, Middle, I: 202, 289;
    II: 195–200, 209

Pliny, II: 162
Plotinus, I: 26, 204; II: 58, 125, 194, 197, 207–18, 219, 224, 226, 229, 235, 250
Plutarch, I: 61, 103, 146, 274; II: 12, 139, 196–99, 255–56
Plutarch Athen., II: 221
Polemon, I: 289
Polyaenus, II: 146
Polybius, I: 46; II: 165
Polycrates, I: 161
Polygnotus, II: 103
Polystratus, II: 146
Pompey, II: 166
Pope, A., II: 271 n. 8
Porphyry, I: 45; II: 111, 194, 207, 208, 216–18, 219, 220, 224, 227, 228, 250
Poseidonius, II: 162, 165, 166–69, 173, 185, 193, 198, 227, 234, 254
Potamon, II: 186
Poulain, I: 308 n. 10
Praechter, I: 12, 48, 137, 159, 164, 301 n. 2, 302 n. 5, 308 n. 30, 2, 309 n. 43, 311 n. 18, 319 n. 2; II: 126, 179, 205, 256, 271 n. 1
Proclus, I: 52, 72, 158, 274, 277, 313 n. 41; II: 166, 221–24, 225, 226
Prodicus, I: 112–13
Protagoras, I: 89, 102, 107–12, 113, 115, 142, 145–46, 147, 167 ff., 174, 244–45; II: 236
Pseudo-Dionysius, I: 187; II: 127
Pseudo-Plutarch, II: 254
Ptolemy Phil., II: 111
Ptolemy Soter, II: 111
Pyrrho, II: 126, 157–58, 186
Pythagoreans, I: 19, 45–53, 54, 65, 70, 71–77 (Zeno's polemic), 81, 90, 92, 97, 105, 184, 222, 271, 272, 289; II: 33, 111, 171, 186, 190–91, 193, 196, 212, 215, 221, 230, 233, 239, 246–47
Pythias, II: 10
Pythocles, II: 145

Remigius, II: 227
Rilke, I: 230
Ritter, C., I: 11, 153, 223, 240, 276, 311 n. 9
Roberts, W. R., II: 100
Robin, L., II: 256
Ross, Sir W. D., I: 11, 74; II: 65, 72, 107, 265 n. 53, 58, 266 n. 33, 268 n. 25
Rubens, I: 16; II: 229

Sallustius, II: 220
Satyros, I: 83
Scaevola, Q. M., II: 165–66
Scepticism, II: 126, 157–61, 163, 186–91, 238
Schaarschmidt, I: 158
Schelling, I: 77, 159, 161; II: 43
Scholz, H., II: 28
Schopenhauer, I: 23, 33; II: 43, 83, 100
Scipio, II: 165
Seneca, I: 26, 146; II: 138, 140, 142–43, 156, 172–75, 179, 181, 182, 183, 186, 235
Septimius Severus, II: 193
Sextius, Q., II: 186
Sextus Empiricus, II: 131, 158, 188–89, 191, 255, 272–73 n. 7–8
Shakespeare, I: 15, 16; II: 229
Sidonius, Apoll., II: 194
Simplicius, I: 65, 70, 84, 274, 310 n. 9; II: 110, 224, 225, 255
Socrates, I: 66, 88, 105–6, 107, 116, 117–36, 137–43 (passim), 151–53 (and Plato), 155, 158, 167–68, 174–75, 186, 189, 197–99, 226–27, 245–46, 286, 316 n. 14; II: 80–82, 85–86, 114, 129, 158, 196, 230, 233–34, 243–44, 246–47
Socrates (Hist.), II: 218
Solon, I: 105, 225
Sophists, I: 101–16, 134, 145, 226–27, 245, 260; II: 157, 230, 234, 236, 237, 243

Sophocles, I: 15, 33, 102, 105, 117, 253; II: 110

Sosicrates, I: 142

Sotion, I: 65, 83, 142; II: 186

Spencer, H., I: 15; II: 83, 93

Speusippus, I: 289–90, 291; II: 10, 14, 39, 88

Sphairus, II: 129

Spinoza, I: 15, 178, 221, 222; II: 133, 134

Stace, W. T., I: 46, 68, 87, 130, 223, 306 n. 11, 312 n. 1; II: 109, 264–65 n. 35

Stebbing, S., II: 28

Stein, H. von, I: 310 n. 18

Stenzel, J., I: 48, 205, 206, 212, 301 n. 2

Stephanus, II: 226

Stilpo, I: 139; II: 129

Stobaeus, II: 254

Stoicism, I: 59–61, 291; II: 81, 124–26, 129–243, 146, 149, 155, 158, 159–60, 161–62, 163, 165–81, 182–83, 185, 186, 189, 190, 193, 196, 197, 199, 200, 205, 234–35, 238, 241–43, 245–46, 248–49

Strabo, II: 172

Strato, II: 169–70

Suidas, II: 196, 207

Synesius, II: 226

Syrianus, I: 123; II: 221, 224

Tascius Vict., II: 194

Taylor, A. E., I: 11, 107, 117, 118, 119, 121–24, 157–60, 165, 182, 198–99, 218–20, 223, 272, 309 n. 49, 312 n. 27, 313 n. 41

Teles, II: 156

Thales, I: 33, 36, 38–40, 42, 43, 57, 65, 68, 79, 93–95; II: 32

Themison, II: 13

Themistius, II: 171, 227

Theo of Smyrna, I: 220

Theodoric, II: 228

Theodorus, I: 143, 144; II: 156

Theodosius II, II: 218

Theognis, I: 33

Theophrastus, I: 40, 42, 81, 89, 272; II: 10, 58, 110–11, 254

Theramenes, II: 96

Thomas à Kempis, II: 173

Thrasea, II: 183

Thrasyllus, I: 158; II: 276 n. 1

Thrasymachus, I: 115

Thucydides, I: 34, 105

Timon, II: 158

Titus, II: 183

Trajan, II: 184, 185, 196

Tzetzes, II: 127

Ueberweg, I: 158

Valentinian III, II: 218

Varro, II: 156, 162, 166

Velasquez, II: 229

Vespasian, II: 183

Vettius, II: 227

Virgil, I: 15; II: 150

Virius, II: 194

Vitellius, II: 183

Vitruvius, II: 162

Whitehead, A. N., I: 288, 301 n. 3

William of Moerbeke, II: 221

Xenocrates, I: 289, 290–91; II: 10, 129, 198

Xenophanes, I: 47, 54, 64; II: 158

Xenophon, I: 105, 120–21, 124, 127, 158

Zabarella, II: 72

Zeller, E., I: 32, 43, 60, 70, 77, 87, 102, 112, 115, 301 n. 2, 306 n. 11, 307 n. 4; II: 166, 262 n. 32

Zeno of Elea, I: 70, 71–77, 89, 102, 114; II: 66, 236

Zeno (Stoic), I: 139; II: 110, 129, 130, 132, 138, 139, 140, 141, 142, 161

Zeno of Tarsus, II: 129